INTEGRATED DEVELOPMENT PLAN FOR INDIA
Goal, Tools and Strategies

Integrated Development Plan for India

Goal, Tools and Strategies

SHANTI SWARUP GUPTA
Vice Chancellor
Agra University, Agra

CONCEPT PUBLISHING COMPANY, NEW DELHI 110059

ISBN 81-7022-411-X

First Published 1992

Shanti Swarup **Gupta** (*b*. 1929)

Published and Printed by
Ashok Kumar Mittal
Concept Publishing Company
A/15-16, Commercial Block, Mohan Garden
NEW DELHI 110059 (India)

Lasertypeset by
Microtech Advance Printing Systems (Pvt.) Ltd.
H-13, Bali Nagar,
NEW DELHI 110015

To

My Wife

PUSHPA

PREFACE

A peep into the recent past shows that so long as the country was under the foreign yoke, there was only one point programme before the nation – How to become free? For this, no sacrifice was considered big enough and practically no attention was paid to either social rejuvenation or economic betterment. Very little time and thought were given to decide in what direction free Bharat would advance.

Having attained Independence, our thoughts, strangely enough, did not go to the basic question, viz., on what road of progress we have to move? What is our ultimate goal? We also forgot our past promises of Village Republics. Instead, under the evil influence of the western thought, we plunged into making an ideal constitution. In the absence of a goal, we compiled the best things of the various constitutions of the western world, and called this Pindora's Box as the Indian Constitution. We gave to ourselves democracy. To decentralise power, we artificially broke India into federating units to make the country a Federation. Unable to rid ourselves of the slave mentality bequeathed to us by our masters, we adopted their Parliamentary form of government. We also accepted the latest fashion known as 'Secularism' and 'Socialism' without bothering whether they go well with our genius and whether democracy and socialism are compatible terms. Where has all this landed us in a short span of forty years? Federating states are continuously being deprived of their rights and the centre has increasingly become more powerful. In practice we have more of a Unitary type of government. It appears the experiment of Parliamentary form of government has also failed and politicians have started talking of the Presidential type of government. Minority governments have made democracy a farce. Today, communal riots, terrorism, demand for new smaller independent States, desire to secede, scant respect for the Rule cf the Law, etc. have made the future of India dark. People have started saying that they never bargained for this freedom.

On the Economic front we were committed to remove poverty, unemployment, uneven distribution of wealth etc. Rudderless, we thought of making a new cocktail by mixing Capitalism and Socialism and calling it Nehruvian Socialism. Forty years of Central Planning has multiplied our problems rather than solving a single one. Today, economics has not only become an important part of life but the whole life. But even then we have more unemployment, more poverty amongst plenty, greater uneven distribution of wealth, scarcities, staggering debts, both internal and international, mounting unfavourable balance of payments and unprecedented rise in prices of two digits, greater regional disparities and corruption.

In social sphere, the less said the better. In our aping mentality, we have lost faith in and given up our age-old value-system, social institutions such as family, marriage etc. and social and national festivals. Today, we have become more dishonest, more intolerant, more hypocritic, more law-breaker, more disrespectful to our elders, more self-centred and more corrupt. Today, bride killing, sex laxaties and sex-crimes, unhappy marriages, broken homes, uncared for old parents and unconcerned children etc. are becoming the order of the day.

A nation has a past, a present and a future. They are all interdependently integrated. Unfortunately in India, our leaders tried to forget our rich past and tried to build a future, cut off from the past and even the present. In this they could neither think of the life as a whole nor fix a goal. This appears to be our misfortune. So, no amount of piecemeal borrowing from the west or from the U.N.O. and its allied agencies, of ideas, technology or money will help us much. We must use these valuables with caution and keeping in mind our goal of life and methodology.

In India, *Dharma* had ever been given great importance. Unfortunately, under the mistaken notion, circulated by our rulers, we equated *Dharma* with religion, which it is not. *Dharma* means nature. For example, the nature of fire is to burn; the nature of water is to flow. Similarly, the people of a nation have a nature. *Dharma* also means Law, justice, equity, fairplay and welfare. So in Bharat, *Dharma*, provided guidelines, a code of conduct, to regulate all facets of life. These guidelines were spelt out under the title of values – human, social and spiritual. They were in keeping with our nature and helped in fulfilling the specified goal. Our seers, therefore, ordained that *Dharma* should control social, political and economic life. It is only then that a fully developed, happy and contented nation can become a reality. *Moksha* from want, hunger, disease, ignorance, indigestion of plenty etc. can be achieved. The scholars wedded to the ideals of ancient India call it "Integral Humanism".

I, as a student of economics, thought of making an humble effort in this direction – to determine a goal and sketch out broad outlines for an integrated happy life. Obviously, freedom, which ought to be value based and decentralisation of power, economic and political, were to be the twin pillars. So, I applied for a major project to the University Grants Commission under the title of 'A New Technique of Area Growth Model for India'. The U.G.C. was good enough to sanction it to me in 1984. Unfortunately being over busy with my duties as the Principal of a first rate post-graduate college and also under a mistaken belief that I can make it an elite college, I could not find time for this work. My dream was put in to its proper place and so I lost no time in seeking pre-mature retirement and devote myself to this work.

The outlines are in the following pages. It is hoped that the details and colour scheme shall be provided by more competent persons.

I am aware that my wife, Dr. Pushpa Lata, in spite of personal inconveniences and mental strain, cheerfully encouraged me all the time in the pursuit of this never ending work. She also helped me with her practical wisdom and commendable grasp of the principles of Economics. I dedicate this book to her knowing it fully well that it is no compensation.

My thanks are due to all my friends and well wishers who helped me in innumerable ways. Prof. Murari Lal, Retd. Principal, who has an oceanic knowledge of ancient Literature and Philosophy, Prof. N.L. Sharma, Head of the English Deptt. (Retd.) who has, besides command over English, wonderful knowledge of almost all subjects, Prof. B.B. Mittal and dear Viniti Gupta, my daughter-in-law, who was ever ready to help me with her scientific knowledge, deserve my special acknowledgements.

I am grateful to M/s Concept Publishing Co., New Delhi, without whose help, this book must not have seen the light of the day.

Date: 11th April, 1992 S.S. GUPTA

CONTENTS

LIST OF TABLES

LIST OF MAPS

PART ONE

THE GOAL

Westerners in their enthusiasm for specialisation started dividing life, which is one, into innumerable segments like economics, politics, sociology, law etc. Not satisfied, they started further sub-division of these segments and in the process the idea of unity of life was totally forgotten. These segments and their sub-parts, started developing independently with different goals or different meaning of a common goal, different fundamentals, different methods, and different strategies. Today we have reached a stage when these differences have become incompatible. For example, democracy in politics and socialism in economics could not walk hand in hand even for a few steps. Again, goal of social-welfare or individual welfare appears to be unattainable. Experts tell us that individual welfare and general or common welfare cannot go together. Following few pages show it.

In order to remedy this evil, a common goal, both for individual and the society, nay the world must be searched.

An effort has been made to search such a goal. It is Anand, *permanent happiness. What does it mean? How it integrates an individual? How it integrates an individual with his society and the world? How all – an individual, the society, the world and its various segments fall in one composite whole in such a goal? An attempt has been made to discuss it all in this section.*

1

FROM WELFARE TO *ANAND*

The wisemen of the world tried to give a goal to the confused humanity. This, in their wisdom, they called welfare. But it appears, this goal has not stood the test of time. A brief review may be worth-while.

I
ON WELFARE

Man's life is an integrated whole and as such his activities should not be divided into separate water-tight compartments – Political, Economic, Social, Psychological etc. But unfortunately this is happening at present. For example, the concept of "Welfare", both of an individual and of society, differs from one discipline to another. Moreover, it is thought that it is not compatible even in one discipline. It is, therefore, proposed briefly to examine the meaning of welfare as it is propounded in the more important disciplines, e.g., Political Science, Economics and Psychology, and have an idea of its utility in life and then try to redefine the new goal.

In Political Science

In Political Science the concept of a welfare state has undergone many changes and even today it cannot be stated with finality that it will not change again. For example, the first stage in the evolution of the idea of a welfare state was to be found when the doctrine of *laissez faire* was at the peak of popularity. It was presumed that the State should protect individual liberty but should not interfere in the least. Mill, Harbert Spencer and others pleaded for the minimum state interference. The state, was considered as a "Joint Protection Company for mutual assistance".[1] It was felt that maximum individual liberty will automatically promote maximum individual as well as social welfare, both of which were supposed to be on good terms then.

The second stage came when public conscience was awakened by the ghastly inhuman conditions of life and work which resulted from the doctrine. Consequently it led to a re-examination of the purpose and foundation of the state. It was realised that unbridled individual liberty led to exploitation and cut at the very roots of welfare. So people like Dalton, Lovett, Thompson, Robert Owen, William Cobbet, Lord Shaftesbury pleaded for State intervention in favour of the weak. Ideas and schemes for the education of the poor, co-operation, labour legislation, abolition of slavery etc. were formulated and pleaded. This also did not take us long on the path of welfare.

The third stage started with Chartist Movement of 1848 which tried to undo political division of society.

The fourth stage began with the theories recommending the widening of the state functions so as to cover almost everything under the sky. The Utilitarians, the Idealists, the Guild Socialists, the Syndicatists, the Anarchists, the Fascists and the teachings of individualists like Green, Duguit etc. contributed in this direction.

The fifth and existing stage began with the end of the Second World War. Now National Health, National Insurance, National Assistance and Children are considered to be four pillars of welfare state.[2]

In Political Science, the concept of the Welfare State has been defined differently by different persons. However, there are certain points on which there seems to be no difference of opinion. First, it is the concept of a truly democratic state. It has nothing to do with a totalitarian state. Secondly, it is of paramount importance that there should be peace, both internal and international. Without the idea of "one world", a welfare state is not conceivable. Thirdly, it should meet the demands of social security. Without a minimum economic well-being, no higher achievements are possible.

T.W. Kent defines a welfare state as "a state that provides for its citizens, a wide range of social services".[3] T.M. Marshall has summed up the concept of a welfare state thus: "It is the assumption by the community, acting through the state, of the responsibility for providing means, whereby all its members can reach minimum standard of health, economic security and civilised living and can share according to their capacity in its social and cultural heritage".[4]

It is, for convenience, described as the welfare state, a state responsible to the material needs of all subjects; providing complete and adequate security against all the sinister contingencies of life, abolishing want and unemployment, giving education up to the University standard (and beyond) to all who desire to avail themselves of it. In short, it will be Santa Claus State.[5] The welfare state is a system of social responsibility for certain minimum standards of individual and communal welfare.[6] In a welfare state, the community at large recognises a collective responsibility towards its weaker or less fortunate members and takes definite action to assist those members.[7]

The concept of welfare state has been ridiculed on several of its aspects.

First, when the concept of a welfare state is interpreted in different ways by different persons – Communist, Socialist of different brands, Gandhian, American – it becomes difficult to understand it and more so to practise it.

Secondly, it has been mainly a theory of re-distribution of existing wealth. And re-distribution of wealth alone cannot promote even material welfare.

Thirdly, the concept is concerned with material well-being and grossly ignores mental, emotional, moral and spiritual welfare.

Fourthly, it restricts individual freedom. Once we concede to the state that right of interference, there will be no end to it and ultimately the individual will become a non-entity. It is a definite path to totalitarianism.

Fifthly, it brings about the worst type of bureaucracy, a top heavy administration, both expensive and inefficient.[8] Barbara Woottan called it *Administrative Elephantiasis*.

Sixthly, Marxists call it a new formula by which the lingering love for capitalism can be preserved by which no problem is solved.

In Economics

Probably, it was Pareto, who, for the first time tried to develop the concept of welfare. He was mainly concerned with the problems of production including exchange but did not bother himself about distribution. It was Pigou, who for the first time, applied his mind towards the problems of distribution alongwith production and shifted the emphasis from individual welfare to social welfare. And in social welfare or general welfare also, he studied only that part which could be brought directly or indirectly in relation to the measuring rod of money. So, Pigou talks of economic welfare and presumes that at worst non-economic welfare remains constant. After Pigou and Marshall, any number of economists have worked on the subject, notable amongst whom are Prof. L. Robbins; Kaldor and Hicks who, under the criticism of Robbins, have propounded the "Compensation Principle"; and Dr. Little, Baumel, Samuelson, Beggson and Tintner, who have developed 'Social Welfare Principle'. Even now economists are not satisfied and a lot of work is being done on the subject.

In spite of all the hair-splitting, mental acrobatics and mathematical gymnastics, the economists have failed to answer several important questions:

1. Man does not live by matter alone. He has a mind, a *Manas* and a soul also which start troubling him more acutely after a level of material prosperity has been reached. It is not known how to measure these non-economic factors and arrive at an integrated welfare picture.
2. Individual welfare is as important, if not more, as social or general welfare. The modern economists, in their over-enthusiasm, have almost by-passed the individual welfare. Most of the present day studies centre round general welfare. Even the idea has been ventured that individual welfare and general welfare, after a limit, become incompatible.
3. Any welfare study, worth its name, should take into consideration, both the production and distribution aspects and only after considering both, should pass a judgement. This immediately raises the problems of inter-personal and inter-situational comparisons. For example, when wealth is snatched from the rich and passed on to the poor, it should be possible to say whether welfare has increased, decreased or remained the same. Both the Compensation Principle and the Social Welfare Principle have tried to answer this question but the success is doubtful.
4. It is presumed that perfect equal distribution of income will result in maximum economic welfare. But equal distribution will adversely affect capital formation and productive incentives and thereby, in the long run, is likely to stop growth of and may even reduce National Income. This will certainly not be conducive to welfare.

5. The concept of welfare embraces many states of mind, but there are no economic states of mind. Hence, the whole concept is subjective and economists have hardly any reliable objective tests correctly to measure it.
6. The concept of welfare is not only subjective but it is also subject to change with time, place and person. Thus, it adds to our already insurmountable problems.
7. Economists have adopted ordinal nature of utility while it should have been cardinal.

These and many more ticklish problems, staring in the face of an economist, make him almost dumb. He is lost in the ocean trying to search the depth and the shore and failing in both.

In Psychology

In psychology no literature is found on welfare. However, literature is available on 'Personality', which includes 'Integrated Personality', and 'Adjustment'. It can be presumed that these concepts are synonyms for 'welfare'.

A. *Personality*

Some authentic definitions of personality may be quoted and examined:

> 'It may be defined as the most characteristic integration of an individual's structures, modes of interest, behaviour, capacities and attitudes.'
>
> – *Muirehead*

> 'Personality can be broadly defined as the total quality of an individual's behaviour as it is revealed in his habits of thought and expression, his attitudes and interest, his manner of acting and his personal philosophy of life.'
>
> – *Woodworth*

> 'Personality is the dynamic organisation within the individual of their psycho-physical systems that determine his unique thoughts and character.'
>
> – *G.W. Allport*

The salient points in the definition of Allport are –

1. Man has two distinct traits – physical and psychological.
2. Both the traits are dynamic. They change with time and place, as also country and society.
3. Family, educational institutions and society, i.e. culture and politics sow and develop the traits through environment.
4. The organisation is important because it integrates several traits such as goodness, frailty, love, hatred etc.
5. Because of this organisation, an individual gets particular ideas and actions which give him a personality.

Morgan and Gillilan have divided personality on the basis of nature in four parts: –

(a) *Elated* – Those, who by nature, are optimist.
(b) *Depressed* – Those, who by nature, are pessimist and remain depressed.
(c) *Irritable* – Those, who lose temper quickly and pick up quarrels.
(d) *Unstable* – Those who are undecided and in disequilibrium.

Prof. Carl G. Jung has classified personality into two parts:

(i) *Extrovert* – Those, who are talkative, materialistic, social, emotional, quick to decide and act, believe in acting etc.
(ii) *Introvert* – Those, who are solitude lovers, hesitating, indecisive, idealist, impractical, thoughtful etc.

B. *Adjustment*

Conformity, in which one surrenders oneself, out of love or complex, and carries on the wishes of others, is not Adjustment. Adjustment is a continuous process which is based on better analysis and understanding of self, of others and of environment. When one changes one's behaviour to adjust with the other's, the other also changes demanding a fresh adjustment. Thus a process of constant interaction occurs.

The world is physical (i.e. physique and health, body chemistry and glands), social (i.e. family environment, education and economic condition) and cultural (i.e. inner refinement concerning truth, beauty and goodness). Without full social adjustment, one may carry on but will be misfit in the society and will make one's life miserable as well as of others. Without psychological adjustments one will develop a split personality and a complex character which will be good to none. And without physiological adjustments it will be impossible even to survive.

The psychologists have tried to develop several tests to measure the degree of adjustments. These tests, even if objective, have subjective elements. Moreover, they do not help much as they do not give guidelines for better adjustments.

C. *Freud : Integrated Personality*

The reputed Psycho-analyst, Freud, has tried to define "Integrated Personality" in a different way. He tells us of three things – Id, Ego and Super-Ego. Id is physical or animal, which is power and usually depends on pleasure principle; Ego is mental or the controller of Id and is based on reality principle, and Super-Ego deals with 'ought to be' i.e. socially approved. It tells of the destination. Freud felt that when there is a harmonious functioning of Id, Ego and Super-Ego, one has an integrated personality. With this ideal combination one has no angularities and no complexes. One is a happy and contented man.

In spite of this brilliant analysis of Freud, which is difficult to understand, one does not get an idea of how to achieve an integrated personality. The whole discussion mainly remains theoretical.

Theory vs Practice

The simple concept of welfare, whether in political science or economics or psychology, faces innumerable, almost insurmountable problems when introduced in practical life. Only one example – Fixing of Minimum Wages in India will prove the point.

A court of Australia, for the first time, defined the idea of Living Wage in 1907.[9]

International Labour Organisation (ILO) conventions from 1928 to 1949 (Nos. 26, 63 and 93) suggested that with a view to protecting labourers, minimum wages should be fixed and for this appropriate machinery should be created.[10]

Royal Commission on Labour, 1931 did not lay down any principle of wage fixation but popularised the belief that higher wages will lead to attract better workers and improve efficiency.[11]

Central Legislative Assembly in 1938 adopted a resolution of 'sufficient wages', i.e. need based wages.[12]

In India, in 1947, to save economy from the wave of strikes and lock-outs, a Tripartite Conference was held which passed Industrial Truce Resolution. The slogan was 'Produce or Perish'.[13]

Minimum Wage Act was passed in 1948.[14]

Fair Wages Bill was introduced in Parliament in 1950 but allowed to lapse.

The framers of the Indian Constitution dreamt of making India a Sovereign Socialist Secular Democratic Republic ensuring Justice (social, economic and political), Liberty (of thought, expression, belief, faith and worship), Equality (of status and of opportunity) and fraternity, to all its citizens.[15] So, they incorporated in the Indian Constitution Fundamental Rights (Articles 12 to 35), which are enforceable by courts and Directive Principles of State Policy (Articles 36 to 51), which are in the 'nature of fundamental in the governance of the country and it shall be the duty of the State to apply these principles in making laws', but are not enforceable by any court.

Article 38 says that it shall be the duty of the State to secure a social order for the promotion of welfare of the people. Thus, the aim is Welfare State.

Article 39 lays down certain policy statements such as:

(a) right to an adequate means of livelihood, and
(b) equal pay for equal work for both men and women.

Article 43 has two parts, the first deals with living wage and second about cottage industries. Here we are mainly concerned with the first part.

This first part of the article prescribes that the State should endeavour to secure –

(i) work,
(ii) a living wage, and
(iii) conditions of work ensuring a decent standard of life and full enjoyment of leisure and social and cultural opportunities to all types of workers, agricultural, industrial or otherwise by either

(a) framing suitable laws, or
(b) setting up an economic machinery, or
(c) any other way.

The experts opine[16] that the framers of the Indian Constitution were probably inspired by similar provisions in the constitutions of other countries such as:

The Brazil Constitution, which aims at securing the objectives of Article 43, by legislation.
The German Constitution, which gives importance to the adjustments in the Economic Organisation.
The Constitution of USSR, which stresses the Economic Organisation and other means.

The Report of the Committee of Fair Wages, 1949, defines three types of wages:

1. *Living Wage* – It is one that enables a male earner to provide for himself and his family not merely the bare essentials of food, clothing and shelter but a measure of frugal comfort including education for children, protection against ill-health, requirements of essential social needs and a measure of insurance against the more important misfortunes including old age.
2. *Minimum Wage* – It must provide not merely for the bare sustenance of life but also for the preservation of the efficiency of the worker. For this purpose, it must also provide for some measures of education, medical treatment and other amenities.
3. *Fair Wage* – It is below living wage and higher than minimum wage. The lower limit of the fair wage must obviously be the minimum wage and the upper limit of the living wage.

It may be noted here that in advanced countries like Australia, New Zealand, U.S.A. and Canada, where the National Income is very high, there is hardly any difference between a minimum wage and a living wage.

It is an accepted view that the minimum wage, in the quantitative money term, is a dynamic concept. With changes in prices, national income, standard of living, efficiency of worker etc., the minimum wage will also go on changing.

With a view to implementing the decision to fix minimum wage, first in organised industry, a machinery was set up. Various Wage Boards tried to do the needful. When the disputes arose, the Tribunals were organised to give their verdict. Finally, the issues went to the Supreme Court. A study of these three sources shows that there is no unanimity in different Boards, different Tribunals and even in different judgments of the Supreme Court. The matter got further complicated when the different Pay Commissions, appointed by the Government, gave new dimensions to the problem. It will be advisable to have a look on how the opinions have differed on a single point.

The Supreme Court laid down a principle of Industry-*cum*-Region basis to determine Minimum Wage. This principle was based on the comparison of wages of various concerns of an industry of a region. Soon it was felt that even in a region it is necessary to differentiate between efficient and large concerns due to their being capital intensive and small or medium concerns with lesser capital and technological base. After sometime, even the insistence on a region had to be given up. In a case of workers of a Bank, obviously, the wage differences could not be permitted on the basis of a region. Thus, this basic principle could not hold ground in different cases.

The Supreme Court enunciated another important principle of capacity to pay. The difficulty arose on how to calculate the capacity to pay. In different cases, different methods to measure came up. Some of the important ones are:

(i) Industry should be able to maintain production with efficiency,
(ii) Elasticity of demand for the product, and
(iii) Industry-*cum*-Region basis.

No single principle could serve the purpose for different types of concerns, of different situations.

Tribunals laid down the principle of financial position of the concern to determine capacity to pay. Some Tribunals took gross profit as a justifiable indicator of the capacity while others agreed more with the Supreme Court principle of production with efficiency. Some took Dividends and Reserves as a better criterion. There appears to be no unanimity on this point also.

The dispute also arose on the size of the family. Textile Labour

Enquiry Committee thought that the wage would be sufficient for the worker, his wife and two dependents. Workers' unions pleaded for three dependents or even four dependents. No unanimity could be achieved.

How to convert the females or children into an adult consumption unit was another problem. Some pleaded that Lusk's co-efficient method should be adopted and others pointed out its defects.

How to calculate minimum needs of food, cloth, rent, medicine, education etc., posed another set of problems. For example, Dr. Ayroyd recommended the criterion of 2,700 calories for each Indian adult of moderate activity. Others disputed it and wanted it to be 3,000 calories. Then the question of food habits – vegetarian or non-vegetarian arose. Obviously, vegetarian food is cheaper than non-vegetarian and even in vegetarian the differences are due to eating habits – rice or wheat being the principal food. Again, disputes arose about cloth requirements. A set of experts recommended 18 yards of cloth per adult consumption unit per annum. Equally other brilliant experts gave different figures. Dispute also arose whether woollen cloth be included or not. Similarly, opinions also differed on rent. Some suggested 7.5 per cent of pay, other 10 per cent, some talked of the prevalent market rent and still others of rent on the basis of floor area provided by the Government to its employees. The idea of study of Family Budgets was also mooted. There appears to be no unanimity.

Another set of problems stared in the face when these quantities of food, cloth, rent, medicine, education etc., were converted into money terms. Third Pay Commission points out these differences in the claims put up by different organisations. They range from Rs. 204.70 to Rs. 347.25 for the same period.

Thus, the innocent looking pious thinking of fixing minimum wages bogged down with innumerable problems. And this was the state of affairs in some selected industries of organised sectors. The problems are likely to become more complex when workers of unorganised sector will be covered by the scheme of fixing minimum wages.

II
ON *ANAND* (Bliss)

The above discussion on welfare has clearly shown the conceptual defects and also the difficulties in implementing it. So, it is worthwhile to search for another goal which may be more fundamental, rational and practicable.

Some Important Ideas

To understand the fundamental, rational and practicable goal of *Anand* (Bliss), which is based on the ancient Indian thought, it is essential to know and understand some important ideas:

1. Man is the central point both as an individual and as a member of a family; of a group of families which is known as society with its various segments such as social, political, economic etc.; of a nation and a group of nations known as World or Family of Nations. Hence, there must be unity in the goals of a man, a family, a society, a Nation and the World. Any variations in goals will create problems, tensions, split personalities, chaos, confusion etc.
2. Man, as is evident, has a body, a vitality or energy, a *Manas*, an intellect and a spirit. All these five essential elements should be taken into consideration while fixing a goal. This goal must be able to bring unity and cohesion among these elements otherwise man cannot remain in permanent peace and happiness.
3. The ancient seers, who were social scientists and great pursuers of truth, found out five *Koshas* (Sheaths) in every man. They are:

   (a) *Ann Mai Kosh* (Material Sheath) – It is said to be lifeless but is essential. Nothing is possible without it.

   (b) *Prana Mai Kosh* (Vital Sheath) – It refers to vitality or energy.

   (c) *Mano Mai Kosh* (*Manas* Sheath) – Indian seers opined that *Mana* is different from mind. It is the originator of all desires *(Kama)* and all types of activities (*Arth*). But these desires and actions may or may not be with a direction and a purpose. However, western psychologists do not give it any separate identity. They think it to be a part of the conscious mind.

   (d) *Buddhi Mai Kosh* (Intellect or *Vivek* Sheath) – Western psychologists are of the view that mind has three parts – conscious, unconscious and subconscious. They know about conscious mind but are almost ignorant about the other two. So, their education and science are mainly concerned with the development of the conscious mind which enables them to take correct decisions. The Indian seers, when they talk of *Buddhi Mai Kosh* or intellectual sheath, take into consideration the development of all the three parts of mind. They feel that without the proper development of all the three, righteous decisions cannot be taken. They give special attention to controlling of *Mano Mai Kosh*, i.e., *Kama* (desires) and *Artha* (activities) in such a way that it may provide happiness.

(e) *Anand Mai Kosh* (Permanent Happiness Sheath) – Indian social scientists said that soul *(Atma)* is a segment of super-conscious *(Parmatma)*. The soul lives in a body and the body is said to be alive as long this soul is in the body. This soul lives some where in the unconscious mind.

The Indian seers opined that an ideal combination of the first four sheaths will open the doors of the last and the fifth sheath, i.e., Permanent Happiness Sheath.

The Indian seers gave to man the goal of permanent happiness, which they called *Anand* (Bliss). This was the result of dynamic and balanced integration of the four sheaths.

If the goal of man is *Anand* (Bliss) or permanent happiness, then the goal of a family, of a society with all its segments; of a Nation and of a Family of Nations should also be *Anand*.

4. Hindu seers have discussed four parts of *Antah-Karan*.

(i) *Manas* (Conscious mind as called by western psychologists) – Ancient Hindu psychologists opined that *Manas* has two main instincts:

(a) *Kama* – It is much more than sex. It refers to all types of desires including sex. Psychologist Freud felt that sex alone is the motivating force of all human activity. He felt that sex may be enjoyed fully. Hindu seers felt that with enjoyment of sex, it should be controlled and sublimated. It should be channellised for higher achievements. That will be a royal road to perfection.

(b) *Artha* – It means all activities – social, political, economic etc. So, *Artha* does not mean matter or matter earning activities alone. Karl Marx, founder of Scientific Socialism, felt that matter alone is the motivating force of all human activities. This thought could not stand the test of time even for three quarters of a century. It has collapsed in its own citadel.

Hindu seers felt that love for sex or love for matter alone cannot make a man happy. The history of modern world proves that the Western thinkers were not correct when they gave undue importance to sex or matter. So, the ancient Indian thinkers' view that love for spirit should be the only motivating force of *Kama* and *Artha*, because it leads to *Anand* (Bliss) or permanent happiness, deserves to be accepted as more near the truth.

(ii) *Buddhi* (intellect) – Ancient seers felt that *Buddhi* (Intellect) is the power of discrimination which monitors the activities of all the three parts of mind – conscious, unconscious and subconscious. This power of discrimination can also be misled and take wrong decision if it is not, what the seers call, *Nirmal* (Pure). To enable it to take righteous decisions, it should be trained, or pass through a mill.

Westerners feel that education of modern science helps in developing intellect and taking righteous decisions. To an Indian seer it appears to be a tall claim. Science helps in searching truth, establishing a relationship between cause and effect and developing a process of reasoning. It mainly remains confined to the realm of conscious mind. It does not touch subconscious and unconscious parts of mind which are store houses of very valuable information and powers. So, modern education and science do not make intellect pure (i.e., *Nirmal*), capable of taking unbiased righteous decisions which may help in promoting human happiness on a permanent basis. Most of the scientific discoveries confirm this viewpoint.

The seers felt that increasing acquisition of Human-values, Social-values and Spiritual-values makes *Buddhi* – all the three parts of mind, active and *Nirmal* i.e., pure and righteous.

(iii) *Chitta* – Western psychologists call it subconscious mind where past experiences are stored. Ancient Indian psychologists opined that past experience can be of two types – good or bad. Good past experiences give us good *Sanskars* and the bad ones, bad *Sanskars*. The *Sanskars* consequently give birth to a good culture or a bad culture.

(iv) *Ahankar* (Ego) – Ancient Indian seers opined that *Ahankar* (Ego) is the conscious realisation of separating or limiting the individual spirit (*Atma*) from the super-conscious (*Parmatma*).

Indian seers-*cum*-social scientists felt that an ideal combination of *Manas*, *Buddhi*, *Chitta* and *Ahankar* leads to the royal road to *Anand* (Bliss), i.e., permanent happiness.

5. Ancient Indian seers were of the view that Man's life is divided into four *Pursharth*, i.e., Activities.

(a) *Moksha* – This is an ideal to be achieved. It means liberation of the soul from the bondage of the world i.e., from the cycle of birth and death. It means union with the super-conscious. It is very difficult to achieve this ideal but it is worth trying it. It is the next higher stage than that of *Anand*, (permanent happiness or bliss). It does not pertain to this world.

(b) *Kama* – As said earlier, *Kama* means all types of desires – sex, material, name, fame etc. It includes traits, attributes, psychological values and even 64 types of *Kalas* (Artistic expressions). *Kama* is the motivating force of all actions. Freud built his model only on one type of desire, i.e., sex.

(c) *Artha* – It means actions or activities. The term includes not only the economic activities but all conceivable activities. Karl Marx's model is based on only one activity pertaining to matter. It is *Kama* which is the motivating force of *Artha*.

(d) *Dharma* – In Hindu philosophy, *Dharma* does not mean sect or religion or rituals or sacraments. It means a code of conduct which develops righteousness in a person. It develops a faculty which decides what is right and just and what is wrong and unjust or evil. This decision taking is not done on the basis of material considerations alone. Life is taken as a whole. So, Hindu seers did not equate their decision-taking faculty with the modern term scientific-temper. They put it on a higher plane and called it *Vivek* which, they felt is developed by imbibing human-values, social-values and spiritual-values.

Hindu seers-*cum*-sociologists, after experimentations, came to the conclusion that when both *Kama* (desires) and *Artha* (activities) are controlled by *Dharma* i.e., righteousness, then one progresses on the path of *Anand* and *Moksh*.

6. Ancient Hindu philosophy broadly classified men, on the basis of their natural traits or basic nature, in three categories:

(i) *Tamsik* – One who is basically self-centred and believes in the philosophy of eat, drink and be merry. He has no love or faith in righteousness and no ethical or moral considerations. He is purely selfish to the extent of meanness. Such persons become dull, idle and are given to inertia.

(ii) *Rajsik* – One who is basically self-centred but also believes in the philosophy of live and let live. A *Rajsik* person is given to passions. He is a better person from the society point of view.

(iii) *Satvik* – One who is not at all self-centred and who believes in the maxim of live for others. A *Satvik* person is basically a philanthropist. He is an asset to the society.

Indian seers opined that the three basic traits come through genes but can also be acquired. They firmly suggested that every one should try to become a *Satvik* man. It will be good for the individual as well as for the society. The onward journey can be made through self-analysis, self-control and training. Eating and living nabits, company, constant watchfulness and efforts go a long way on the march from *Tamsik* to *Satvik* life. It is here that Hindu Philosophy of *Karma*, i.e., freedom to act becomes important.

Indian *Rishis* opined that the man's actions (*Artha*) can also be classified in three categories of *Tamsik*, *Rajsik* and *Satvik*. By constant endeavours, man can give up *Tamsik* or *Rajsik* actions and acquire *Satvik* actions. He can make it a second nature.

7. Indian *Rishis* always talked of five dimensions – length, breadth, height, time and spirit or light. This spirit or light, they thought, is a constituent of the infinite – *Sat* (Existence), *Chit* (Subconsciousness) and *Anand* (Bliss or permanent happiness).

   Till recently, scientists were mainly concerned with space and therefore they talked only of three dimensions – length, breadth and height. Scientist Einstein, through his theory of Relativity introduced the fourth dimension of time. Scientist G. Fainverg in 1967 and Dr. Sudarshan of Texas University, U.S.A. in 1968 confirmed this fourth dimension, i.e., time. This has radically changed the scientific theories and thinking.

   Suppose this time dimension can move both ways – forward and backward. Further suppose, it moves backward and we are confronted with our forefathers. Will it not establish the existence of the fifth dimension of spirit? Will it not revolutionise the present scientific thinking and scientific theories?

8. Ancient Hindu scholars talked of three *Shariras* (Bodies). They are:

   (a) *Sthool-Sharir*, i.e., Gross organs of activity made up of main five basic elements – earth, water, fire, air and ether (*Akash*). The modern science has discovered more than 128 elements.

   (b) *Sukshma-Sharir*, i.e., Subtle body. The organs of the subtle body, i.e., wisdom are:

      (i) Five *Gyanandriyas* (Senses of Knowledge) – Nose, tongue, eyes, skin and ears.

      (ii) Five *Karmendriyas* (Senses of Action) – Anus, Sex, organ, hands, legs and speech.

      (iii) Five *Prana* (Breaths) -- Breathing, excretion,

digestion, blood circulation and nervous system.

(iv) *Manas* – It includes *Kama* (desires) and *Artha* (Actions).

(v) *Vivek* (Intellect) – This is different and superior to scientific temper.

(c) *Karan-Sharir*, i.e., Causal Body. Ancient Hindu *Rishis*, through experiments reached the inevitable conclusion that super-conscious is the cause of every thing. It is this super-conscious which creates nature, which, in its turn, creates flora, fauna, acquatic-animals, birds and human-beings. They further reached the conclusion that the soul, which is a tiny part of super-conscious, resides in the tiniest part of body known as *Karan-Sharir*. This is located some where in, what the modern psychologists call, unconscious mind.

The Hindu seers felt that western way of life is primarily based on the principle of exploitation because they want to conquer nature instead of working in co-operation with it. Urbanites, i.e., urban industries and urban population are exploiting the ruralites i.e., agriculture and rural people. In towns, more powerful people and larger industries are exploiting masses and also small scale industries. A country exploits another. The vicious circle goes and no form of economy – capitalist, socialist, mixed – can minimise this exploitation till the fundamental approach will remain the same. Similarly, no form of Government – Democratic, Fascist, Socialist – will be able to deliver the goods. A complete change in thinking and way of life is needed.

More About Sheaths

The five sheaths discovered by Hindu *Rishis-cum*-Social Scientists are the key points to achieve permanent happiness. It is, therefore, desirable to know more about them.

The five sheaths, as stated above are:

1. *Ann Mai Kosh* (Material Sheath).
2. *Pran Mai Kosh* (Vital or Energy Sheath).

3. *Mano Mai Kosh* (*Manas* Sheath).
4. *Buddhi Mai Kosh* (*Vivek* or Intellect Sheath).
5. *Anand Mai Kosh* (Permanent Happiness Sheath).

These sheaths are found in every man but are in different stages of development. They are interdependent too. A person should make conscious efforts to develop them in the desired quantities and mix them in an ideal proportion. When this is achieved, permanent happiness or bliss comes automatically.

A brief description of these sheaths is given below:

1. *Ann Mai Kosh* (Material Sheath)

In the evolution of the world, first came the matter in the form of Sun, Moon, Stars, Land, Mountains, Rivers, Ether etc. Modern science agrees with it and classifies them as solids, liquids and gases.

The Hindu seers discovered that matter is essential in many ways. First, it helps in making bodies of flora, fauna, amphibians, mammals, birds, human-beings; it makes every thing which has life. They discovered five basic elements of nature — earth, water, air, fire and ether. The permutations and combinations of these elements, they thought, produce all types of bodies. For example, water and stone (earth) produce moss. The modern scientists agree with them though they have discovered more than 128 elements todate.

Secondly, the seers called the body, *sthool-sharir* (gross organs). The ancient Hindu *Rishis* opined that matter is essential to keep the body get going. The plants, the animals, the birds and even the human bodies need food, water, air, shelter, etc., which are provided by the matter. So, the importance of the matter cannot be under-estimated.

The Indian *Rishis* believed that in spite of the importance of matter, over emphasis on matter is not good. It is not conducive to permanent happiness. The western scientists, philosophers, sociologists, economists, political scientists, nay all types of thinkers, do not subscribe to this thought. To them matter and happiness are directly related. However, a stage seems to have come when this concept is meeting a challenge in its own citadel. U.S.A. is an affluent society. It is at the peak of material prosperity but the people there are far from being happy. People have to induce sleep by taking pills. Dreaded diseases such as cancer, blood-pressure, heart ailements,

AIDS etc., are daily taking increasing toll. Love, faith, confidence and other noble values have already become casualties. Wife doubts her husband, and *vice versa* and parents have no time for children and so is the converse. Majority of crimes are committed by teen-agers. There is hardly any family life. Matter and more matter have made life miserable.

One thing more. The Indian seers seem to ask several questions. For example, if body is made of matter alone, how is it that every one has different colours and different sizes? How is that some one is born normal and healthy and some one, born with deformities? Why every child has some inborn traits inherited from his parents or even grand parents? These differences show that body is not made of matter alone. There is some thing more to it. These wise seers explain this phenomenon with the help of theory of genes and theory of vitality or energy. Westerners seem to agree. Dr. Hargovind Singh Khurana of U.S.A. got Nobel Prize for his work on genes. Several scientists, all over the world, are working on the inner vital organs of human body and discovering startling things which are confirming the views of ancient Indian *Rishis*.

2. *Pran Mai Kosh* (Vital Sheath)

Ancient Indian seers said that *Ann Mai Kosh* (Material Sheath), i.e., body, which they called *Sthool-Sharir* (gross organs) is made of matter. Inside this *Sthool-Sharir* (gross organs) is another body known as *Sukshma-Sharir* (subtle body). This *Sukshma-Sharir* (subtle body) is also made of matter but has five important organs:

(i) *Gyanandriyas* (Senses of Knowledge) – According to *Rishis*, they are five – eyes, nose, tongue, ears and skin.
(ii) *Karmendriyas* (Senses of Actions) – Seers said that they are also five – Anus, sex organ, hands, legs and speech.
(iii) *Prans* (Breaths) – They too are five – Breathing, excretion, digestion, blood circulation and nervous system.
(iv) *Manas* – This includes *Kama* (desires) and *Artha* (activities).
(v) *Vivek* (Intellect) – This is different and superior to scientific temper.

These five components of *Sukshma-Sharir* (subtle body) are the most important parts. They exist, as *Rishis* opined, in all living beings, including flora and fauna. The only difference is the stage of their development.

These five components are mechanical, i.e., functional. They function in a most scientific manner. The question arises, why do they function? What makes them work?

It is an admitted fact that none can move, not to say of functioning, without what Indian seers called *Prana* (Energy). The modern scientist may agree to call it energy.

According to physics, energy is of six types:

1. Sound
2. Heat
3. Light
4. Magnetism
5. Friction or mechanics
6. Electricity — hvdro or thermal or atomic.

The energy which makes the components of *Sukshma Sharir* function, appears to be of a different type of energy than these six types. For example, like electricity, it does not repulse or give shocks.

Ancient Indian seers gave a few characteristics of *Prana* energy:

(i) Energy can be associated with any body (or its part, or organ) but it has a separate existence and identity.
(ii) Energy can be transferred from one body (matter) to another.
(iii) One type of energy can be converted into another type of energy.

The modern scientists will readily agree that these characters of *Prana* energy are found in the six types of energies also which they know of. In spite of these similarities in character, which probably are due to the process by which energy is produced, there are a few dissimilarities.

Modern scientists have found out, though in an imperfect way, that the food which we eat, through digestion process, takes the form of blood. In Blood, which has fats, carbohydrates and proteins are burnt with the help of oxygen which is provided through respiration system. This gives energy which we find in cells. In this process carbon dioxide is also produced whose retention in the body is harmful. Hence, it is exhaled out into the atmosphere through respiratory system.

The Indian *Rishis* had laid great emphasis on the type of food which one should eat. Their insistence on *Satvik* food and *Satvik* habits may have some good relation with the quality and quantity of human energy produced, or energy requirements, or both. Similarly, the seers' insistence on deep breathing and *Pranayam*, a technique to control intake, retention and outtake of breath, which means taking oxygen and expelling carbon dioxide, might be influencing the generation of energy. Modern science is agreeing to the importance of *Pranayam*.

It is quite revealing and interesting that science is finding out these things today which ancient Indian *Rishis* were saying long back. A few illustrations will be sufficient.

(a) *Mind* is a very complicated part of the human body. Psychologists tell us that it has three parts – conscious, unconscious and subconscious. For the perfect functioning of this most complicated machine of human mind, energy is needed. This energy is generated in the mind itself. Where it is generated, is yet not known. The maximum which science has been able to do is to invent an instrument known as E.E.G. (Electro-Encepholo- Graphy) which can record the current of the mind and help in diagnosis of the disease.

(b) *Heart* is a type of pumping set which pumps blood in arteries. It regulates the flow of blood which is the life line of the whole body. Naturally, the heart must also be working with the help of energy. Recent researches have shown that in the right auricle of the heart, there is a tiny generation set which is known as Pace-Maker. The medical science has invented an instrument known as E.C.G. (Electro-Cardio-Graphy) to measure this energy and through it to diagnose heart disease.

(c) *Eyes* are just like a camera. The image of the object is formed on Retina, the innermost layer of the eye. This image is conveyed to the brain through optic nerves. The energy required for their perception and communication is readily provided partly by the cells of optic nerve, which have energy and partly by the brain. The energy of the eyes are measured by the instrument known as E.R.C. (Electro-Ratino-Graphy).

(d) Human body is full of cells. They have electric charge. Extensive studies in cytochemistry have established that all the cells have charged ions.

(e) Human body has also innumerable Genes. They are carriers of parental characters and they are inherited by subsequent generations. This phenomenon is termed as heredity. The whole of this activity including reproduction and inheritance of genes is accomplished with the help of energy. This energy is provided by cells.

(f) Harmones play an important role in the human body. The functions of harmones are known – they help in normal functioning of digestive system, circulatory system, excretory system, respiratory system etc., through chemical reactions. Normally, they function with the help of energy.

(g) Enzymes are also important for the human body. They also use energy.

Such instances can be multiplied.

Energy is also found in all living beings: may they be flora or fauna or birds. Here are some examples:

(i) Bats are able to know the location of objects with the help of their particular type of energy. Bats, zoologists tell us, emit magnetic rays to locate objects. Science has taken the idea from bats to develop radar system.

(ii) Electric Ray Fish produces mild electric current which is used to keep away her predators.

(iii) Sea Gulls fly to safe places before the sea storm comes. They are helped by energy currents of some type.

(iv) Termites keep the entrance of their nests in a particular direction with the help of some kind of energy, may be magnetic.

(v) Certain birds migrate from one place to another with the change of weather. They mostly travel by night. It is a settled opinion of the scientists that these birds receive direction with the help of magnetic energy.

(vi) Owls, Frogs, Snakes – all use special types of energy to locate their preys.

Examples can be multiplied.

Scientists of different fields are working in this new sphere in U.S.A., Italy, France, U.S.S.R. etc. The School of Nancy, the School of Charcot and the School of Mesmarist of U.S.A. have become well-known centres.

Hindu seers felt that the life currents in vitals move through subtle media of ethers.

The functions of this *Sukshma-Sharir* (subtle body) or functional body can be made more efficient if energy from which they are operated can be made more efficient, i.e., its frequency and voltage are regulated to desired specifications. How can it be done? Indian *Rishis* have given a full strategy starting with *Satvik* food to *Satvik* thoughts to *Satvik* actions and some exercises, various forms of which are called *Yoga*, *Dhyana*, *Sadhna* or *Tapa*.

3. *Mano Mai Kosh* (*Manas* Sheath)

Besides the *Sthool-Sharir* or *Ann Mai Kosh* (Material Sheath) and *Sukshma-Sharir* or *Pran Mai Kosh* (Vital Sheath) or functional body, there is another body which deals with emotions. This is called *Manas Kosh* or *Manas Sheath*.

This *Manas* Sheath is somewhere located in the mind. This is found in more developed form in a human being than in animals, birds or even plants. Western psychologists call it conscious mind.

Manas Sheath has two main parts or emotions:

(a) *Kama* – It means all desires including sex, wealth, fame, salvation (*Moksh*) etc.

(b) *Artha* – It means all activities – material and non-material, good or bad, social, political, religious, spiritual etc.

Kama or desires lead to *Artha* or activity. This combination is the key to human happiness or unhappiness. Till recently, it was a considered opinion that all physical ailments are due to imbalances or phlegm, wind or gas and bile, or seasonal changes, or infections etc. Hence different types of medical sciences – Allopathy, Homoeopathy, Unani or Aurvedic, tried to treat a sick person according to their own systems. However, recent researchers are assigning increasing responsibility to emotional factors. Fear, anger, hatred, envy, jealousy, feeling of insult, insecurity etc., are responsible for several physical problems which cannot be cured by any system of medical science. Headache, migrain, lunacy, nervousness, blood pressure, skin diseases, deformities in wombs, lethargy are some such diseases. On the other hand, good thoughts, respect, confidence, happiness, satisfaction, fearlessness, non-anger, love, auto-suggestion etc., help to improve health and impart younger looks. Hence, greater importance is now being given to psychological treatment.

Scientists have recently invented an instrument known as E.M.B. (Electrical Stimulation of Brain) which is used in brain-washing. The experiments on animals have been quite successful. Due to this instrument it became possible to make cats get afraid of rats.

Indian seers were of the confirmed opinion that man must try to control *Kama* (desires) and sublimate them. Then, he should also try to control his *Artha* (activities) for material advancement and direct most of them to help others. This gives self-satisfaction and inner happiness. This control, the seers opined, was a control of *Dharma* over *Kama* and *Artha*.

There is not one but several methodologies to achieve this desired goal. Development of concentration power through *Yoga* or *Bhakti* (devotion) or social service is one way. It is an accepted fact that concentration checks disintegration and concentrates powers so that they become more effective. It also improves efficiency. To develop concentration, one must develop determination.

It is here that the role of *Satvik* food, *Satvik* thought, *Satvik* actions, nay *Satvik* life becomes important.

4. *Buddhi Mai Kosh* (*Vivek* or Intellectual Sheath)

Ancient Hindu *Rishis*, who were great discoverers had found out that *Buddhi* has great powers. If it is properly awakened, it sharpens the memory which can remember the events of past lives and foresee future events; the ears can hear the past and future voices and eyes can see future. It can solve the most complicated problems in a minute and guide man to correctly differentiate between right and wrong, from the wider point of view. Till recently even the Indians doubted in the efficiency of the awakening of *Buddhi*.

Psychologist Freud has given three classifications of mind:

(i) The Conscious – It gives awareness of inner and/or outer environment.

(ii) The Subconscious – It pertains to mental activities of which the individual is not aware.

(iii) The Unconscious – That portion of the psyche which is a store house of memories which are not directly accessible to consciousness, but may be brought into consciousness.

The western psychologists know much about the conscious mind and many number of experiments have been made to know this part of mind. However, their knowledge till recently was almost negligible about the subconscious mind and still less about the unconscious one. Now they are trying to know about these two minds, specially the unconscious one and the findings are encouraging.

The Indian seers were of the opinion that the conscious mind is mainly concerned with *Ann Mai Kosh* (Material Sheath), *Pran Mai Kosh* (Vital Sheath) and *Mano Mai Kosh* (*Manas* Sheath) i.e., worldly things and individual gains. It helps in the development of an integrated personality through the interplay of Id, Ego and Super-ego. Here, acquired knowledge is confined to matter only. This science develops an analytical power to decide what is right and what is wrong for him or his material world. He takes a narrow view. This we call scientific knowledge and scientific temper.

The western psychologists are, at present, busy in knowing more about unconscious mind. It is now certain that this part of mind is not concerned with the blood circulation system, respiratory system, digestion system, or any other system concerned with the keeping of the body and mind functional. The medical science has now realised that in the head, there are some centres of magnetism, they are affected by the North Pole as well as South Pole. The hair when combed quickly, create a magnetic effect on the comb.

The psychologists feel that the unconscious mind has tremendous powers to know the past and to foresee the future, help in solving complicated problems and communicating with other worlds through various senses. This mind becomes more active when the conscious mind is resting, i.e., man is sleeping or when through selected methods, it is made active. A few instances, to prove its powers, can be cited:

(i) Cats are able to know that a building will be destroyed shortly. So, they change their abode well in time.
(ii) Goethe has written in his autobiography that one night, in his sleep, he felt that a severe earthquake had come in Sicily. After sometime, it proved to be correct.
(iii) J. Swift wrote in one of his books that *Mangal* Planet has two moons and the speed of one moon is double than that of the

other. This premonition proved to be true in 1877 when Naval Observatory of Washington verified it.

(iv) James Watt was worried on how to make round lead balls for guns. In sleep, he got a clue. He dreamt a storm, rain and round shells hitting his head. When the melted drops of lead were dropped in the water, the process of making round balls was invented.

(v) Iliyas was desperately trying to make a sewing machine. He had developed everything except a needle. One night he dreamt that horsemen, with spears, who had eyes in head, had come to kill him. This premonition gave him an idea of how to make a needle with an eye.

(vi) Neils Bohr, in his dream got an idea of the structure of Atom-nucleus and the rotating electrons.

(vii) Henry Fehar collected information of about 69 mathematicians. He reached the conclusion that 51 mathematicians got hints in their sleep on the basis of which they could complete their problems.

All these were the wonders of the partly active unconscious mind.

Awakening of the unconscious mind can change the basic character of a man, develop memory and other senses. Here are some illustrations.

(a) French Psychologist Prof. Delgoda, bypassing a current on Temple of a timid animal, Loo Loo, could make him a fearless animal.

(b) Canadian Dr. W.J. Penfield bypassing a current at a particular part of a man could develop his memory to the extent that he could remember even his past life which was stored in a part of his mind.

(c) Dr. J.V. Rhyne has discovered that without the means of communication, thoughts can travel and influence another man, even when he is at a distance. We sometimes get an idea that a particular visitor will arrive and it proves to be true. We sometimes feel bad and expect some bad news and they come.

Indian scriptures mention a number of persons who had succeeded in awakening this part of their mind, partly or fully, and therefore came to have enormous powers which we call supernatural, Savitri, Anusuia, Damyanti, Gandhari, Sudama, Karna, Kabir, Tulsi, Arvind, Gandhi are some such names. They were not seers who had renounced the world and withdrawn to forests.

How to awaken this part of mind? *Rishis*, past and present, have mentioned a number of methods. Some are:

(i) *Yoga* or *Tapa* or *Sadhna* which includes *Satvik* way of life.
(ii) Social service.
(iii) Developing determination and concentration powers through various methods.
(iv) Adopting human values, social values and spiritual values and go on increasing their quantities.

Obviously, this awakening of mind gives much wider conception of right and wrong than the scientific knowledge and equips a person to have more comprehensive judgement.

Rishis called this awakening of *Chetna* (consciousness) as the fifth dimension. One can imagine how much this fifth dimension of *Chetna* will change the picture of what we see, hear, do, like or dislike.

5. *Anand Mai Kosh* (Permanent Happiness Sheath)

Ancient Indian *Rishis*, who were social scientists, great discoverers and seers had discovered that life comes in a body because of soul; when this soul leaves the body, it stops functioning and the cells stop producing energy. This soul (*Atma*) and super-conscious (*Parmatma*) are one and the same; life, or soul or spirit, is indestructible; the soul leaves a body to enter into another body after a time-interval and this process goes on till it achieves *Moksha* (salvation) i.e., Soul (*Atma*) and super-conscious (*Parmatma*) become one.

Western thinkers, to begin with, did not accept the existence of spirit or soul. However, the recent researches have forced them to have a second thought. Some experiments deserve mention:

(a) Some Para-Psychologists, after mesmerising a person, recorded the occurrence of two or three or even a dozen earlier lives by taking him back to past lives. These readings have withstood the test of authenticity.
(b) Scientific researches are increasingly becoming introverts. For

example, study of Atom revealed that Atom is a miniature of solar system; Electrons, Protons and Neutrons form one Atom in which electrons rotate in a set pattern around the nucleus of an Atom which is formed of Protons and Neutrons; the splitting of the Atom releases tremendous energy etc. The questions may be asked; what makes the electrons move? From where does come the tremendous energy when Atom is splitted? The Western scientists have yet to offer an answer. The Hindu seers answer it with the help of their theory of soul and super-conscious, which they also sometimes call as light.

(c) Botanists have discovered that plants are not lifeless, they have life. Not only this. They can feel various sentiments and react to them. Efforts are being made to utilise them in protecting buildings and catching thieves.

These and many more researches have reduced the vehemenct antagonism of scientists to the existence of soul.

According to Hindu *Rishis*, *Anand* (permanent happiness) starts when the soul (*Atma*) starts realising that it is a part of the super-conscious (*Parmatma*) and begins to integrate with it. With every step towards integration, *Anand* goes on increasing.

This process of integration starts when there is a proper mixture of the four human sheaths, viz., matter, vitality, *Manas* and *Buddhi*, which are also interdependent. For example, matter is essential but too much importance of matter will be harmful for the development of vitality sheath. Then both matter and vital sheaths are important but *Kama* (desires) and *Artha* (activities) must be channellised towards the goal of permanent happiness. This can come only through the development of *Buddhi* (mind) specially its subconscious and unconscious parts. This alone can give powers for taking the correct decisions (not so the present scientific knowledge). When this is achieved, a stage is set when soul (*Atma*) starts realising the existence of super-conscious (*Parmatma*) and the process of integration starts. This opens the door of permanent happiness or *Anand*.

Thus, the Hindu view of evolution is wholestic and not confined merely to material development or evolution. Permanent happiness cannot be ensured when we confine ourselves only to a lower stage of development i.e., matter.

NOTES

1. Margaret Spahr, *Readings in Recent Political Philosophy*, 1949, pp. 272-73.
2. D.L. Holeman, *The Welfare State*, 1953, p. 14
3. T.W. Kent, *Welfare State*, 1950, p. 2.
4. T.H. Marshall, *Citizenship and Social Classes*, p. 11.
5. Edited by Herbert G. Marx Jr., *The Welfare State*, 1950, p. 10.
6. M. Bruce, *The Coming of Welfare State*, p. 2.
7. S.C. Shurmay, *Income and Economic Welfare*, p. 142.
8. D.L. Hobman, *The Welfare State*, 1953, p. 2.
9. V.V. Giri, *Labour Problems in Indian Industry*.
10. *Ibid*.
11. K.N. Subramanian, *Wages in India*.
12. *Ibid*.
13. V.V. Giri, *Labour Problems in India*.
14. *Ibid*.
15. Preamble of the Constitution of India.
16. K.C. Markandan, *Directive Principles in the Indian Constitution*, pp. 183-90.

2

ILLUSTRATION FROM INDIA'S PAST

After the foregone theoretical discussion of the various stages of development in the preceding chapter, a valid question may be posed and that is: Has India ever tried to put in practice this theoretical model? If so, with what results?

It may be stated without fear of contradiction that the last stage, namely *Anand Mai Kosh* (permanent happiness sheath) is attainable only by the individuals and not by the masses. However, the confirmed view was that one step forward on the path will promote human happiness. Hence, repeated efforts were made to take the masses move on this path of permanent happiness by giving matter a low priority and development of Human-values, Social-values and Spiritual-values top priority so that more and more people may be able to develop their *Buddhi* (intellect) control *Kama* (desires) and *Artha* (action) and enjoy happiness. It was this insistence on the development of integrated personality that has kept the Hindu civilisation alive even today when other old civilisations have become non-existent.

In very early Vedic period, a good number of saints, who lived in forests with their disciples, had reached the fifth stage of *Anand Mai Kosh* (permanent happiness). The atmosphere in their hermitages had become so pure that peacocks protected snakes from the sun-rays and tigers and sheep co-existed peacefully. They were the pace-setter for the masses.

In early Vedic period, *Varun* (3000 B.C.), known as the Lord of Waters, had not only himself acquired the fifth sheath but had succeeded in taking bulk of the people of the society towards that goal. He insisted on spiritual life and righteousness. He had developed techniques to locate wrong doers and punish them promptly if they did not correct themselves. Life was simple. Every one tried to imbibe more and more of Human-values, Social-values and Spiritual-values and matter was given the importance that it deserved.

In Vedic period itself, a change came when Indra took over command. He believed in the philosophy of material enjoyment. The whole society followed him. So, most of the people became unhappy. Envy, jealous, hatred, in-fights became the common scenes. Life became miserable.

Rama, the son of king Dasharath of Ayodhya, is known as an incarnation of Lord Vishnu, which was nothing but an insistence on the path of spirit, righteousness and discipline. He tried to remove the imbalances and re-establish the well tested way of life in which there was a proper admixture of matter, *Pran* (vitality), *Manas*, *Buddhi* and Spirit. He provided social, political and economic organisations conducive to attainment of the goal of *Anand* (permanent happiness). He admirably succeeded in taking society on the spiritual path. He took his message to the farthest corner of South India and in doing so had to punish those who refused to be corrected. Thus, he integrated North and South. Rama hardly preached. He insisted on righteous actions and strict discipline. His impact was so great that even today, he is remembered and people dream of *Rama Rajya* where happiness dominated.

In the period of Rama, several individuals had attained the fifth stage. King Janak, Vishwamitra, Valmiki and dozens of individuals had attained unimaginable super-powers and lived in the stage of *Anand* (permanent happiness).

Time rolled on and unfortunately another spell of change came when materialism tried to re-establish its supremacy. But this could not last long. Krishna came on the scene to check the rot. He again advocated the royal road to *Anand* (permanent happiness) by giving a low priority to matter, more vigorous development of *Pran* (vitality), control over *Kama* and *Artha* and development of unconscious mind so that soul (*Atma*) may meet *Parmatma* (super-conscious). He preached *Geeta*, organised people through dance, drama and flute and punished the wrong doers. He did not spare even serpent *Kali* and killed him by dancing on its hood. He got his own clan-men killed when they went on wrong path.

Soon after the war of *Mahabharata*, Yudhishthir became the king and society was taken on the path of righteousness (*Anand*).

Decadence again set in. Lord Mahavir and Lord Buddha (600 B.C.), who had achieved the stage of permanent happiness, tried to reform society and purge it of its evil practices. They preached the moral and ethical aspects of life, instead of spirit, which, for a time, eclipsed the corporate life of the vedic society. They preached heterodox views of society resulting in creating chaos, confusion and disbelief in the minds of a sizeable section of the community. Very soon there was a reaction against this crisis of faith. This shows how deep the *vedic* way of life and philosphy had taken roots in the Hindu society. However, it may be said to the credit of these two religions that they too did not unduly emphasise the importance of materialism.

In the Gupta period (A.D. 300-400) heroic efforts to go back to the *Vedic* values were made. But it was not that easy. So, the efforts of revival, unwillingly resulted in the birth of a new *Dharma*. It was neither fully *vedic* nor fully *Buddhist*. It was *Puranic Dharma*. (A.D. 300-400) which set up new models and absorbed even *Buddhism* which took refuge in *Mahayana*. But *Mahayana* was more or less the same *Puranic Dharma*. *Vedic* gods, who were formerly propitiated by *Yagya* now began to be worshipped through idol in the temples. It was believed that the formless gods had entered the idols and sanctified them.

Puranic religion gave us multiplicity of gods, goddesses, temples and monastries. They created a fresh problem by removing the focus on one single spirit and throwing up a number of hillocks undermining the supremacy of Mount Everest. The vision got blurred. But in *Puranic* way of life also, *Atma* remained the focal point and material persuits were considered not that much important.

Shankaracharya (A.D. 800) appeared on the scene and once again focused peoples' attention on *Advaita*, or non-dualism and succeeded in reconciling the diverse and seemingly conflicting sects in Hinduism. The royal road to spirit was broadened and properly lighted but this philosophic approach did not appeal to masses and the emphasis shifted to *Isht Devtas* (Individual Gods). This gave rise to a number of *Acharyas* like Ramanuja, Madhava and Vallabh, who preached worship of *Avtars* (Incarnation of God). Even in this multiplicity of ways of life, the goal appeared to be not the material prosperity but the advancement of the royal road to spirituality.

Menace of scourge of Jihadi invaders, who broke down temples and idols, gave rise to a very large number of saints who tried to reconcile the two concepts of a god without attributes (*Nirgun* and *Nirakar*) and a god with attributes (*Sagun* and *Sakar*). But this dispute of mode of worship or types of gods did not lose sight of the ultimate goal of *Anand*, the Permanent Happiness. However, with the impact of Muslim culture, the love for material prosperity started gaining momentum. Slavery and cruelty perpetuated by the state and life style of rulers acted as an impetus. But in this period also, several saints achieved the fourth or fifth stage and preached people the path of *Anand*.

With the advent of the Christian British, there was again heart searching among the Hindus and sects of reformers arose. Among them the main were Raja Ram Mohan Roy, Swami Dayanand, Ram Krishna Paramhans, Vivekananda, Lokmanya Tilak, Arvind Ghosh and Mahatma Gandhi. Most of these men had sufficiently progressed on the path of *Anand*. These reformers tried to fight against several social evils that had crept into the Hindu society but failed to arrest the ever increasing lust for the god-gold, which was restrengthened with the materialistic life style of Britishers coupled with an inferiority complex. The whole society, willy-nilly, was slipping away from the path of *Anand*.

Gandhi was a saint who thought that to talk about spirituality in a slave country where majority of people were not able to have even two square meals a day was like putting the cart before the horse. The first need was to get the country liberated from the foreign yoke. So, he threw himself heart and soul into the freedom movement. Gandhi said that those who consider politics to be incompatible with *Dharma* know neither *Dharma* nor politics. He tried to spiritualise politics. This is unfortunate that he did not live with us after freedom was achieved. However, a careful reading of his speeches, writings and conversations will show that he too, like seers, wanted material progress to the level it is able to satisfy the essential requirements of life and thereafter he insisted on spiritual advancement. To him Human values, Social values and Spiritual values were paramount. Truth, simplicity, non-violence, love, bread labour and God were the corner stones of his way of life.

After the death of Mahatma Gandhi, his heirs were too much influenced by the western philosophies of democracy, which is another name of capitalism, and socialism, which have even failed in the country of its origin. The result is hot pursuit of materialism which is another name of running away from *Anand*. The last forty years of planning prove that in spite of the so-called material advancement, not a single problem of the country could be solved and people have become less contented and more restless. Peace and happiness seem to be leaving us.

I
GOAL OF AN INDIVIDUAL : *ANAND*

A man has two dimensions. In vertical dimension, as per Hindu philosophy, he has a body (material), vitality, a *Manas, Buddhi* (Intellect) and spirit and at the horizontal plane, he has a family, a society which has several segments like religious, political, social, economic, legal etc., a nation and as such this nation too is a member of the Family of Nations. So, to be in the stage of *Anand*, there must be an ideal equilibrium – horizontal, vertical and also horizontal-vertical. Till this ultimate equilibrium is not achieved, efforts must be made to have a dynamic equilibrium.

Vertical Equilibrium

The Indian psychologists tell us that the human organism has five important parts – the body (matter), vigour or energy, the *manas*, *Buddhi* and the spirit.

These parts are arranged in an ascending order, the body being at the lowest and the *Atma* at the highest level. To make an individual to be really and permanently happy, i.e., in a state of *Anand*, there must be an equilibrium or balance among all these parts (vertical) and this balance should be dynamic.

The Body (Matter)

A person can never be happy if he is not physically fit. To be physically fit, one must be able to meet one's basic needs and have a balanced diet. Experience has shown that with increase in material acquisitions, the balanced diet becomes the first casualty. In such conditions one is prone to switch over to food that has more of taste value than nutrition value and generally becomes an addict to alcoholic drinks and drugs. So, neither starving conditions nor reckless dietary habits are conducive to good health. Besides this, a knowledge of what to eat and what not to, is essential.

To be healthy, besides a balanced diet and a proper living condition, one must also have clean and regular habits. Time has shown that with material prosperity these two things are the first likely to be neglected. For example, one starts sleeping late and waking late. One is not regular about one's food or rest or anything. Speed and more speed becomes the motto of life. Eventually health is ruined. So, it is essential to have clean and regular habits, i.e., healthy habits.

Regular exercise and physical fitness are directly related. By exercise, one does not necessarily mean hard exercises alone. It simply means that those exercises may be selected and done in that measure that may keep the body fit. With age and state of health the forms of exercises should change.

Medical facilities are also essential because human body is bound to catch one disease or the other. But medical treatment should be such as to cure the disease and not to suppress it or to create adverse side effects as modern allopathy seems often to do.

Modern science has recently discovered the importance of ecology. Hence, to keep the human body fit, it is essential that there should be the least pollution of different types – noise, water, air, atmosphere etc. To minimise it, we have started talking of ecological balances and pollution control. We have yet to realise that villages and small townships are better places to live in than big cities.

Besides meeting the body needs of a balanced diet healthy habits, proper exercises and medicines, man also needs two more things. First is shelter. He must have a place where he can live safely from the extreme weather hazards and wild animals. Secondly, he should have minimum clothing to protect himself against weather and also to make him presentable in society.

Vitality or Energy

Human body has thousands of cells which are full of energy. These cells are life for all the vital functional parts of the human body like heart, mind, lungs, digestive system etc. To keep the body in good health, it is essential that the quality and quantity of the energy or vitality of these cells should be improved so that the functional organs of the body are able to perform their duty better. The energy or vitality of these cells mainly comes from two sources – food that we eat and the oxygen that we inhale. The ancient Hindu seers, therefore, attached great importance to a simple but healthy living which they called, in their wisdom, *Satvik Jeewan*. Modern science has yet to make experiments to deny or confirm the truth of this *Satvik Jeewan*, which encompasses in itself good food, proper exercise, control of senses, good thoughts, good reading habits, good company and good actions. The whole life is to be made orderly.

The Manas

Western scholars do not think that *Manas* has a separate identity from mind. However, the Indian psychologists consider it as an important constituent, independent of the mind. It has two parts – *Kama* (Desires) and *Artha* (Actions). Both these organs may tempt man in thoughtless multiplication of desires and activities. Indian psychologists feel that *Manas* is like a restless bird, the more it gets, the more it wants, regardless of what is good and what is bad, since it does not have that discerning faculty. So, it is essential to keep it under control and direct it towards healthy channels. If it is not kept under a proper check, it will certainly mislead the conscious mind and body to wrong channels and bring more harm than good. How *Manas* can be kept under control and applied to useful things is a different issue.

The Mind

The saying is that 'a healthy mind dwells in a healthy body'. But to think that no attention should be paid to develop the mind and the whole focus should be on the development of human body alone is a fallacy. Development of mind is equally important.[1] Conscious mind can be developed through education, formal and informal. However, the ancient Indian scholars tell us that there is a difference in academic excellence (*Gyan*) and rational outlook (*Vivek*). One may be a giant as far as academic achievements are concerned but one may be a dwarf in the worldly affairs. So, mind should be developed on right lines so that it may be able to differentiate between right and wrong in a whole time perspective.

Psychologists opine that the mind has three parts – conscious, subconscious and unconscious. It is the development of the conscious mind alone that the Western educationists have been trying to develop, ignoring the other two parts. In contrast, the Indian seers attached greater importance to the development of the other two parts. The modern science has now also started realising that the subconscious and unconscious parts of mind are capable of doing wonders. However, they are still not sure of the methods by which these two parts of the mind can be awakened. The Hindu *Rishis*, it appears, had developed certain techniques to awaken them. They prescribe *Yoga* or *Tap* or imbibing more and more of Human values, Social values and Spiritual values or even doing real good social service. These methods help in the awakening of the subconscious and unconscious parts of the mind and integrate and develop the human personality. This gives a better faculty of judgement.

The Soul

Modern science is not that vehement in denying the existence of Soul (*Atma*). However, it has yet no opinion about super-conscious (*Parmatma*). The Hindu seers not only believed in the existence of Soul and Super-conscious but had demonstrated the powers of this Soul-force. They also believed that it is possible to attain ***Moksha***. Even in the twentieth century, India produced a saint of Arvind's stature who had immense super-natural powers.

Vertical equilibrium or integration means that man must make conscious efforts to have a healthy body, healthy cells, control *Kama* (Desires) and *Artha* (Actions), develop conscious mind and awaken subconscious and unconscious mind and make sincere efforts to keep spirit in meeting the super-conscious i.e., *Moksha*. When man succeeds in awakening of all the three parts of mind he enters the sphere of *Anand* (Permanent Happiness).

II
HORIZONTAL INTEGRATION

Man is called a social animal. He cannot live in isolation. He first makes a family and thereafter a society. This society develops several segments like religious, social, political, economic, legal, etc. The Nation follows soon after. And with the rapid means of transportation, the world becomes narrow and it becomes essential to have a Family of Nations. This horizontal expansion of an individual – family, society with different segments, nations and world must have common goals and common basic governing principles. What could they be?

The goal of a man's life, as discussed earlier, is *Anand*

(Permanent Happiness). So, the goal of a family, a society, a Nation and the world can also be nothing else except *Anand*, i.e., Happiness. This happiness can come only through love. Love and self-sacrifice seem to be interchangeable terms.

The Family

In ancient India, joint family was the rule rather than an exception. This family was a workshop to produce a quality-oriented man who believed in simple living and high thinking. He aspired to have an integrated, balanced and developed personality. He was given an atmosphere in which he imbibed, in a natural way, Human values, Social values and Spiritual values. Not only this. The family acted as a natural social insurance against ill-health, accident, death, old-age etc.

In this family, elders loved youngers and readily made self-sacrifices for their happiness. On the other hand, youngers respected their elders and had an immense faith in them. Discipline was insisted upon. Ill-will, jealousy, hatred, mutual suspicion etc., had no place in life.

Thus family atmosphere taught to love even enemies, animals, plants and the world as a whole.

The westerners might not be able to understand or appreciate this mighty Indian institution of family where parents and other elders had all the time for the children and in return children never considered their parents as a burden. The relationship between daughter-in-law and mother-in-law was sweet. Even today, this family is keeping the Indian society intact though deficiencies and deformities have crept in and self-interest has started raising its ugly head.

The Society

A society is a functional operative unit of a definite territory, normally called a state. It is a group of organised individuals or families. It works as a whole. The interests of each of their component members or component units are subordinated to those of the entire group. A criminal is destroyed or segregated because he is a disturbing factor. Men go to war and get killed so that society may be protected and enriched. In exchange of this curbing of individual freedom, society is expected to shape an individual properly and encourage him to play his role in terms of his potentialities and achievements. Society also provides the individuals with basic security, comfort, education, equipment, opportunity etc. It shapes his desires, actions, thoughts, ideals etc. It guides him in human relationship, which exists between different members of a family and also outside family.

Hindu seers insisted that the individual is very important and he should have maximum freedom to develop his potentialities but they also insisted that social norms cannot and shall not be normally by-passed by an individual. They evolved a unique method to make them complementary and supplementary to each other. This unity of thought and action was achieved by having common goals, common fundamental guiding principles and a unique strategy.

The goal of an individual was *Anand* (Permanent Happiness). The goal of the society was also to maximise happiness of all its members. The duty of the society was to help the individuals to maximise their happiness as per their genes, nature, potentialities and opportunities. Society tried to provide right directions and maximum opportunities to the individuals.

The ancient Hindu social-scientists insisted, on the basis of long experience:

(i) That material prosperity and individual or group happiness march together for two or three steps only and thereafter part company. So, matter should not be given undue importance. Its place should be given to *Anand* (Permanent Happiness).

(ii) That the recognition of a man should not be on the basis of his material prosperity or academic achievement but on the basis of Human values, Social values and Spiritual values that he has imbibed. The higher a man treads on the path of righteousness, viz., Truth, Love, Non-violence, Purity, Patience, Forgiveness, Non-stealing, Self-control, Control of *Kama* and *Artha*, Non-anger, Knowledge of Soul (Faith in super-conscious), Patriotism, Discipline etc., the more he should be respected. It is for this reason that these seers who had renounced the world i.e. family and material persuits and started devoting all their time and energy to self-discipline and social service were given the highest respect by the society. Their word was law and even a king, the symbol of material prosperity and state authority, could not venture to defy them.

(iii) That the *Kama* (Desires) and *Artha* (Activities) should be subordinated to *Dharma*, which was nothing but a code of conduct based on Righteousness leading to *Moksha*, i.e. salvation from the cycle of birth and death.

(iv) That soul and super-conscious are one, that soul never dies, that soul leaves a body to take birth in another body and so on. On the basis of this, the logical inference was: love all human beings, nay even birds, animals, plants etc., who have a soul.

The Hindu *Rishis* had developed several strategies for the society by which it helped in motivating people to the righteous path of *Anand*. One of the important strategies was of *Ashram-Vyavastha*. In *Ashram-Vyavastha*, the life span was divided into four equal parts. The first part was known as *Brahamcharya* in which every child was compulsorily sent to a school to learn reading and writing. Together with this formal education, he was taught the meaning of Human values, Social values and Spiritual values and also given practical lessons in imbibing these values. In this *Ashram* he was taught, through logic, the cardinal truths about Hindu way of life, such as matter is not important, soul and super-conscious are only important; Soul never dies, it only changes bodies; one has control over means and not ends; one has to, as per Newton's Law, bear the consequences of every act individually. What is *Anand* and how to achieve it, the ultimate goal of life should be *Moksha* (a release from the pangs of the cycle of birth and death etc.) Love is the key to this salvation etc.

In the second part of life called *Grahasth*, the individual was asked to marry, have a family, help in production of material things and lead a life as prescribed by the society. This gave him the opportunity to test the validity of the cardinal principles which were taught to him as a student. This self-experience strengthened the conviction in the theoretical knowledge and confirmed its utility and practicability.

The third state of *Vanprasth* required that elders should start leaving family responsibilities and pass them on to the younger generation. They should increasingly devote themselves to self-development and social service. This will minimise tensions caused by generation gap.

The fourth and the last stage was of *Sanyas*. Here the physical strength becomes minimum. So, one was expected to leave even social service and devote all the time and energy to self-development.

This goal, fundamental principle and strategy of the society kept the society united and helped the individuals to develop their integrated and balanced personality towards the goal of *Anand*.

This society also gave a political, economic and cultural set-up, which helped in the promotion of the aim of maximum happiness, i.e. *Anand*.

A. *The State*

The Hindu *Rishis* assigned a very limited role to a state. The state or the ruler was expected to be an expert of the Hindu *Dharma* i.e. to know what was the goal of the society and what were the basic fundamentals of life (To be *Dharmagya*). He was also expected to practise this *Dharma* in his own life (To be *Dharmatma*). And to ensure that the subjects follow the path of *Dharma* (To be *Dharmapalak*). Defence, Law and Order, Justice and other functions of the present day state were assigned a comparatively low priority.

The Hindu seers saw to it that the country is divided into innumerable *Jan-pads* (District States in the modern terminology). The idea behind it seems to have been that every *Jan-pad* should be a viable unit but its resources and powers may not be big enough to enable the ruler, to exploit masses.

The Hindu seers made the institution of the ruler normally hereditary. They believed in the theory of genes and therefore thought that it will normally help in making a noble and capable man as a ruler. The political set-up was so designed as to check the evils of the present day democracy and at the same time to curb the freedom and powers of the ruler. Besides the team of Ministers, incharge of various departments, in which King did not usually interfere, there was a saint-Guru, called *Raja-Purohit*. The verdict of this saint-Guru was final. The King could not afford to disobey him because he commanded the respect of the entire society. This ruler could even be removed by the people if he became self-centred.

This philosophy of a state and the set-up of the state helped the masses in developing their integrated and balanced personality on the path of *Anand*.

B. *The Economic Life*

In ancient India, matter was considered essential, first in forming a body and thereafter maintaining it. But thereafter it's role ended. So, the economic life – production, consumption, exchange etc., as we call it now, had low priority. The aim was not, in the modern terminology, "a higher standard of living", which actually in the Gandhian sense, is a "complex standard of life". It does not seem to be quality but quantity oriented. So, the emphasis was on a few things but of a higher quality which may help in the promotion of *Anand*.

The emphasis was on simple living and self-sufficiency. The village was the primary unit of production, both of agricultural and industrial goods and also of consumption. Towns were few. They were either a seat of power or pilgrimage or trade. This decentralisation of economic life, automatically minimised the powers of exploitation and left sufficient energy and time for more useful works, both social and personal.

C. *The Cultural Life*

The cultural life was so designed as on one side it will satisfy the natural urges of people and on the other hand sublimate them. The whole cultural life was to help people in the onward movement towards *Anand*.

Music, dance, drama and other forms of fine arts were developed to give enjoyment. But with enjoyment, the silent purpose was to tune people with the rhythm of nature. It revealed to people the beauties of nature. It made them lovers of nature. And nature is pure, it is love, it is truth, it is benefector of people, it is rhythm and it is discipline. All this promotes permanent happiness.

Social functions and National functions were designed, with several purposes. They reminded of the stories which showed the victory of virtue over evil, good over bad. They gave the lesson of patriotism and discipline. They strengthened the basic concepts of the Hindu way of life.

Thus, in brief, the whole society was geared up to promote *Anand*.

The World

The Indian seers aimed at maximising *Anand* of every individual of the society. It built up its edifice on the foundation stone of love of soul and super-conscious and self-sacrifice. It preached that life or soul in everyone, irrespective of country, sex, colour, religion etc. is connected with super-conscious and so is the same. Thus, love got universalised. These seers announced that the whole word is a family (*Vasudhaiv Kutumbkam*). It implied that all the people of the world should unite to achieve more and more of *Anand*.

When the aim of an individual, a society and the world as a whole will be to achieve **permanent happiness** through love and self-sacrifice, **through Human values,** Social values and Spiritual values, then **automatically in this new world,** there will be no place for narrow selfishness, **exploitation,** hatred, envy, jealousy, imperialism, wars, colour prejudices etc.

Horizontal equilibrium or integration means that an individual, a family, a society with its different segments and the world – all must have a common goal to maximise *Anand*. The ancient Hindu model shows that it is possible and desirable. This is possible if the Human values, Social values and Spiritual values become the basis of integration. Sacrifice of the individual for the sake of family, sacrifice of the family for the sake of the group, sacrifice of the group for the sake of the nation and sacrifice of the nation for the sake of the world and sacrifice of the world for the soul and super-conscious should be the motto. All these are concentric circles. The narrower circle sacrifices for the sake of the bigger or broader circle. This is the only royal path to *Anand*.

III
GROWTH AND *ANAND*

Economics started its journey from the study of wealth, moved on to welfare and from welfare to choice making. Now it is concentrating on growth, as it is considered as an important part of welfare. But what is growth? How does it affect an individual, a society and the world at large? The economist does not worry much about the two ends – individual and the world and is mainly lost in the development of society and that too, only its material aspect.

The wisemen of ancient India never lost sight of any of the three – individual, society and the world. They believed that all the three are equally important and should grow together. They also realised that growth should be in promoting permanent happiness, which, in their wisdom, they called *Anand*. They insisted that increase in material prosperity should not be the goal as it is only a tiny segment of human life. The other segments – political, social and religious — are equally important, if not more.

With this background, the aim of Economics, nay, the whole life, may be summed up in the following words:

Economics in close collaboration with other segments of life, and with maximum freedom, tries to develop life in such a way (based on self-realisation) that there is maximum dynamic vertical integration of a man and also horizontal integration with various segments of life and all progress towards *Anand*, i.e. none lives in either misery or excessive luxury (in economic terms) and all have the opportunities of optimum development of their respective personalities in an integrated and balanced way.

Perfection is defined in Hindu Philosophy as an integration of *Sat*, *Chit* and *Anand*. *Sat* is material existence. *Chit* is consciousness and *Anand* is the supreme goal or enactment of the soul and the super-soul.

NOTE

1. Psychologist Tichner tells us that mind has two parts — one depends on past experiences and the other on present experiences. On the other hand, psychologist Freud divides the mind on the basis of actions – conscious, subconscious and unconscious.

3

SOME IMPORTANT VALUES

Value and Principle or Theory are interchangeable words.

Indian seers, for the betterment of man and his society, evolved a number of values or principles. These values are classified under three categories: Human values for individual's upliftment, Social values to promote social goal and Spiritual values to help individual to achieve the highest goal of life. But this classification does not mean rigid compartmentalisation. In fact one helps the other.

Indian seers clearly saw that matter is destructible while soul is permanent. But they also realised that matter is essential because the body is made of matter and to maintain this body till it lasts, matter is needed. They also saw that man is a social being, he cannot live by himself. Hence, the ancient social scientists, known as *Rishis,* evolved values which while helping the individual in his advancement on the path of *Moksha*, i.e. salvation from the pangs of birth and death, will also help in the better functioning of the society. They also invented these values which primarily will help society in improving qualitatively but, at the same time, contribute the betterment of an individual. So, individual, society and salvation were interlinked while formulating these values. Matter was given a secondary importance and the soul, the highest.

The total number of these values vary from time to time. For example, *Manu*, the great law-giver, has given ten values while defining Hindu Dharma. In *Geeta, Bhagwan* Krishna gives about 20 values and at other places the number goes up to two dozen. This shows that values can be added, subtracted, moulded and emphasis changed as per need of time, place and society or individual. There is no rigidity or finality about them. For example, Lord Buddha and Lord Mahavir gave a very high priority to the value of non-violence and tried to make individual or human value a social value. Mahatma Gandhi made this value a tool for winning political freedom. Again, no specific mention is found of the value of self-sacrifice in the earlier literature but Lord Rama seems to invent it and use it as a social value. When step-mother queen Kaikai manipulated fourteen years exile for Rama, who was going to be enthroned the next day, and kingdom to her own son, Bharat, the whole atmosphere got surcharged. Anger and violence should have been a natural corollary. But Rama used the new technique of self-sacrifice. He praised his step-mother and gladly agreed to make the supreme self-sacrifice. Rama's behaviour gave a surprise to all, Bharat rebuked his mother, who started looking pigmy in her own eyes, and refused to accept the throne. One sacrifice encouraged the other sacrifice, and in the process both the brothers became immortal. This individual self-sacrifice, while it uplifts the moral fibre of an individual, it also inspired the whole society to follow suit. Life becomes pleasant and happier.

Indian seers attached too much importance to these values. Actually, Hindu *Dharma* is nothing except a bundle of these values – human values, social values and spiritual values. Hence, these seers advised people to subordinate their desires and actions to *Dharma*, i.e. these values. According to them this was a sure path to happiness and *Anand.* Following the dicta of these values will not create a paradox which todays Western economists and political scientists face, viz., individual welfare and social welfare do not go together.

It will be better to discuss here a few values or principles. *Rishi* Manu, who codified several aspects of Hindu way of life, has mentioned ten values. These values integrate the personality of a man and at the same time uplift the society.

Manu says:

धृतिः क्षमा दमोद्रस्तेयं शौचमिन्द्रियनिग्रहः ।
धीः विद्या सत्यमक्रोघो दशकं धर्म लक्षणम् ।।

– (*Manu* : 6.92)

[i.e., *Dharma* has ten characteristics — patience, forgiveness, control of *Manas,* non-stealing, purity, self-control, education, knowledge of soul, truth, and non-anger.]

Right from the days of *Vedas,* through *Puranas, Smritis* etc., down to Gandhi, any number of saints and scholars have written on these ten values and probably there is very little left which can be added. Westerners, on their own, have also written on some of these qualities. So, the importance of these values is not in dispute. The real need of today is to remind the modern man of the meaning of these ten values in simple but logical way and impress upon him to imbibe them to save himself and the world. A more important thing is to tell an average man how to cultivate these ten values. Psychologists and philosophers have a role there.

The considered opinion of the writer of these lines is that these ten values have no overtones of Hindu *Dharma* and so cannot and should not be branded as communal. Further, cultivation of these ten values by themselves should solve the problem of national integration in India.

One will realise, after reading these ten values, that the well known vices like anger, fear, envy, hatred, ill-will, jealousy. violence, cruelty, theft, exploitation, uneven distribution of income etc. will automatically give way when these values or virtues are imbibed by an individual and a society.

A brief narration of these ten values first and thereafter some others is attempted below :

I
SHAUCH (Purity)

Purity is a human value which is the easiest to practise.

Indian seers insisted on the cleanliness of the body, the house, the clothes, the water, the food, the surroundings, the atmosphere, and even the thought and action. Since values and *Dharma* were interchangeable terms, it became the dictate of the *Dharma* to get up early in the morning. Soon after getting up, the first duty was to go to toilet, wash the eyes, brush the teeth and clean the mouth. Thereafter, the next duty was to role the bed, sweep and dust all the rooms and wash with water those places like kitchen, bathroom, toilet etc. which are potential breeders of mosquitoes, flies and other pests. The third duty was to take physical exercise. And the next duty was to take bath and wash all wears. All this was done under the garb of *Dharma* or Human value — a perfect lesson in personal hygiene which includes fitness also.

Drinking water can be a carrier of diseases. So, *Rishis* suggested techniques, again under the garb of *Dharma,* to make water pure.

They invented cheap earthen pot, which has porousity, for storage of drinking water. Modern science agrees that the earthen pot is killer of pests. And it was suggested to put a few leaves of *Tulsi* which is now accepted as a medicinal plant.

Indian seers divided food under three categories – *Satvik*, *Rajsik* and *Tamsik* and insisted that mainly *Satvik* food should be taken as it is health giving. This classification, one can venture to say, was very scientific as it was based on many factors such as purity, health or energy giving contents etc. These seers opined that there is a very close relationship between food, thought and action — a sphere where western researchers have yet to make a beginning.

The concept of purity and the present day adulteration do not go together.

The *Rishis* gave greatest importance to the purity of the atmosphere. They were convinced that health and atmosphere have direct relationship. So, under the name of *Dharma,* they succeeded in persuading the people to grow trees and plant *Tulsi* in the compound and daily water it. Modern science admits that *Tulsi* is a medicinal plant and trees are purifiers of the atmosphere. *Yagya* was considered another method to purify the atmosphere. The modern science is yet to issue a certificate to it though it has recently partially accepted its capacities to invoke rains.[1] Nevertheless modern scientists are busy these days with their new found environmental studies which Indian seers had studied long back.

Indian seers gave the greatest importance to the internal purity, i.e. purity of thought, action and behaviour. They connected it, on one side with food habits and living habits and on the other with reading and doing habits. Today none will dispute the adverse effect on thought, action, behaviour and health of cinema, TV and pornographic literature.

Thus, purity was a very important human value for keeping body and mind healthy.

Western way of life is based on the love of matter. Hence, to begin with, there was very little consciousness of cleanliness or purity. But slowly the concept is developing and Western people are taking to it in a big way. It was only recently that they realised the importance of purity of environment. However, even now, they have not been able to classify eatables and to understand the importance of pure thoughts and actions.[2]

II
ASTEYA (Non-stealing)

Asteya, i.e. non-stealing is a social value.

This value of *Asteya*, (Non-stealing) has its roots in the basic philosophy of Hindu *Dharma* i.e. matter is destructible while soul is permanent. But the seers had also the clear vision that matter is also essential to keep the body healthy and get going. So efforts were made not to abolish matter but to reduce attachment to it. This basic philosophy was strengthened with the social needs which required non-stealing to run the society smoothly. Hence, any number of stories were coined to show the evils of theft and advantages of being honest. Efforts were made to make honesty or non-stealing a second nature. Today, the Western societies also want people not to steal but the goal is achieved not through trying to change the human nature but by fear of punishment. In Islam, this fear is almost terrifying. Hands or legs can be chopped-off or one can even be killed by throwing stones at him. The difference between the two approaches makes a very great difference. In one, the results are not permanent and in the other they are not only permanent but they come easily also.

Indian *Rishis* did not stop at non-stealing. They went a step further. They insisted that even the lost things when picked up should be returned to its real owner *via* state or *Panchayat*. The Western states also expect a similar behaviour from their citizens.

A more far-reaching interpretation was given to this value of non-stealing. Followers of Hindu *Dharma* were told that since material things are not lasting, therefore, the mentality to hoard them beyond a reasonable limit is also a type of theft. The logic was obvious. The more one has, when resources are limited, less the others will be left with. This will encourage, in modern terminology, uneven distribution of wealth leading to further exploitation. When the thinkers and governments of the West are keen to reduce these inequalities with the help of either fiscal and monetary policies or through abolition of private property, the ancient Indian *Rishis* tried to strike at the very root of the mentality of hoarding. It is apparent that where the Westerners are failing, the Indians succeeded admirably. The reason is apparent. When one wants to give matter predominance, the other wants to abolish its importance.

The concept of non-stealing was also extended to the realm of ideas. The Westerners also agree with it and so the copyright laws have been made. But here too, the difference is clear. In one, efforts are made to check the evil with the help of laws and fear and in the other, efforts are made to change the very nature of man with the help of *Dharma*, psychology, etc.

III
DHI (Knowledge confined to matter, i.e. Education)

Dhi, or knowledge of matter or education is a human value.

Indian *Rishis* divided knowledge into two groups :

(a) Knowledge of material sciences including various subjects of arts, fine arts, commerce, science, law, education etc. The Westerners call it education.
(b) Knowledge about soul, which Westerners have now started realising.

The knowledge of the first type i.e., *Dhi*, in modern terminology, is education. Modern psychologists think that the mind has three parts — the conscious, subconscious and unconscious. *Dhi* or education helps in awakening the conscious mind only.

Indian *Rishis* thought that mental development through *Dhi* is essential. It is also essential because it helps in producing material goods which are so essential for life. But its real importance lies in that it is a gateway to the real knowledge, which they called *Vidya*, the spiritual knowledge. Modern science, it appears, is now entering this realm of knowledge.

Modern science is nothing but a search for truth, an attempt to establish relationship between cause and effect. Till recently scientists were mainly involved in studying the external aspects of things but now they have started going introvert. The result is that they are searching new truths and discarding old laws. Newton's Law of Gravitation has been replaced by Eistein's Law of Relativity. Similarly, upto sometime back it was said that matter is indestructible and the smallest particle is atom. Now the scientists tell us that an atom consists of electrons, protons and neutrons; a splitting of an atom generates tremendous energy which might be used for constructive or destructive purposes; and an atom is a miniature solar system. The ancient Indian *Rishis* said that atom has also life (life and light are synonyms) and matter is destructible while life or soul is permanent. Can this truth be denied today in the light of new scientific discoveries? Again, there was a common belief that plants have no life. Sir Jagdish Chandra Bose was the first scientist who tried to make a deeper study. He came out with the startling revelation that there does exist life in plants. And now Western scientists are going further deeper. For example, Backster has proved that plants can think, act and even communicate. Scientist Vogel established that plants can anticipate and react. The experiments are afoot to use plants to catch thieves.

These few examples will show that *Dhi* i.e. education in the modern sense is essential to scientifically know the second category of knowledge, i.e. knowledge about soul and also to produce material goods without which life will become difficult.

It will be pertinent to point out here that in the realm of knowledge, *Dhi* is at the lowest ebb and *Vidya*, i.e. knowledge of soul is at the highest. In between the two is *Vivek* in which the subconscious and unconscious minds get awakened. This is a higher stage of scientific knowledge which is limited to the awakening of the conscious mind only.

IV
VIDYA (Knowledge of Soul)

To know about soul and to master it, is *Vidya*.

Indian seers talk of *Manas*, which is a source of desires and actions. *Buddhi* controls *Manas* and helps in achieving *Anand*. The modern psychologists have now started talking of three parts of mind — conscious, subconscious and unconscious. They know quite something about the conscious mind but are almost ignorant of the other two parts, i.e. the subconscious and unconscious. They, however, agree that these two parts of mind are almost like an iceberg and have great potentialities. Indian seers, it appears, had lot of knowledge of these two parts of mind and they had also learnt the art of awakening these two. Their considered opinion was that the soul or *Atma* resides somewhere in this unconscious mind. To reach it, one has first to handle the conscious mind i.e. control it and thereafter awaken the other two parts of mind which will first give *Vivek*, which is something higher than intellect or scientific temper and secondly pave the way to realise and reach *Atma*, the soul, the source of *Anand*.

To know about soul is *Vidya.*

It is a human value and also a spiritual value. But this value has far reaching effects on social life.

Indian philosophers have given six types of philosophies, known as *Darshan.* They are *Sankhya, Yoga, Nyaya, Vaishshik, Mimansa* and *Vedant.* All of them have dealt with soul but the most illuminating and vivid discussion on soul is found in *Vedant.*

Indian *Rishis* had discovered several things about soul such as soul is a reflection or miniature of all powerful supernatural phenomenon which we call Almighty God; the difference in a living and a dead body is that one has a soul and the other none; soul never dies, it only changes bodies; the time interval between leaving a body and entering into another may be short or long; and can even be freed from the pains of repeated births through noble deeds; freeing the soul is called attaining *Moksha* i.e. becoming one with the Almighty like a drop meeting the ocean and losing one's identity etc.

Westerners till recently did not attach much importance to soul and they felt that there is no relationship between education and spirituality. But as they are moving to new spheres of knowledge and their researches are taking them more and more to the introvert aspects, they have stopped denying the existence of soul and the different ideas about soul given by the Indian seers. They are even prepared to accept some sort of relationship between education, training and soul.

Some scientists, independently, made some experiments in UK and USSR. They selected a few models and hypnotised them. They, instead of taking them forward, took them backward and asked questions about their previous lives. The recorded statements were found to be correct. This forced them to believe in the Hindu theory that soul is indestructible, it is permanent and it repeatedly takes birth in different bodies.

V

SATYA (Truth)

Satya is a social value. A society of liars can never progress.

Saints, philosophers and sociologists of different countries, belonging to different religions and different times have pleaded for truth. But what is this truth?

Indian *Rishis* felt that unanimism between seeing, thinking, hearing, talking and acting is truth. To say what one thinks or sees or listens is truth. To do what one says, or thinks is truth. Gandhi, in his own inimitable style said:, "Generally speaking, observing the law of truth is merely understood to mean that we must speak the truth. But we in the *Ashram* understand the word *Satya* or truth in a much wider sense. There should be truth in thought, truth in speech and truth in action."

Truth is of two types — Absolute (i.e. Fundamental) and Relative. Absolute truth is one which does not change with time and place. This is often related to natural phenomena. The relative truth is one which changes with time and place. Gandhi said, "What may appear as truth to one person will often appear as untruth to another person." Newton propounded the Law of Gravitation. To him it appeared to be truth. Einstein found out that instead of Law of Gravitation, the truth is the Theory of Relativity. The example of six blind people standing around an elephant and describing him was a relative truth. They all were speaking the truth but the elephant was much more than what they individually were feeling and telling.

Indian *Rishis* have tried various socio-psychological techniques to convince people of the utility of truth. People were made conscious of the evil effects of being a liar because it can give only very short term benefits. Even techniques were developed which helped a person to imbibe the habit of truth.

One will have to accept that Western societies are, by and large, believers in truth. Probably, their opulence and also the social structure, which is individualistic, do not require them to hide things and so to resort to untruth.

VI

INDRIA-NIGRAH (Self-control or *Brahamcharya*)

Indria-Nigrah is a social value. Normally, a loose person is not permitted inside the house.

There are five senses — ear, nose, eyes, tongue and organ. To have a control over them is, *Brahamcharya.* Gandhi while explaining the meaning, said:

". . . Let us remember the root meaning of *Brahamcharya. Brahamcharya* means *charya* or course of conduct adopted to the search of *Braham* or truth. From this etymological meaning arises the special meaning, *viz.* control of all senses. We must forget the incomplete definition which restricts itself to the sexual aspect only."

Gandhi, giving the action strategy said:

"Control of the Palate is the first essential in the observance of the vow. I found that complete control of the palate made the observance very easy, and so I now pursue dietic experiments not merely from the vegetarian's but also from the *Brahamcharya's* point of view. As a result of these experiments I saw that the *Brahmachari's* food should be limited, simple, spiceless and, if possible, uncooked."

Again,

"A *Brahmachari* must need control his palate. He must eat to live and not for enjoyment. He must see only clean things and close his eyes before anything unclean. A *Brahmachari* will likewise hear nothing obscene or unclean, smell no strong, stimulating things. . . . The third step is to have clean companions — clean friends and clean books . . . the last and not the least is prayer."

As is apparent this value of self-control is the outcome of the basic philosophy that matter is not important and the soul and its salvation is important. Westerners believe in matter and they have no love for soul. Hence, they do not believe in spiritualism. Their philosophy is materialistic – eat, drink and be merry. Obviously, in this philosophy, self-control or *Indria-Nigrah* will hardly have any place. To them multiplication of wants, higher standard of living and happiness are interchangeable terms. But now, it appears, they too have started realising the futility of this love for matter. In spite of unthinkable affluence, the people are not happy.

Islam went a step further than Christianity in its love for matter. The Prophet emphatically denies any utility of celibacy or not to marry or to sleep on floor or not to eat this thing or that thing etc. He asks his people to refrain from observing these restrictions and to enjoy what merciful *Allah* has given them.

VII
DHRITI (Patience)

Dhriti is a human value though it has a social importance also.

Normally people lose their calm, composition and balance of mind in slightest adverse circumstances. Not to do so is *Dhriti*.

Psychologists tell us that facing the difficulties with calmness and balance of mind awakens the powers and gives strength to meet the challenge of adverse circumstances better.

There is a difference between anger and impatience. Anger is normally spontaneous while impatience is not, and anger subsides quickly while impatience lingers on.

Patience and satisfaction are closely related. When one is satisfied with one's family members, friends, achievements etc. then patience comes naturally.

Indian seers, who were psychologists par excellence, have invented methods by which one can acquire *Dhriti* (Patience).

In the West, much importance is not paid to patience. There, the emphasis is on impatience — to get everything done fast. Speed and more speed is their way of life. This, it appears, is again based on the basic difference of love for matter and love for spirit. With love for matter, its acquisition and enjoyment, at the earliest, are bound to get priority. This will not leave much scope for patience.

VIII
KSHMA (Forgiveness)

Kshma is a human value though it has social importance also.

When a person injures another person — physically, mentally, monetarily, emotionally or in any other way – then the natural reaction is to get provoked, to retaliate and to seek vengeance. Not to do so and forget the incident as non-important and have no ill-will against the doer is forgiveness.

This restraint, this feeling to sit tight and not to seek vengeance should not be out of fear or realisation of one's weakness or temptation or calculations of some expected future gains. Forgiveness presupposes strength to seek vengeance but even then to exercise better self-control and a desire to be good to others.

Forgiveness, on one side, saves energies which might have been wasted in anger and retaliation and on the other hand generates new emotions. The person who forgives feels relaxed and self-satisfied that he has done some good job and consequently his personality gets integrated. And the other person, who after acting in a wrong way, expects a reaction, but does not get it, soon gets perplexed and loses self-confidence. He gets a split-personality.

Ancient Indian *Rishis* developed an action plan to develop the faculty of *Kshma* (Forgiveness). Today, psychologists and social scientists should try to make these methods relevant to the changed conditions.

In Christianity, lot of emphasis has been laid on mercy. But there is difference between forgiveness and mercy. In mercy, one is not injured physically, emotionally or monetarily and so the question of retaliation does not arise. Here, seeing the adverse circumstances of a fellow being, one is filled with a different type of emotion and so proceeds to help him. This is mercy.

Mercy, though good, divides into the mercy doer and the mercy receiver. Both develop complexes. It is not good.

In Islam, the scope of mercy and forgiveness is the minimum. It teaches revenge. Even the most loyal are not to be spared. The maxim seems to be that fear and the greater fear of punishment or reprisal will only keep people on the Islamic path.

IX
DAM (Control of *Manas*)

Indian seers talk of *Manas*, *Buddhi* and *Anand* as separate identities. By *Manas*, they mean a place from where all the desires and all the actions originate. The *Rishis* compared this *Manas* with a restless bird. They said that the more it gets, the more it wants. So, they wanted it to be controlled. According to these *Rishis, Manas* is controlled by *Dam*, i.e. *Buddhi*.

Western psychologists divide mind in three parts — the Conscious, Subconscious and Unconscious. According to them the conscious mind is a place from where all the desires and actions originate and which also receives signals and gives directions to the various organs of the body. Mind also, through knowledge and training, can be made to take scientific and judicious decisions and control emotions.

Thus, it appears, *Manas* and the conscious mind are one and the same thing.

The ancient seers felt that *Manas* is controlled by *Dam*. This *Dam*, or *Buddhi* helps mind in taking important, just, rational and beneficial decisions. An example can be given to clear the point.

If after a person has eaten to his full capacity, some delicacies come, his *Manas* will send signals and try to persuade mind to order hand, mouth etc. to enjoy these delicacies. If mind is prevailed upon, it will result in over-eating and consequently to illness. But if *Buddhi* is not led away and takes a judicious decision, *Manas* will be controlled and man will be saved from physical ailments.

Indian seers pleaded for the desirability of controlling *Manas* and opined that continuous, systematic and scientific control of *Manas* can help in changing its basic character of restlessness. This will elevate a person.

X

AKRODHA (Non-Anger)

Akrodha is a human value.

Every one gets angry at one time or the other. This anger may be justified or not.

To control anger and the non-existence of anger are two different things. When there is cause of getting angry but even then there is absence of anger, it is non-anger. It certainly needs a great self-control, a very different attitude.

Western psychologists admit that anger is not a good thing. It might lead to serious consequences such as murder, or other heinous crimes or raising of blood pressure leading to heart attack or paralysis. They opine that in anger one loses self-control and even starts trembling. The voice gets loud and hoarse and language faulty. The mind loses all control. And when the anger subsides, the weakness takes over. One feels exhausted.

Indian *Rishis* felt that the most difficult thing to achieve is *Akrodh*, i.e. non-anger. However, they have presented techniques by which a state of non-anger can be achieved. It is for the modern psychologists to make a contribution in this field.

These ten values or principles, as per *Rishi* Manu, were not final. Some more, which are equally important, deserve mention. They are :

A. *Aparigraha* or Renunciation.

B. *Ahimsa* or Non-violence.
C. Fearlessness.
D. Discipline.
E. Patriotism.

Of course, this will also not exhaust the list but it will give a fairly good idea of the values of Hindu *Dharma*.

A. *Aparigraha* (Renunciation)

It is a human value which has great social importance.

Aparigraha, i.e. renunciation means that on the basis of theoretical knowledge, acquired as a student or reading or hearing, and practical experience of life, one is convinced that happiness in possessing more and more material things and acquiring even power, name and fame are of temporary nature and the lasting happiness comes only by loving soul, i.e. *Atma*, which is permanent. So, when a man, out of conviction, of his own, starts leaving or minimising possession of worldly things, power, name and fame, it is known as renunciation.

The difference between *Aparigraha* (Renunciation) and *Asteya* (Non-stealing) is apparent. *Asteya* means not stealing or not accumulating wealth beyond a reasonable limit. *Aparigraha* means go on leaving use and possession of wealth and power, as per ones capacities. Prof. J.K. Mehta called it as going on reducing wants till one reaches the stage of wantlessness or zero want.

When a head of family, out of his own sweet will, starts renouncing power and passing it on to his sons, probably most of the family problems created out of the so-called generation gap will vanish. Life will become more peaceful and worth living.

In the West, a person is retired after achieving a particular age. It is presumed that his health, memory, working capacity etc. have deteriorated leaving him a less efficient worker. The retired person adjusts to this situation, willy-nilly. On the same analogy, one can conclude that if one, realising these obvious limitations, willingly starts retiring and passing on the responsibilities to younger generation, it will relieve the burden and make one happy and at the same time, the youngers will start respecting and loving him. The whole atmosphere will become a happy one.

B. Ahimsa (Non-violence)

Non-violence is basically a social value.

Non-violence is a noble instinct, which can be developed if efforts are made in the right direction. This integrates one's personality and keeps one on the path of righteousness. The virtue has been acclaimed and even practised by the great men of the world — Socrates, Jesus, Buddha, Mahavir, Mahatma Gandhi, to name a few, and strongly recommended by several religions — Taoism, Christianity, Judaism, Buddhism, Jainism etc.

The three words — violence, anti-violence and non-violence — are very different from one another. Violence is the use of force, physical or mental, to achieve selfish interests. Richard B. Gragg includes pride, anger, killing, wounding, fighting, exploitation, tempting to evil etc. in the category of violence. According to Gandhi, "Exploitation is the essence of violence".

Anti-violence is dimetrically opposed to violence. It indicates, in the words of K.G. Mashruwala, "Love, forgiveness, friendliness, peace, kindliness, civility, frankness, service, protection, philanthrophy, generosity and so on". Benevolence, i.e. generosity and unselfishness are the keynotes of anti-violence. It is thus a thing which can be practised only by the saints, and that too after great efforts. An ordinary man in the ordinary business of life can hardly think of it.

The term non-violence or *Ahimsa* gives the impression of being a negative doctrine. But it has two aspects, one is negative and the other positive. In the negative sense it means refraining from violence. In the words of Gandhi. "*Ahimsa* does not simply mean non-killing *Himsa* means causing pain to, or killing any life out of anger, or from selfish purpose, or with the intention of injuring it. Refraining from so doing is *Ahimsa*."

Gandhi poisoned a calf to end his suffering when death was inevitable. It was not violence.

This negative aspect of non-violence aims at maximum human welfare as it attempts to reduce killing, pain, anger, selfishness etc. from the world.

In the positive form, non-violence means, in the words of Gandhi, "the largest love, greatest charity".

This positive aspect of non-violence is to convert even an enemy to one's own side so that aggression and fear may go from this world and man may be able to lead a happier and more peaceful life. This aspect of non-violence will end imperialism and colonialism, wars, local or world, and exploitation. World will become a happier place to live in.

Non-violence can be of three types — Enlightened non-violence, Passive non-violence of the weak and Passive non-violence of the coward. Enlightened non-violence can be practised by a brave person who can raise the plank of his morality to a very high order by accepting non-violence as a creed. Gandhi said, "Those who accept non-violence as a creed would never surrender their sense of humanity and brotherhood even in the midst of conflict of interests and would even try to convert and not coerce their adversary".

A person who practises Passive non-violence of the weak adopts it as a policy to achieve some desired end and normally gives it up after the fulfilment of the purpose for which it was adopted. Gandhi said after 1947 that "there was no such thing as non-violence of the weak. Non-violence and weakness was a contradiction in terms".

Passive non-violence of the coward is no non-violence. One adopts it out of one's helplessness. Gandhi said, "Cowardice and *Ahimsa* do not go together any more than water and fire".

Famous psychologist, Richard B. Gragg in his book, *Power of Non-violence*, has said that like a violent army, it is possible to raise an army of non-violent soldiers which can be more effective than the army of violent soldiers.

India mainly won its Independence with the help of non-violent, non-co-operation movement. This shows its utility in the sphere of politics.

Today, economics has become our master. Gandhi has therefore demonstrated the utility of non-violence in the sphere of economics. For example, Gandhi called mass production with the help of technological superior and still more superior machines as violence because they lead to exploitation. So, he was against the ever increasing use of machines. And in the positive aspect of non-violence, he expected producers to help the labourers in improving their lot and consumers in getting quality goods at a reasonable price. Gandhi tried to construct a structure of production which may be non-violent, i.e. beneficial to all.

The value of non-violence can be adopted as a policy or as a creed. Those who have nothing to do with morality and are engrossed with quick material gains adopt it as a policy and so it is short lived.

On the other hand, those who have not much love for material prosperity, and insist on love of soul, will adopt non-violence as a creed. It is for this reason that in the West, non-violence has not much utility. Unfortunately, they forget that violence breeds more violence.

C. Fearlessness and Boldness

Fearlessness and boldness are individual traits. They may be called human values. But it is possible that a person may be very bold and fearless in his personal affairs but may prefer to remain silent or indifferent in matters of social importance. Hence, socialisation of this value is needed. Then, it becomes an important social value.

Fearlessness is a negative word. One who is not fearful is fearless. And positive aspect of fearlessness manifests itself in bravery and boldness.

Fear is an emotion, a state of tension or disequilibrium in which an individual perceives the situation he faces as calling for moving away from the source of stimuli. He serves an urge to escape or avoid the source of threat. The inverse emotion to it is fearfulness.

Psychologists tell us that emotional processes basically and fundamentally are perceptual processes, i.e. personal perception or social perception. Earlier psychologists considered only conscious perception process but now both conscious and unconscious perception are taken into account.

There is a difference between fear and anxiety. Fear is a reaction to something in the real world while anxiety is a reaction that seems unjustifiable or out of all proportions to the actual danger that is apparently involved. Fear is more dramatic and intense while anxiety is more diffused, vague and of lower intensity.

Fear provoking stimuli start with childhood. These stimuli are : loud noise, strange people, strange places, people or things coming upon the child suddenly etc. As the child grows, these fear provoking stimuli decline and their place is taken by new ones. These new fears are more intense and more numerous. Darkness, high altitude places, sudden displacement, being alone, snakes, painful past experiences etc. are some causes of fear. And adolescent fears are more imaginary such as ghost, possible accident, ill-health, ridicule etc. Mainly these fears relate to self (bodily injury, illness, death) and status (failure, being ridiculed, forbidden sexual attitude, rivalry).

Characteristics of fear stimuli are its sudden and unexpected appearance leaving hardly any opportunity to adjust to the changed condition or novelty of strangeness of occurrence such as a person dressed in an unusual awe-inspiring way.

Response to these stimuli may be either to withdraw from the object or to cry, hide face, hold breath etc. The other response may be to act bravely to hide the fear. It may also lead to rage.

To control fear, it is not desirable to divert from the object of the fear. One should either (i) try to be forewarn of the fear and equip oneself with the skills that will be of specific aid to deal with fear, or (ii) try to reassure oneself of the harmlessness of the feared object.

Fear comes when one is afraid of losing something, mainly material things. Excessive love for matter is behind this psychology. On the other hand, fearlessness automatically comes when one does not bother to lose material things as they are considered unimportant. Fearless- ness and faith in super-conscious go together.

D. Discipline

Discipline is necessary for individuals as well as for a group or the whole society.

Man, as the Indian *Rishis* have said, has body, mind, *manas* and soul. Discipline helps an individual, through training to control, develop and bring in unison the body, the mind and the *Manas*. Discipline gives an individual regular and good habits, sweet manners and orderly behaviour and makes them his second habit. It helps in the development of concentration power. Discipline cultivates in a man the qualities of courage, dutyfulness, conscientiousness, co-operation, group feeling etc. It also helps in bringing under control the instinctive urges. Thus, discipline develops the personality of an individual to the maximum with a view to achieve a set goal.

It is not necessary that even a disciplined individual will always behave in a disciplined way. For example, a soldier may lose his discipline. Again a disciplined member, as a member of a crowd, may become indisciplined. A crowd has the potentialities to awaken self-interest or passions and break up the discipline of an individual. And when this happens, the crowd becomes mad and a source of chaos, inefficiency, waste, immobility etc. Thus, collective discipline is very much needed from the social or the national point of view.

Scholars — psychologists, philosophers, educationists, military scientists and sociologists – have given their independent views on how to inculcate and develop discipline, both individual and social, amongst the people. The sum and substance of their writings can be summarised as below.

An infant should be taught discipline through nature, i.e. through pleasure and pain.

A child (4 years to 12 years) needs authoritative discipline i.e. through fear of punishment and temptation of reward.

An adult (12 years to 16 years) needs social discipline, i.e. self-discipline or self-regarding discipline.

Thus, methods of teaching and inculcating discipline shall change with age and maturity. It should go from repressive discipline to emancipationistic discipline *via* impressionistic discipline.

Indian seers felt that discipline comes in a natural way, through family, school, neighbourhood, college and university, society and work-place. However, some Westerners opine that compulsory military training (not like N.C.C.) goes a long way in producing a disciplined nation. But this type of discipline is not self-discipline. The best form of discipline is self-discipline.

The basis of individual or collective discipline should not be self-centred but patriotic and for social good.

E. Patriotism

To understand the meaning of patriotism, one must understand the meaning of the State, the Nation and the Nationality.

1. *The State*

Machiavelli is credited for giving the concept of State in early sixteenth century. According to him, state has "the power which has authority over men". This idea describes the nature of the state, not the end of the state which is a question of political philosophy and not political science or political sociology.

Max Weber, R.M. Maclever and C.H. Page, Horold J. Laski, F.M. Watkins, and dozens of other authorities have emphasised this power of coercive aspect of the state. For example, Geoffrey K. Roberts defines state as "a territorial area in which a population is governed by a set of political authorities, and which successfully claim the compliance of the citizenry for its laws, and is able to secure such compliance by its monopolistic control of legitimate force".

The constituent elements of a state are population, territory, government and sovereignty. A brief narrative of these elements is desirable.

(a) *Population*: The state is a human institution. The population is therefore an essential element of the state. But this population should be united by the conditions of interdependence, consciousness of common interest and general regard for a set of common rules of behaviour and institutions.

It is not necessary that the population of a state should belong to a single race, religion, language or culture. Homogeneity of population is not considered as an essential feature.

(b) *Territory*: A state comes into existence only when its population is settled in a fixed territory.

Today a state has to meet its international obligations. It cannot do so till it has a settled territory over which it has an authority. It is given recognition by other states only when it has a fixed territory.

Territory symbolises the sphere of sovereignty of the state. Territory provides the natural resources for the sustenance of the population of the state and provides for a sense of security and opportunities for its citizens. It is this territory which is an object of sentimental attachment which unites people.

(c) *Government*: J.W. Garner defined government as "the agency or machinery through which common policies are determined and by which common affairs are regulated and common interests are promoted". In other words, the authority of the state is exercised by the government, but the state and government are not synonyms. The government may rise and fall but the state may continue. A state loses its identity only when it is over run by an alien power. Then it becomes a colony of the imperial power.

(d) *Sovereignty*: Sovereignty denotes the final authority of the state over its population and its territory. It is this sovereignty that a state declares — through the agency of the government, its laws and decisions and issues commands which are binding on all citizens. It is also by the virtue of its sovereignty that a state deals independently with other states.

Modern authorities of Political Science differentiate between State, Nation and Nationality. It will be profitable to know these differences.

Nation: Nation is a concept, an abstraction.

Nation refers to people living in a defined territory, inspired by a sense of unity, common political aspirations, common interests, common history and common destiny.

State: When sovereignty is added to this concept of nation, it becomes a State.

It is possible that a nation may be living in more than one State. For example, after World War-I, Austrian nation was spread out in two States — Austria and Poland. Again, it is possible that more than one nation may be residing in one single state. When U.S.A. was discovered, people of different nations started migrating to U.S.A. and settling down there. In Africa, even today, people of more than one nation are living. In U.S.S.R. also, people owing allegiance to different nations are residing. With loosening of central control, they are trying to exert themselves. In India, Muslims form a separate distinct politico-cultural group which has different interests, different ways of life and different political aspirations from the Hindus, So, the Indian leaders talk of making a composite culture.

It is possible that there may be a nation without a home. Jews were a nation but they had no state till the end of World War-II when Israel was carved out and handed over to them. The Muslim nation of India got Pakistan after getting India divided and still they are not satisfied.

Nationality: Nation, as said earlier, is a concept. Reply to this concept is nationality.

Nationality usually denotes a set of people inspired by a feeling of unity based on common race, language, religion, culture, geographical compactness, common political aspirations and historical develop- ments.

Scholars opine that there is no one single source of nationality.

Unity of blood, speech, geography are some reasons. Anthropologists and historians now generally consider that a sense of nationality is primarily the product of historical experiences and cultural traditions. Common habits, i.e. conduct and beliefs which are embodied in social customs and political rules are valued by the group as a whole. Preservation and advancement of cultural values strengthen nationality.

With this background, it will be easier to grasp the meaning of patriotism and differentiate between the Western and Indian view-point.

Western View

In the West, patriotism and nationalism are synonymous words.

In the beginning of the civilisation, people lived in clans and roamed about in search of food. Later on, they settled down in villages and towns. Thereafter the concepts of city-states, military monarchies or world empires grew. The concept of Nation, Nation-State and Nationalism developed quite late. Naturally, therefore, Hans Kohn, the ablest contemporary student of modern Nationalism, points out that the new creed "as we understand it, is not older than the second half of the 18th century".

"Nationalism is an advanced form of ethnocentrism, in which the limits of social cohesion are coterminus with the bounds of the language and culture of people in a large community inhabiting extensive territories. Ethnocentrism implies friendship with the members of the 'in group' and hostility towards members of all 'out groups'."

Wars against alien groups played an important role in attainment of awareness of one's own identity, i.e. national personality. Anglo-Saxon England attained a national personality only when it resisted Danish invasion. France became a Nation-State after the "Hundred years War" and resistance against the English invaders. In Spain, constant warfare against the Southern Saracens gave birth to Spanish nationalism. Dutch nationalism flourished after the long struggle against Spanish rule. Swiss nationalism emerged out of conflicts with Austria. Sweden became a nation through conflicts with Russians and Poles and Germans. American nationalism was generated by the War of Independence. Italian nationalism attained maturity after conflicts against Austria. The German nation became a unified state through conflicts with Danes, Austrians and Frenchmen. Instances can be multiplied.

Industrial Revolution strengthened the bondage of nationalism.

Imperialism and thereafter wars for independence strengthened the feeling of nationalism.

Nationalism, it appears, is taking the place of religion.

Under the spell of nationalism, out of the three great catch-words – liberty, equality and fraternity—only fraternity, i.e. national solidarity has been fully achieved and liberty and equality are still distant dreams.

Keeping this historical background in mind, one can define nationalism or patriotism of the West as allegiance to the Nation-State above all other allegiances and a loyalty requiring, if need be, the supreme sacrifice on the altar of patriotism. This nationalism or patriotism has more to do with the preservation of territorial integrity, solidarity, independence and sovereignty of the Nation-State than with the protection of religion, race, culture, value-system etc. This concept, from the Indian point of view, is more materialistic than spiritual.

The Indian View

India, till the advent of Britishers, was not a Nation-State. As such nationalism of the western type did not exist here.

India, from times immemorial, was divided into hundreds of *Jan-pads*, i.e. District Republics. They were independent and not federated as India is today. There was no central government. India had also different ways of life — food, language, dress, customs, etc. at different parts — north, south, east, west and central. In spite of these diversities, India was one — its soul was one. For example — Rama, Krishna, Buddha, Mahavir and a score of others, were worshipped all over India. Sacred books — *Vedas, Smirtis, Puranas, Geeta, Ramayana, Mahabharata, Dhammapad* were read and respected at every nook and corner of India. Valmiki, Vashistha, Vishwamitra, Sandeepan, Draunacharya were great teachers known throughout India. Nalanda, Magadh, Taxila, Ujjaini, Kashi etc. were famous seats of learning which attracted scholars from all over India. Four *Dhams — Badrinath, Puri, Dwarka* and *Rameshwaram* and dozens of *Tirths* (*Dharmik* centres), though scattered all over India were centres of attraction for every Hindu. This unity in diversity was the handy work of patriotism of Indian brand.

Ancient Indians were taught to love and respect their country as mother.

We love and respect mother because she gives us birth and thereafter feeds us. It is said in Hindu scriptures that elements — fire (or heat), earth, air, water and ether – go to make body. Even science seems to accept it. These five elements we get from Mother India. Again, Mother India provides us all that we need for survival. Economists tell us that land consists of everything that is *above land* like Sun, heat, air; everything *on the land* like rivers, mountains, standing crops; everything *in the land* like fertility and everything *below the land* like water, minerals etc. All these free gifts of land help us to get all the material goods we need. It is a source of our survival, physical fitness and material prosperity. We love and respect Mother India as a token of gratitude and are prepared to protect its territorial integrity and sovereignty even at our life's cost. This is one aspect of patriotism, which, from Indian point of view, is of lower level.

There is a difference between man and animal. Man does not live by food alone. For him social atmosphere, which creates human values, social values, ideals, culture, traditions, customs etc. become more important. The social atmosphere, values, traditions, culture, ideals etc. are given by the great men of the land, in a course of time. Hence patriotism of higher order means to love and respect the great men of the country, the human and social values which they gave and the customs, traditions, ideals and the resultant culture which they helped in making. This patriotism means inculcating these ideals, values, culture etc. in one's own life and preparedness to lay down one's own life in protecting them.

This patriotism does not mean conservatism or remaining static. Life is dynamic. Death is static. Hence, with time, ideals, values, traditions, customs, i.e. culture must go on growing and changing. But the only condition is that the change should have roots in the land, it must be in keeping with the cultural flow of the country. It should not be blindly imported from foreign lands and forcibly grafted on the country. It will create a hybrid thing which will be suicidal. This extra-territorial loyalty, in matter of culture, is not patriotism, in the same way as extra-territorial loyalty in matters of territory is not patriotism.

Patriotism, therefore, means giving greater importance to the territorial integrity of the country, its great cultural heritage — value system, customs, traditions etc. – and the great men of the land, belonging to different walks of life, who went to evolve the country's culture than to one's own life. Preparedness to protect all of them, honour them and try to imbibe their preachings in one's own life is patriotism. Paying lip sympathy or doing exactly opposite to it is treachery.

APPENDIX I

POWERS OF YAGYA

Yagya, a technique to pray, was given to humanity by the *Vedas*. It appears that, in the garb of *Dharma*, *Yagya* serves multiple purposes. For example it was to please the super-natural powers, it was to purify the atmosphere and, as now Principal Har Prasad Sharma claims, it can cause rain and also stop it. Principal Sharma, in a period of eleven years 1979 to 1990 has performed thirteen *Yagyas* to cause rain. According to him, the results of his *Yagyas* were as below:

1st *Yagya*	Vrindavan (Dist. Mathura)	Jan. 1979	- successful
2nd *Yagya*	Vrindavan (Dist. Mathura)	May 1979	- successful
3rd *Yagya*	Mathura	June 1979	- successful
4th *Yagya*	Etah	Sept. 1979	- successful
5th *Yagya*	Vill. Chata, Mathura	Sept. 1981	- successful
6th *Yagya*	Vill. Kharota, Mathura	Jan. 1982	- successful
7th *Yagya*	Vill. Khaira, Mathura	Sept. 1982	- successful
8th *Yagya*	Vill. Celoni (Haryana)	Oct. 1982	- partially successful
9th *Yagya*	Mathura	June 1987	- successful
10th *Yagya*	Mathura	May 1988	- successful
11th *Yagya*	Ajmer (Rajasthan)	June 1989	- successful
12th *Yagya*	Vill. Jheenga (Mathura)	Oct. 1989	- failed
13th *Yagya*	Vill. Kotda (Ajmer)	May 1990	- successful

The 10th *Yagya* at Mathura was partly financed by the Department of Science and Technology, New Delhi. In this *Yagya*, scientists of the Indian Institute of Tropical Meteorological, Pune and of observatories of Mathura Refinery, Taj Complex in Agra and satellite imageries at Palam, New Delhi, participated. *The Hindustan*

Times, New Delhi, in its issue of June 2, 1988, wrote :

> "At the time of writing, changes in wind circulation were reported and an easterly wind had set in. There was a little change in the temperature and chances of scattered dust and thunderstorm were there. However, scientists are in no hurry to attribute the changes in atmosphere to the *Yagya*. . . ."

It is unfortunate that Indian scientists are not bothered to scientifically assess the powers of *Yagya* to invoke rains, or to stop them or to purify the atmosphere. The seers claimed that in *Yagya* fire wood of particular trees only are used and pure *ghee* along with *Havan Samigri* is offered. These things generate smoke which has the qualities of both a germicide and purifier of the atmosphere, i.e., corrector of the proportion of oxygen, carbon and other gases.

In America, recently a university, known as *Agnihotri University*[3] has been established in California to make scientific studies of the different aspects of *Yagya* such as power of the words and the pronunciation of *Yagya Mantras*, the power of the Sun, the power of *Havana-Agni*, the power of feelings etc.

A Geologist, Dr. Garry Lane, has invented an instrument to measure the path and power of the words, their pronunciation effect etc. He has discovered that the sound waves can travel through solids as well as ether. Further, the sounds of *Yagya Mantras*, specially the *Gayatri-Mantra*, because of extraordinary rhythm and sound effect, have some different powers. They move upward in a circular motion and can easily carry the particles produced by *Havan-Agni*. In *Havan*, wood of specified trees is used for fire and *Ahuti* of pure *Ghee* and *Havan-Samigri* is offered. All this produces special type of gases and particles. The sounds of *Mantras* take these particles and gases with them to Ino-sphere and universe. It has been observed that they have the potentiality to create commotion.

Studies have also revealed that the Sun can create good or bad atmospheric affects in Ino-sphere. It has been observed that when *Yagya*'s sound carrying *Havan* gases and particles reaches Ino-sphere, the Sun creates baneful effects for humanity. For example, rainfall may be induced. Again, the atmosphere will be purified. Dr. F. Falling thinks that the two world wars, increasing vehicular traffic, industries, etc., have so much polluted the atmosphere that man is increasingly suffering from the diseases like cancer, blood-pressure, leukaemia etc. The Sun, with the help of *Yagya*'s sound, gases and particles by purifying the atmosphere can minimise the evil effect of this pollution.

Studies on "Power of Feeling" are yet in infant stage but it has been revealed that they also move in waves like sound and have magnetic qualities.

APPENDIX II

FOOD, HEALTH, THOUGHTS AND DEEDS

Indian seers repeatedly said :

What you eat, so your health
As your health, so your Thoughts
And as your Thoughts, so your Actions

Thus, they establish a direct relationship between food, thoughts and deeds. These seers give more importance to stamina than vitality. The seers, in their wisdom, divided food, thoughts and deeds into three categories:

1. *Satvik* – The best for health, thoughts and actions
2. *Rajsik* – Inferior to *Satvik*
3. *Tamsik*– The worst for health, thoughts and actions.

An idea of the food, in each category, can be had from the following illustrations:

1. *Satvik* – Cow's milk, curd, some vegetables, fruits, fresh cooked vegetarian food, honey, etc.
2. *Rajsik* – Fried food, most of the sweets, spicy food, butter, ghee, dry fruits, etc.
3. *Tamsik*– Meat, egg, wines, intoxicants, non-vegetarian food, tea, coffee.

It will be a fruitful exercise to try to discover the truth of these categories.

I
FOOD AND HEALTH

The science of Allopathy has found out that every human being, as per age, weight and work, requires certain amount of calories, vitamins, minerals, fats, proteins, carbohydrates, etc. Table A.1 gives this relationship:

TABLE A.1: Recommended Dietary Allowances for Indians

Group	Particulars	Body wt kg	Net energy Kcal/d	Protein g/d	Fat g/d	Calcium mg/d	Iron mg/d	Vit. Retinol	A µg/d β-carotene	Thiamin (β_1) mg/d	Riboflavin (β_2) mg/d	Nicotinci acid mg/d	Pyridoxin mg/d	Ascorbic acid µg/d	Folic acid µg/d	Vit. B-12
Man	Sedentary work		2425							1.2	1.4	16				
	Moderate work	60	2875	60	20	400	28	600	2400	1.4	1.6	18	2.0	40	100	1
	Heavy work		3800							1.6	1.9	21				
Woman	Sedentary work		1875							0.9	1.1	12				
	Moderate work	50	2225	50	20	400	30	600	2400	1.1	1.3	14	2.0	40	100	1
	Heavy work		2925							1.2	1.5	16				
	Pregnant woman	50	+300	+15	30	1000	38	600	2400	+0.2	+0.2	+2	2.5	40	400	1
	Lactation:															
	0-6 months		+550	+25						+0.3	+0.3	+4				
		50			45	1000	30	950	3800				2.5	80	150	1.5
	6-12 months		+400	+18						+0.2	+0.2	+3				
Infants	0-6 months	5.4	108/kg	2.05/kg						55µ/kg	65µ/kg	710µ/kg	0.1			
						500								25	25	0.2
	6-12 months	8.6	98/kg	1.65/kg				350	1200	50µ/kg	60µ/kg	650µ/kg	0.4			
Children	1-3 years	12.2	1240	22			12	400		0.6	0.7	8	0.9		30	
	4-6 years	19.0	1690	30	25	400	18	400	1600	0.9	1.0	11		40	40	0.2-1.0
	7-9 years	26.9	1950	41			26	600	2400	1.0	1.2	13	1.6		60	
Boys	10-12 years	35.4	2190	54			34			1.1	1.3	15				
					22	600		600	2400				1.6	40	70	0.2-1.0
Girls	10-12 years	31.5	1970	57			19			1.0	1.2	13				
Boys	13-15 years	47.8	2450	70			41			1.2	1.5	16				
					22	600		600	2400				2.0	40	100	0.2-1.0
Girls	13-15 years	46.7	2060	65			28			1.0	1.2	14				
Boys	16-18 years	57.1	2640	78			50			1.3	1.6	17				
					22	500		600	2400				2.0	40	100	0.2-1.0
Girls	16-18 years	49.9	2060	63			30			1.0	1.2	14				

TABLE A.2: Nutrition Contents

Sl. No.	Items (per ounce)	Protein (g)	Fat (g)	Carbo-hydrates (g)	Calcium (mg)	Phos-phorus (mg)	Iron (mg)	Vita-min A	Vita-min B	Vita-min C	Vita-min D	Vita-min E	Vita-min K	Nicoti-nic acid (mg)	Ribo-flavin (mg)	Calo-ries
1		2	3	4	5	6	7	8	9	10	11	12	13	14	15	16
Satvik																
1.	Cow milk	0.9	1.0	1.4	34	25	0.1	Tr	5	1				0.1	57	18
2.	Curd	0.8	0.8	0.9	34	25	0.1	Tr	Tr	—				—	17	14
3.	Skimmed milk	1.0	Tr	1.4												11
4.	Carrot	0.3	0.1	3.0	23	8	0.4	568 to 1221	17	1				0.1	6	13
5.	Cauliflower	1.0	0.1	1.5	8	17	0.4	4	31	19				0.3	23	11
6.	Grapes	0.2	0.1	2.0	6	6	0.1	—	11	9				0.1	6	9
7.	Bannana	0.3	0.1	6.1	3	14	0.1	Tr	14	1				0.1	9	22
8.	Guava	0.4	0.1	4.1	3	11	0.3	Tr	—	85				0.1	9	19
9.	Mango	0.2	0.1	3.3	3	6	0.1	1353	—	4				0.1	14	14
10.	Lemon	0.4	0.3	3.1	25	6	0.1	7	—	18				0.1		17
11.	Green vegetables (Average)	0.2	Tr	1.4												5
12.	Wheat flour	3.4	0.5	20.5	11	91	2.0									100
13.	Dal (Average)	6.7	0.7	15.9												100
14.	Rice	0.1	0.2	22.2	3	5	0.6	1	17					0.7	34	100

(contd.)

TABLE A.2 *(Contd.)*

1	2	3	4	5	6	7	8	9	10	11	12	13	14	15	16
Rajsik															
1. Ghee	—	25.0				171				0.4					225
2. Butter	0.1	24.0				205									218
3. Khoa	4.1	8.8	5.8												124
4. Almonds	5.9	15.2	3.0	65	140	1.0	Tr	23	—	—	—	—	0.7	—	170
5. Cashew nuts	6.0	13.3	6.3												174
Tamsik															
1. Eggs	3.8	3.9	0.2	20	74	0.9	255	Tr							51
2. Meats (Average)	6.4	0.7	—	3	54	0.2	Tr	14	1				1.6	D	32
3. Wines															
4. Chillies (Dry)	4.5	1.7	8.9										11		74

The western allopaths tell us that excess or deficiency of various nutritive contents is not health giving. In either case, one or the other disease takes over the human body. For illustration purposes, Table A.3 has been prepared:

TABLE A.3: Nutritive Intakes and Diseases

Sl.No.	Item	Diseases, if Deficient	Diseases, if Excess
1	2	3	4
1.	Vitamin A	Night blindness, xerophthalmia, bitot's, spot, keratonalacia	Hyper vitaminosis A, i.e., Loss of appetite, headache, itching on skin, swelling on long bones, enlargement of liver.
2.	Vitamin B_1 (Thiamin)	Beri Beri	–
3.	Vitamin B_2 (Riboflavin)	Stomatitis, Chilosis Glossitis, Leisons	–
4.	Vitamin B_3 (Niacin)	Pellegra, i.e., Dementia, Dermititis, Diarrahoea	Burning sensation
5.	Vitamin C	Scurvy (Bleeding of Gums)	–
6.	Vitamin D	Rickets, Osteomalacia	Loss of appetite, Nausea, Vomiting, dullness, calcification of lungs and kidney
7.	Vitamin E	Per oxidation of poly unsaturated fatty acids takes place and yellow and brown pigments are formed. Degeneration of cellular and sub cellular membranes	–
8.	Vitamin K	Inadequate intestinal absorption, lack of digestive and Bile juices, Intestinal obstruction, no blood coagulation, no synthesis of prothrom bin	–
9.	Fat	Phrynoderma due to deficiency of essential fatty acids, Dryness, Thickening of and Toad skin, desquamation	Atherosclerosia due to excess cholesterol
10.	Protein	Kwashiorkar, Marasmus Prdine and calary deficiency	–
11.	Calcium	Defective and slow bone growth, Tetany	Stunted growth, stones (Renal) Metastatic Calcification Myxoedema
12.	Iodine	Goitre in adults, cretinism in children	

(Contd.)

(Contd.)

1	2	3	4
13.	Sodium	Involvement in dehydration	Cramps, oedema, Hyper-Natremia
14.	Potassium	Hypo-Calemia (Injury to myocardium and kidney)	Hyper-Calemia (cardiac depression, central Nervous system depression, mental weakness
15.	Cobalt	—	Polycythemia (increased number of red blood cells in blood), Cardiomyopathy (nausea, vomiting, anorexia, peripheral neuropathy)
16.	Iron	Anaemia	—

On the basis of these studies, allopaths admit of a direct relationship between food and health. So, they talk of a balanced diet.

It appears the Indian seers went a little deeper in their studies than the modern scientists have gone. The following points are interesting and revealing:

1. The nutritive contents given in Table A.2 are of food in raw form. One normally does not take eatables in raw form. They are cooked, sometimes fried, sometimes spices are added and sometimes they are taken after twelve hours or twenty four hours or even more. What happens to the nutritive contents? The western scientists have yet to make in-depth studies of these changes. So, they make a general statement that the nutritive contents do deteriorate when food is cooked or fried or preserved. They do not indicate the quantum of deterioration. They do not even venture whether the deterioration will be at a uniform rate of all the nutritive contents. So they do not object to the tinned food so popular in the west.

   In contrast, it appears, Indian seers made indepth studies of all these aspects before categorising food into three – *Satvik*, *Rajsik* and *Tamsik*. They even taught the house ladies to cook different eatables at different temperatures and durations and what spices to add to minimise the bad effects of certain eatables. They insisted on eating freshly cooked food because, in their opinion, even *Satvik* food becomes *Tamsik* after a time-interval.

2. Table A.1 gives us an idea of the body requirements of different nutritive components. But it has not made any serious studies of what to eat and how to eat to get a balanced diet. They have not even ventured to answer some ticklish questions. For example, a particular eatable may give more calories but very little of other nutritive contents. And the other eatable may give less calories but most of the other nutritive contents. Which of the two is to be preferred and why? Again, two foods may give almost equal calories but one may be difficult to digest and the other easily digestible. Which of the two is good for health? Probably, Indian seers made all these studies and on the basis of these studies divided food into three categories and developed the science of cooking.
3. Western allopaths lay emphasis on vitality and their concept of a balanced diet, it appears, is based on this. Indian seers, while recognising the importance of vitality gave more importance to stamina. On what stamina depends has not been discovered so far by the Westerners. The Indian seers, it appears, gave the classification of food on the basis of a proper mix of vitality and stamina.
4. Table A.2 gives the nutritive values of different eatables of one ounce weight. Table A.1 gives the nutritive requirements on the basis of age, sex, etc. An ordinary male adult needs 2500-3800 calories per day. With simple arithmetic, it means that one must take 25 to 30 ounces of wheat or *dal* or rice (unboiled) or 10-15 ounces of *ghee* or butter or more, 50 ounces of eggs, or meat, or approximately 200 ounces of cow milk, curd, guava, mango, carrot etc. And if one wants to eat more than one item, the mix must be such that it may give the required calories.

   Now if one adult male decides to consume only one item, say rice, to get the required quantities of calories, he will have to consume 25-30 ounces of rice. This quantity will give him the following nutritive values, when the requirements are different:

Item	*Will Get*	*Requirements*
Protein	2.5 - 3.0	60
Fat	5.0 - 6.0	20
Carbohydrates	555 - 666	N.A.
Calcium	75 - 90	400

Phosphorus	125 - 150	N.A.
Iron	15.0 - 18.0	28
Vitamin A	25 - 30	600
Vitamin B_1	-	1.2 to 1.6
Nicotinic acid	17.5 - 21.0	16 to 21
Riboflavin	850	1.4 to 1.9

This shows that there is either excess of a few things or deficiency of others. It implies man is likely to get different diseases as Table A.3 reveals. It also reveals that wheat and pulses are better food from the point of a balanced diet.

Western science, it appears, has not studied the problem from this angle. Probably, Indian seers studied it from this angle also before dividing eatables into different groups. Probably, according to them, this necessitated cooking, frying, adding spices and taking a number of eatables at a time.

5. Indian seers tell us that the human body has five functional organs – heart, which circulates blood, brain, which controls the nervous system, lungs, which purify blood, digestive system and excretion system. These five functional organs themselves generate electricity necessary for their functioning. Modern science agrees with them. Further, the raw material used to generate this electricity is food that we eat. Thus, quality of raw material eaten, and the quality of electricity generated should have a direct relationship. An inferior quality of coal will not enable engineers to produce electricity, which may give good current, stable voltage etc. On the same analogy, it can be argued that the food we eat will affect the quality of the energy generated by these functional organs. The western science has not studied this aspect of the problem. Indian seers while classifying food into *Satvik*, *Rajsik* and *Tamsik*, it appears, took this aspect also into consideration.

The following conclusions can be drawn from Table A.2.

(a) *Satvik* food has the lowest calories, *Tamsik* has higher calories and *Rajsik* the highest.
(b) *Satvik* food has almost all the nutritive values, *Tamsik* has less number of nutritive values and *Rajsik*, the least.

(c) *Rajsik* food has highest fat contents followed by *Tamsik* and thereafter *Satvik*.
(d) *Rajsik* food has highest protein contents followed by *Tamsik* and thereafter *Satvik*.
(e) Most of the *Rajsik* and *Tamsik* foods have almost no calcium but most of the *Satvik* foods have calcium.
(f) Seers say and the doctors agree that the easiest to digest is *Satvik* food, followed by *Rajsik*, and *Tamsik*.

It can be concluded that health depends on what we eat. It may further be added that the Indian seers' classification of eatables into *Satvik, Rajsik* and *Tamsik* was more scientific. The western scientists have yet to make the indepth studies to either accept their version or refute them. However, the Westerners have also realised that the non-vegetarian food is harmful for health. They are learning it in a big way. The Indian seers called it *Tamsik* food.

II
FOOD, THOUGHTS AND ACTIONS

It is an admitted fact, both in the east and the west, that actions follow thoughts. The feeling of hunger first comes to mind and thereafter the action of eating follows. What is to be taken for a change comes first in ideas, thereafter, the preparation of that menu follows. What to wear, first comes in thoughts and then the action follows. Instances can be multiplied.

The modern Indian saint, Mahatma Gandhi, established the relationship between food, thought and action. How to observe *Brahamcharya* (celibacy or control of all senses) Gandhi said:

> "Control of the palate is the first essential in the observance of the vow. I found that complete control of the palate made the observance very easy, and so I now pursue dietic experiments not merely from the vegetarian's but also from the *Brahamcharya's* point of view. As the result of these experiments I saw that the *Brahamchari's* food should be limited, simple, spiceless, and if possible, uncooked."

(Autobiography, p.152).

NOTES

1. Department of Science and Technology has financed Principal Har Prasad Sharma of Mathura to perform these *Yagyas*. The scientists themselves studied the atmospheric changes that this *Yagya* invoked and thereby caused rains. See Appendix I.
2. See Appendix II.
3. This description is on the basis of an article published in a Hindi Magazine, *Akhanda Jyoti*, Mathura, U.P., India.

PART TWO

THE TOOLS

4

THE FAMILY — THE IGNORED BUT IMPORTANT UNIT OF PLANNING:

An Indian View

In the modern world, a family is a nuclear unit, consisting of parents and their children, living together under a common roof. This nuclear family in on the verge of disintegration in the West as hardly any love and confidence are left between husband and wife and parents and children.

A family has the potentialities to produce value-oriented men and women capable of reaching a stage of *Anand* (i.e Vertical and Horizontal integration) and building a new world, more peaceful, and more useful. So, it will be profitable to go a little back and trace the origin and development of the institution of family.

Clan or Tribe : The Original Joint Family

Fedric List, gave five stages of economic development. The first stage was Savage Stage or Hunting Stage in which an individual lived individually. It gradually gave place to the Pastoral Stage where people had learnt to live in groups, known as clans or tribes. The clan had learnt the art of catching wild animals, taming them and living on them. In search of fodder this clan had to move from place to place. The clan mainly consisted of blood relations, having a common ancestor. But some others were also admitted to it. It was a usual practice for one clan to attack another clan for capturing their animals and ladies. So, ladies were taken captives and the rest of the members of the conquered clan were slained because they consumed what they produced, leaving no surplus. These ladies were gradually made mistresses. But with passage of time, shortage of labour was felt and man became more productive and so even the males of the conquered clan were not murdered but taken as slaves.

These clans or tribes got tired of their nomadic life. By a fluke of luck and through Nature's process of evolution they had also come to know the art of growing plants. The wise men of the clan had also noticed the periods when the seeds sprouted. This was associated with their observation of the phenomena of astronomy. So, slowly clan after clan started settling down at one place, which later on was called a village. They took to cultivation. This was the beginning of the third stage of economic development known as Agricultural Stage.

By this time the clan had not learnt to thatch huts or construct houses. So, they lived under the roof of the open sky. Because animals were the main food, whose ownership was common and roasting of an animal was not difficult, the common kitchen remained as such. The wise men in the clan were few. They knew prayers by heart and had learnt astronomy and geography. Therefore, the prayers and religious functions remained common. The people of the clan were worshippers of Nature. The Sun, the Moon, the Stars, the Wind and the Water etc. were their gods. They too were common. And the strongest or wisest man of the clan was the leader whom others obeyed. Thus the institution of a joint family germinated.

Splitting of a Clan : Rise of Joint Family

This clan gradually learnt to thatch huts. The size of a hut was small. Only a small group of people could live in it. The clan got splitted into small groups, consisting mainly of parents and children. But the huts were raised in a compact area. All the members of a clan lived in a small area but the seeds of separation were already sown and this gradually reduced the importance of the clan and increased the importance of the family.

As the family grew, new huts had to be raised in close vicinity. These clusters of huts, consisting of children of a grandfather, were, for identification sake, given the name of a Joint family of an individual person. This was the rise of more closely knit Joint Family.

Nuclear Family

With the advent of Industrial Stage these Joint Families started getting splitted into nuclear families due to a number of factors. Wants multiplied and so in search of work people had to move out of the villages. Faster means of transport and communications helped in this movement. Materialism increased and with it selfishness. Selfishness and joint living could not go together for long.

Disintegration of Nuclear Family

Now a stage appears to have come in the West where due to excessive materialism, love for self, shortage of time and lack of will, love and sacrifice, which were the binding factors of even a nuclear family, are fast disappearing. Parents have no time to devote to their newly born children and so, when these children grow up, they have no consideration for their ageing parents. Mothers in distress find it difficult to live with sons though daughters, due to their soft nature (not love) may tolerate them. Even this nuclear family is disintegrating.

This brief narration shows a close link between the family and the traits of the members of a clan.

Malthus is credited with the title of the Father of the Science of Demography for he, for the first time, realised the importance of the population of a country and made a study of its quantitative aspects. Thereafter, a number of studies of population have been made and now the Family Planning, in the quantitative sense alone, has come to stay with us.

Probably it was Robert Owen (1771-1858) who thought about the quality of a man and through his experiments of Labour Reforms, Colonies and Labour Exchanges, tried to change the quality of man by changing his environment. His dictum was that none was born good or bad but the atmosphere made him so. Marx also realised this truth and tried to create a new man of his liking by designing a new socio-politico-economic way of life. Marx's success or failure is being debated today, even in Marxist Russia and China. But the trend seems to be clear.

The western economists never saw a man in his entirety. He was seen in parts as social man, political man and economic man. And as an economic man also, only his labour part was considered important and so only those factors that make a labour efficient were studied. Some time back a phase started in which expenditure on education, which was considered as a welfare activity earlier, was regarded as an investment because it produced intellectual labour, technocrats, bureaucrats, engineers, scientists etc., which were important components for increasing productivity. And now an economic man is seen as a distinct capital known as Human capital. Probably, the day is not far off when *man* as an integrated whole with all his social, political and economic components will assume the central place.

In ancient India, the philosophers, the psychologists, the economists, the political scientists and the sociologists considered the question of how to develop an ideal society in which everyone was, physically fit, intellectually sound, emotionally balanced and integrated, economically contented, politically fully safeguarded and socially virtuous. Thus, they thought every man will be happy and will have the greatest effect in making others happy and contented.

The Indian saints, who were philosophers, psychologists, educationists, sociologists, political scientists and economic experts, — all rolled in one – spelt out the following maxims and tried to build a unique society and a way of life which has no parallel even today.

(1) Life is one. It should, therefore, have common fundamentals on which its various parts — social, political, economic, moral etc. – should be built up. This will avoid frictions among various parts of life and help in making and developing an integrated and balanced personality of man.

(2) The fundamentals selected should both be philosophically sound and sufficiently dynamic to accommodate time and space changes.

(3) Every human being has not the same level of intelligence, education, adaptability, foresight etc. so, to persuade people to follow a way of life, they should be emotionally awakened and wedded to it. They must be convinced that it is for their good, and in the interest of their posterity, the society and the nation. Obviously, a number of strategies will have to be used simultaneously to achieve this end. For intellectuals and highly educated sections, the technique of explanation, logic and scientific truths will have to be used and for the less favoured, mainly the tools of faith and informal education will have to be invoked.

(4) The aim of life should be to develop the faculties of a man and make him contended and happy. That man is the richest who has perfected his life and has the greatest effect on other peoples' lives. In the words of Indian seers, the aim should be to achieve *Anand*, i.e., permanent happiness which comes with

vertical and horizontal equilibrium of a man.

(5) Material things are not lasting. They soon change form. So, their possession and consumption also cannot give permanent enjoyment, satisfaction and happiness. Moreover, the repeated consumption of one material thing, which for the first time gives immense thrill, soon starts losing charm and quickly degenerates into a routine and drudgery. Hence, satisfaction, or contentment, or happiness cannot be maximised simply by multiplying the quantity and variety of the possessions and consumption of material things though they may satisfy ego.

(6) Human body to exist efficiently, needs a minimum package of material things. Till this level of material possession is reached, the consumption of material things and satisfaction remain directly proportionately related. But beyond this level, the increase in consumption of material things increases total satisfaction but at a diminishing rate and after a limit the relationship becomes inverse. After full quota of bread is eaten, any further eating of bread will lead to vomiting tendency.

(7) It is a common experience that when one gives to a needy person one's material things, in spite of the decrease in the quantum of material possession, a peculiar feeling of satisfaction or inner happiness is strongly felt. It gives a thrill and a sense of fulfilment and pride. It shows that helping others and inner satisfaction are directly connected. So, one should try to curb attachment and develop a feeling of detachment from the worldly possessions.

(8) In spite of this limitation on consumption, an individual, the society and the country need material goods. So, they should be produced and in their production each individual should contribute. It is a sacred duty of everyone towards one's own self, one's family, society and the country. The items of goods to be produced and their quantity or number must, of course, depend upon several factors such as the size of the population, its requirements and availability and exploitation of resources.

(9) A family is a closely knit association of its members. The atmosphere of this family is a great educator. The atmosphere of a family mainly depends upon the inter- and intra-personal relations of the members — Mother and children, Father and

children, uncle-aunt and nephew-nieces, brothers, sisters, husband and wife, etc. If these relations are built on the foundation of values – human values, social values and spiritual values – then the family will remain united and will progress. Children will grow up to be virtuous men and women.

(10) Seeds of human values, social values and spiritual values which ennoble a man's own life and that of others are:

- (i) Truth — It includes honesty
- (ii) Non-stealing — Not acquiring other peoples' things by questionable means.
- (iii) Knowledge of Matter — Today we call it education
- (iv) Knowledge of Soul — Today we have very little conception of it.
- (v) Purity of body, material goods, atmosphere, thought and action.
- (vi) Contentment — A virtue which may lead to reduction in possession of wordly things out of one's own sweet will.
- (vii) Forgiveness — It includes love and mercy without which one cannot learn to forgive.
- (viii) Self-control over five senses — ears, eyes, nose, tongue and skin.
- (ix) Control of *Manas*
- (x) Non-anger
- (xi) Patriotism leading to universal love (not internationalism)
- (xii) Bravery and fearlessness—It includes good health.
- (xiii) Non-attachment leading to detachment i.e. socialism by self.
- (xiv) Discipline
- (xv) Modesty

These values will automatically lead to democracy, par excellence, in political life and socialism in economic life — nay in the entire life.

To a modern man it may appear difficult to think of all men possessing these virtues or values. But all these values can be acquired by an average man, if he has a will and is given a proper atmosphere. In ancient India this experiment admirably succeeded and even afterwards, without any conscious efforts on the part of the society and the state, it continued to function automatically for centuries with the force of traditions and conventions. Of course, how much a person will be able to acquire these individual values depends upon his nature and capacity which cannot be changed quickly. But it is an historical fact that the quantity and quality can be improved with sustained efforts.

The ancient Indian sociologists adopted a very simple strategy to produce virtuous MAN pulsating with these human values.

Unlike the Western thinkers, the Indian philosophers attached greater importance neither to an individual, nor to the society but to the family. They realised that the family is a factory which produces MAN. Both, the quantity and quality of MAN depends on the nature of these small factories. Of course, these philosophers were bright enough to realise that the limitations of quality orientation of a child depend, to a great extent, on genes inherited by him. Further, the family alone can lay the foundation and sow the seeds. These qualities, to blossom, also need care, watering and manuring with the socio-politico-economic climate of the country. So, ancient Indian saints tried to develop a way of life which was quality oriented. History testifies to that they admirably succeeded.

Ancient sociologists were good psychologists also. They knew that a child has an impressionable mind and he learns several things from observation. The family atmosphere based on inter- and intra-personal relations, customs and traditions — a type of informal education — therefore becomes very important. In this, love, sacrifice and respect played a prominent role. So, a new-born was given greatest attention and love by the mother, closely followed by grand-parents, sisters, brothers etc. And the father was assigned the role to discipline the child. But this discipline enforcement was humane.

A child sees and hears things carefully and wants to imitate them. So, the family atmosphere was so designed that a new-born child may not find and hear vulgar things, which may pollute his innocent heart and mind. On the other hand, through pictures, short stories, songs etc. he was given the very best ideas of life. The prayers and the religious *Sanskars* were designed to play their formative role. And the playmates were also carefully selected. A close watch was kept on them also.

When a child grew, he was sent to an educational institution. The atmosphere of the educational institutions, specially that of primary schools was healthy and clean. This played a vital role in strengthening the virtues taught at home and in making a noble and virtuous man.

Whatever little was left, was taken care of by the social atmosphere which was so designed as to help and guide the youth on the virtuous path and to frown and punish on his doing wrong things.

The way, through which a virtuous man with above-mentioned values was produced, with the help of a family in ancient India, is a marvellous piece of original planning. The tool of the family atmosphere, mainly depending on the inter- and intra-personal relations of its members, was harnessed to do the job. To know, how a particular value was inculcated in a child, the family atmosphere will have to be vertically bisected. It is likely that in such a vertical analysis of the family atmosphere, one particular thing may be found common in different value studies. This is inevitable. It simply shows multi-effects of one thing on the child's personality.

To illustrate the originality and effect of the family atmosphere in the development of a child's personality three value studies are taken here as illustrations. They are:

1. Good health
2. Patriotism
3. Socialism

I
GOOD HEALTH

The primary importance in any scheme of family planning will naturally be to produce a healthy man with a healthy body and mind. How to do it? Indian social scientists thought that the important ingredients of a sound body and mind are: (i) cleanliness of the house, (ii) cleanliness of the body and clothes, (iii) cleanliness of the atmosphere, (iv) physical exercise, (v) balanced nutritive diet, (vi) health giving habits, and (vii) good thoughts. All these ingredients (for a non-knowledgeable person) were made a way of life in Indian families. This miracle was probably done in the following way:

(a) *Cleaning the House* : It was made the first duty of the house wife, probably first in the name of pleasing God but later on by tradition, to sweep each and every place of the house religiously, dust off walls and articles, wash those places which were likely to become more dirty like courtyard, kitchen place, bath-room (if any), etc. In those days the houses were of mud, with earthen floors. So, the floors were also to be daily or bi-weekly or weekly plastered with cow dung, which was considered to be a disinfectant. Similarly, the males were required to clean the cattle and even wash them regularly.

(b) *Cleaning the Body and Clothes* : It was made obligatory, to reply to call of nature soon after getting up. Nothing except fresh water could be taken to make bowels move. Thereafter, one had to clean one's teeth, wash the eyes and take a bath. It was very essential to wash one's all clothes daily, because with dirty clothes or body, even the daily meals could not be taken. And, to begin with, it was all enforced as *Dharma* entailing fear of punishment of the all knowing and all pervading God. This soon became a force of habit and tradition.

(c) *Cleaning the Atmosphere* : People were made to cultivate a habit to offer prayers soon after taking bath but before eating anything. Nothing could be taken without offering prayers. And while praying, to please God or Goddess, incense like *Dhoopbati,* Jostic *(Agarbati), Gugul,* Camphor *(Kapoor)*, were burnt and offered. Modern science admits that the smoke of all these is an anti-pollutant, it kills the little germs of the room without any side effect as of DDT.

After prayer, one was to offer water to *Tulsi* plants, which was a must, in every house. Science admits that *Tulsi* is a medicinal plant. So, a number of *Tulsi* plants were anti-pollutant.

Every family was required to perform *Yagna* on every religious day and otherwise too. The smoke of Mango *(Aam)* wood, pure *ghee* and *Havan Samigri* purifies the atmosphere.

(d) *Physical Exercises* : It was made obligatory for every young boy and girl, over and above his and her strenuous routine of life to take some physical exercise, either in the morning or in the evening. Different types of exercises, both indoor and outdoor, such games, athletics, gymnastics, wrestling, yogic exercises, horse riding were introduced and developed. Regular competitions of physical agility were organised. The habits thus acquired continued even with the advancement of age. Today, the modern science is gradually realising the importance of *yoga* as preventor and curer of diseases.

(e) *Balanced, Nutritive Diet* : Only recently modern science realised the importance of diet. And very recently a debate was started on non-vegetarian food and its bad effects. However, ancient Indian saints realised the importance of food long back. They classified it into three, namely *Satvik, Rajsik* and *Tamsik*. Mainly milk and milk products such as curd etc., honey, selected fresh fruits, vegetables, pulses and cereals were placed in *Satvik* category of food. This food also deteriorated in quality with time, place, season etc. and became *Rajsik* and thereafter *Tamsik*. Meat food, wines and other intoxicants were placed in the worst category of food, i.e. *Tamsik* food. It was the considered opinion that 'as the food so the body, thought and action'. So, great importance was attached to food. People were advised to stick to *Satvik* food.

Not only the selection of eatables was important but the methods of cooking them was also considered equally important. Tasty food with a quality to improve health was the motto. So, experts decided as to which eatables will be taken raw and which boiled and at what temperature. The invention of *Roti* (bread) is in itself a superb invention in the realm of cooking. No lighter cereal food has been invented even today. Not only this, several spices — Black pepper, Asafoetida *(Heeng)*, Cumin seeds *(Zeera)*, Coriander *(Dhania)*, Turmeric *(Haldi), Ajvain* etc. were discovered which have medicinal properties. Which of them in which quantity will be added with which vegetable and pulse mainly to reduce health hazards but also to add its health giving properties was a marvellous piece of research. Modern science has yet to study their properties and effect on health. Not satisfied with this, the ancient philosophers went still further. They thought "prevention is better than cure". So two steps were taken:

(a) Fasting, once a week, and on pretext of different

religious days, was popularised. If some knowledgeable person has inclination and time to do some little research, he will soon realise that most of these fasting days are connected with seasons. For example, rainy season which is the worst for health, has major share of these fasting days.

(b) Leaving salt or sugar or fat or cereals or some other eatables for a few days in a year.

Today's medical science agrees that both these strategies will prevent the diseases such as blood pressure, heart-trouble, diabetes etc.

(f) *Health Giving Habits*: The family tradition and customs made it obligatory to follow a few habits which were health giving. Some of them are:

(i) To wash hands and mouth before and after eating any thing. It prevented decay of teeth and chances of getting infection.
(ii) Early to rise and early to sleep.
(iii) To use earthen pot or copper utensil for storing water. Both purify water.
(iv) To drink or eat in silver utensils, if possible. Silver has a purifying effect.
(v) To put *Tulsi* leaves in drinking water.
(vi) To sit erect, to walk erect and to sleep on wooden cot. This prevented diseases like spondalitis.

(g) *Good Thoughts* : Health and mental contentment or psychological satisfaction are closely related. The modern scientists and psychologists agree to it. Ancient Indian sociologists had realised it long back and so they tried to create a family atmosphere in which there will be hardly any scope of fear for the future, brooding or worrying and mental prostitution. The atmosphere was healthy, assuring insurance for the future. Several steps were taken in this direction:

(i) Inter- and intra-personal relations of different family members were based and developed on love, sacrifice duty, respect, tolerance, forgiveness, forbearance, etc. Thus, an atmosphere was created in which 'live and let live' was successfully practised.

(ii) Prayers, devotional and folk songs, dances, games — all contributed to making a robust out-look.

(iii) Faith that whatever He does is for good, Man has a right and duty to act but results are not in his control and the result of each and every act, good or bad, will be awarded, act-wise, the result may be instant or after a time-lag.

II
PATRIOTISM

No country can become independent and thereafter remain independent for long until majority of its people are great patriots. Further, without independence a nation cannot plan its own way of life and strive for either social or political or economic development. Realising this truth the philosopher-sociologists of ancient India gave to its people a way of life in which seeds of patriotism were sown automatically with the birth of a child and were watered and manured thereafter. This miracle was done with the following strategy:

> To love the country, one must know the country, its culture its great men, its value system and be proud of all of them. This pride comes when one has a sense of belonging to the country.
> To develop this feeling, attitude and temperament, a child was initially trained to develop a sense of belonging to the family and to take pride in the family. When this is achieved, love and duty, which are two facets of a coin, take care of themselves and can easily be socialised or broad based.

After the child has learnt to love the family, this love is gradually broad based i.e. socialised. In the next step this sense of belonging and pride is extended to the *mohalla* (locality) then to village, city and thereafter to the educational institution and the teacher. Ultimately it is extended to the country and then to the world.

Today Japan is successfully following this strategy.

A child is ignorant of the pangs the mother underwent when it was in womb. That period cannot generate a feeling of love for mother. So, it was made a normal thing in the Indian families that the child will be fed with the mother's milk as long as possible. Mothers were not modern (or foolish) enough to stop feeding the child for their own body shape. A mother, in this process, developed intense love for the child and brought up the child at the cost of great personal sacrifices. She also became a playmate of the child. Child's playmate activities gave her great joy. The attachment increased. The child saw it, realised it and so loved its feeder, playmate, benefactor and protector. Mutual love developed and soon the child silently started adoring the mother as an embodiment of love and sacrifice. The seeds of a sense of pride and belonging were sown.

Other members of the family, old and young, due to family atmosphere, found time and got pleasure in playing with the child. The child became a toy and the burden of bringing up a child was shared by all. The child also responded and soon developed intimacy, love and regard for all the playmates. Sense of belonging and pride was thus broad based.

It became customary for the mother and old ladies of the family to narrate short stories of patriotism, greatmen of the land, brave, protectors of the poor, the down trodden and the needy. Lyrics with these themes were also sung. The stories and songs made an impression on the heart and mind of the child. It was assured that these stories related to some greatmen of the country and were a historic truth. Thus, a child started knowing and adoring greatmen of the country.

To mould a life and to make a great patriot and humane being many great efforts and sacrifices are needed. This also needs a proper atmosphere. So, each family by custom and tradition was made a model of simplicity, hard labour, honesty and it vibrated with an atmosphere of respect for elders, love for youngers, discipline, patriotism, humility, sacrifice etc. The inter- and intra-personal relations of a family were great educator and taught how to live unitedly. This, with passage of time, helped in keeping the country united and developed unity in diversity.

It was to give a sense of belonging and pride in the family that at the time of ceremonies and also when introducing oneself a person customarily gave out one's own name along with the name of father, grand father and great-grandfather.

A child was also trained to give the name of his village (town) while introducing himself. This was to inculcate a sense of belonging and pride in the place of birth and residence also.

A child was trained to respect the teachers who were given greater importance than even the parents. The institutions like the present convent schools naturally became dear and respected ones. It also sowed and nurtured the seeds of patriotism, on the intellectual and emotional planes.

Thus, a deep sentiment of love, respect, sense of belonging and pride for family, for village, for educational institution and teachers was cultivated in children and it soon included the country also. This attachment was strengthened by calling the country our mother. Like the mother, the five elements of the country help in the formation of our body and also give us food, shelter and everything enjoyable.

The family atmosphere taught children to respect saints. These saints normally were of roaming type. So when they spoke and gave religious sermons, they always gave illustrations from the lives of great-men of different parts of the country and also described history-geography of different parts of the country. In other words, they helped in knowing the country and its people. A reading of *Ramayana* and *Mahabharata* will bear it out.

The family tradition required, in the name of *Dharma,* that a person should visit holy places. These holy places by design were scattered all over the country. While visiting these places, one naturally saw whole of the country and came to know the people.

III
SOCIALISM

The Indian brand of socialism is much superior to the Western type of socialism of today, which is fast cracking and is on the way out. This was based on inner conviction and was followed in a natural way. There was no compulsion and no split of personality. And this inner conviction and naturalism was inculcated through family atmosphere and later strengthened by educational institutions. An idea can be had from the following truths popularised in the ancient families in India:

(1) The barometer of goodness and greatness is not wealth but virtue. Virtue can be seen and realised by others only through actions. So, good and virtuous actions are, in fact,

measurement of one's greatness.

(2) One can control actions and not the results. The result depends upon innumerable variables and factors, some of which may be beyond a man's power to control. So, one should concentrate on good actions without worrying about results.

(3) Good actions always bring good rewards and bad actions are bound to land one in trouble. Gandhi, in his inimitable style asked how one can expect to eat mangoes, after sowing Babool seeds. Newton's third law — for every action there is an equal and opposite reaction — supports this hypothesis. Good deeds are bound to give good results. The results may be immediate or take time depending upon several known or unknown factors. A ball thrown towards the sky is bound to return to earth but the time and place interval depend upon the force by which it has been thrown up, the angle at which it has been thrown, the gravitational pull at that place, the atmospheric pressure, velocity of wind etc.

(4) Next to virtue, age is to be respected. Age represents experience, which is a great asset in social relations.

(5) Love for Matter, beyond a limit, is not desirable. Atom is the smallest particle of matter which has independently existed. This atom can be splitted into neutrons, protons and electrons. Atom when splitted generates tremendous energy. This energy or light is life which helps neutrons, protons and electrons to move and act as a miniature solar system. So, instead of Atom, i.e. matter, light i.e. life or *Atma* is more important and so it should be respected and loved instead of matter.

These truths, along with several others, were taught to each member of the family through inter- and intra-personal relations of the family members, traditions and customs. The visible impact of seeing was naturally more deep on family members and therefore they followed the path in a more natural way. Some of these traditions and actions were :

(a) Elders' actions were not guided by selfishness but were based on love, sacrifice, duty and other human values. The youngers also imitated these virtues and in addition gave respect to the elders. Love for matter was not allowed to stand in these ennobling inter- and intra-personal relations.

(b) Members were taught to respect virtues. A teacher, who was virtuous par excellence, was the most respected person in the country. Not only did students and guardians respect teachers but even the all powerful king, the symbol of authority, power and wealth, left his throne, when a teacher entered his court and he carried out his wishes happily.

(c) Youngers, irrespective of status and caste, gave priority of passage to an elder. They were supposed to salute him first. Even otherwise his advice was final.

(d) Daughters-in-law paid respect to their mothers-in-law even when they were more educated or wealthy.

(e) Detachment from worldly possessions was a *sine qua non*. *Ashram Vyavastha* was designed to give practical shape to it. After the age of 50 years, one was expected to slowly give up income earning activities voluntarily, pass on responsibility to youngers and devote increasingly more time and energy to doing social good, gratis. And after a few years' training and practice this aging man completely gave up income earning activities and also charge of family leadership. The present days complexities of generation gap had no legs to stand in such a set-up.

(f) It was a common practice in every family that a guest was supposed to be a very important person, irrespective of his status and relationship. His requirements were met first. The instances are not wanting. When the house lady was about to start taking her meals if a guest came, she offered her food to the guest and herself went without food.

(g) By the force of custom, everyone was supposed to offer, before starting eating, some food to cow, crow and dog. This was out of love for the animal world.

Thus, a real socialism, by free will, developed.

CONCLUSION

The above description from the real life of ancient India will convincingly show that FAMILY can be a potential unit of planning in producing a VIRTUOUS MAN. And man is the pivot for whose good we need planning and this planning, howsoever perfect, cannot be successfully executed without his co-operation.

The modern Indian planners will do good if they try to produce a virtuous man in the light of the past experience. They can, of course, make necessary changes in virtues and harness more modern techniques. The help of the mass media, for example, can go a long way. The Indian masses will be able to pick up this approach quickly as it is almost in their blood and the results will also be spectacular. But efforts will have to be made to retain the best and good things of the past, find out deformities which had crept in and try to persuade people to give them up.

5

ON FORMAL EDUCATION

Human capital, till recently ignored, is the most important single factor in the life of a nation. No developmental planning has chances to succeed fully, if it is not based on the correct assessment of this single factor. India's past forty years of planning do bear out this fact. Thinkers have now started realising that planning of human capital, if not precedent to, should at least go hand in hand with economic planning.

Education, both formal and social, is recognised, world over, as an investment because it assists in the speedy and all round development of the people and, in turn, of a country. It is therefore, essential that due care should be exercised while preparing an educational plan.

GOALS OF INDIAN EDUCATION

If formal education has to play its vital role of producing a new man and through him a new and developed nation, the goals of education in the country will have to be determined.

The aim of Education in India should be to develop all the faculties of students in a coordinated and balanced way so that an integrated man can be produced. By all the faculties is meant physical, emotional, intellectual, moral, spiritual and social. Nature does not bestow on everybody equal capacities and talents. Every student has different levels of capacities. Consequently achievements of all the students cannot be of the same magnitude; they must differ from student to student. Education should only help a student to achieve the optimum within the limitations of his own natural capacities so that he may be able to lead a more useful and a more happy life and also contribute fully to the development of the country.

It is surprising that more than 40 years have passed after independence and yet the goals of Indian Education could not be determined.

The aims of Education in India can be spelt out as below:

Physical Development

The primary aim of education should be to help students in the development of their physique. A healthy body does not mean that one should become a *Rustom-e-Hind* or a Gama. It simply means that education should enable an individual to improve his health, in accordance with his natural constitution so that he may be able to lead a life normally free from ailments and be capable of withstanding the normal strains of life. To achieve this, regular physical exercise, daily cleanliness of body, living and working places, regular habits which imply self-control and self-discipline and good eating habits are *sine quo non*.

Ancient Indian saints, differentiated between vitality and stamina. The speed with which a person could do physical work was known as vitality. The duration for which a person could do physical work at constant speed was known as stamina. The Indian saints gave greater importance to increasing people's stamina. The whole idea was to produce a healthy person who could do physical work for longer durations at a constant speed.

With the physical fitness, new traits can also be developed. For example, discipline, fearlessness and boldness and courage should be developed in a student by giving him a psychological treatment and training in arms. Again, it often happens that when we see an injustice committed we do not like it but we have not the courage to interfere. This hitch can be overcome through proper training. The outlook of student will have to be broadened and he be made more bold.

Intellectual Development

Literacy is the first step towards intellectual development. So, education should provide a sound literary knowledge to the students.

Knowledge is infinite. Not only that. It is also expanding at a tremendous rate. No individual, howsoever brilliant, can acquire all this knowledge within the narrow span of his life. So, specialisation, in the broad groups viz. science, arts, commerce, law etc. started. When it became impossible to cope with the rapid expansion of knowledge of a group, the specialisation of individual subjects started. Soon, specialisation of a subject was replaced with the specialisation of a tiny branch of a subject. And now even a branch is further splitted up. A ridiculous situation has been reached when an expert of a tiny part of a branch of a subject is not able to claim that his is the last word even in that tiny part of knowledge. And in the bargain, he has lost all concept of unity of knowledge. He knows hardly anything outside his limited sphere. This must be remedied. Education should give broad knowledge alongside the tinkering of specialised knowledge.

The capacity to grasp and assimilate knowledge differs from person to person and also from age-group to age-group and place to place. The intelligence quotients of a grandfather and his grandson are admittedly different. So is the case of a resident of a town and that of a village, and of one country and the other. Hence the courses should be designed according to the intelligence quotient of recipients of education. They should not be uniform for all parts of the country.

Knowledge should not only improve the capacity to think, argue, understand and analyse. It should also help in better solving the problems of real life. So, the intellectual development should develop scientific temper and, more important, commonsense to solve practical problems of life.

The great men of every country have insisted on truth. And what is this truth? Truth means unison in speech, action, hearing and seeing. This observance of truth and search for truth should be the goal of every education. This does not only help in developing a scientific temper but also brings about a qualitative change in life.

Social Development

Man is a social being. To keep the society going, the unbridled instinct of self-interest has to be curbed and kept under control. The saints and sociologists have, therefore, evolved codes of conduct. These codes of conduct differ from country to country, depending upon what is considered good or bad in a country. India is a country with its roots in the ancient past. She has her distinct culture, traditions and human and social values. Today these norms of behaviour are called values. Some of them are: truth, love, self-control, non-stealing contentment, forgiveness, control of *Manas*, non-anger, hardwork, fearlessness, discipline, modesty, non-attachment, self-sacrifice, and above all, a strong spirit of patriotism. Education in India should help in the development of these norms of personality, character and behaviour among the students. It should not only explain the meaning of these terms but give an insight into how to acquire them and go on increasing their quantities.

Man lives in his family, which is the smallest unit of the society. To learn the art of social adjustments, a beginning is to be made from the family. The students should be taught family values, family traditions, family inter-personal relations and they be so groomed as to imbibe all of them. One should be taught the ideal ways of behaviour with one's grandmother, grandfather, mother, father, uncle, aunt, brother, sister, wife. Once one picks them, they should be broad based to include neighbours, teachers, friends etc.

Social adjustment depends upon psychological equilibrium. It is a common experience that when luck is not in an obliging mood, one is likely to lose one's equilibrium. And with disturbed equilibrium, social relations are the first casualty. So how to face adverse circumstances coolly, calmly and take an objective view should be an essential part of education.

The personal, family and social adjustments require both theoretical and practical knowledge. So, in ancient India a student was taught the theoretical meaning of different human and social values, traditions, customs, ideals etc., the logic behind them and their importance in life. Together, with this theoretical knowledge, he was also given practical training. In this direction teachers and seniors provided an example and then with constant exercise it had the desired effect.

Love for the Country, the World and the Universe

Today, on the one hand, inter-dependence of the countries is increasing and on the other, separatist tendencies are also becoming pervasive. Nature has not been fair and just with each country while distributing resources. The expanding knowledge and technical researches are daily tracking out new items of consumption, making it all the more difficult for a country to remain self-sufficient. Thus, inter-dependence is increasing. On the other hand, in the name of protecting national interests and/or ideology (capitalism, communism, socialism, Islam, Christianity etc.) the world is getting divided into blocs.

The real education should inculcate in the students a love for the people of the world through the love of their family, their country and country-men. Just as education, through moral lessons, teaches subjugation of self-interest to the social and national interests, similarly, it should also teach love for the world through patriotism. In patriotism one makes sacrifices first for the family, then for the nation. Once this tendency takes roots, then the next step can easily follow. Patriotism can certainly help in developing a sense of universal brotherhood without sacrificing reasonable national interests.

Spiritual Development

Western educational system is purely materialistic. The result is that excessive self-interest has become the dominant instinct. This is not conducive to promoting happiness or welfare.

Indian thinkers were wise enough to give a new dimension to the functions of Indian education, viz., spiritual development.

Spiritualism means the search for truth. The ancient saints realised that material forms are short lived and are incapable of providing a permanent and real or inner happiness. Their studies revealed that everything is functioning in a set order. The search of this truth was called spiritualism.

Till recently science had been busy in studying the surface of its objects but now it has taken up deep studies of the inner side also. Thus, Indian religion and modern science are meeting at several points in their search for truth. Now they are starting realising the existence of soul, that the soul never dies, that the soul takes rebirth after a time interval and that it is possible to free it from the cycle of birth and death.

Education should make students aware of this cardinal truth.

In summing, up, it can be said that the aim of Indian Education, in keeping with our old culture, civilisation, value system and also the will of the people, as defined in the Indian Constitution, should be to help the students, according to their individual capacities, in developing themselves physically, intellectually, socially, spiritually in an integrated balanced and dynamic way and thus to make them useful citizens of the country and the world.

It may be added that these qualities may be developed to the full, in the end-products, at the last stage of education. How much of each of these qualities will or can be developed, at the primary and secondary stages is to be decided by the experts.

6

TOOLS OF MASS MEDIA

Education is of two types – formal and informal. Formal education begins when the child starts going to a school and ends when he finishes his studies which may be either in a school, or a college, or a university. So, it is for a period of time, imparted by teachers, has a syllabi and an examination. It gets him a degree which is a pre-requisite for a job. It makes a man more knowledgeable in various subjects. It should, as discussed earlier, help in an integrated and balanced growth – physical, mental, emotional, moral, spiritual and social of the student and give him a scientific temper.

Informal education, on the other hand, begins with the birth of a child and continues till his death. There is no time schedule, no class-room, no formal teachers, no fixed syllabi, no examination and no degrees. Mass media – Radio, TV, Press, V.C.R. – can be a powerful part of informal education. It can be harnessed to make a desired environment conducive to a balanced and integrated growth of human personality.

Recently scientists have claimed that they have discovered a new branch of knowledge, which they call environment. This branch deals with pollution also. Botanists, zoologists, geologists, chemists, physicists and even mathematicians seem to be enamoured of this new find. They, however, do not know that long back social scientists had realised the importance of environment and its effect on man. For example, in ancient India, they had harnessed the family atmosphere in producing a good member of the society imbibed with several virtues. Formal education only strengthened it and widened its scope. In England, Robert Owen also propounded the thesis that none is born good or bad but the atmosphere makes him so. He tried, first through Labour Legislation and thereafter establishment of colonies, to produce a good man. Lenin in U.S.S.R. tried to translate the thesis of Marx and thereby produce a new man who will have no love for private-property and help in making an ideal society, a classless and stateless society. It is another thing that the last two experiments seem to have failed.

It is a pity that when everybody recognises the importance of the powerful mass media – Press, Radio, TV, V.C.R., Film shows, documentaries etc., no systematic efforts have been made to spell out their objectives and harness them in making a new man, an ideal man. A small attempt is being made here to give the possible aims of the mass media, specially with a view to producing an enlightened and virtuous man who will himself be happy and will have a healthy effect in making others happy.

The aims can be:

To Provide Entertainment

TV, radio, cinema, V.C.R. etc., to begin with, were considered a good source of entertainment. Even today people primarily purchase radio, TV, V.C.R. etc., for entertainment and also as a status symbol. It is unfortunate that people did not realise that a simple source of entertainment, without a proper aim, can degenerate into eroding finer instincts and values, cheapening the tastes and encouraging crimes. U.S.A. is experiencing the evil effects today. TV and cinema, specially have become the most dreaded things because of their bad effects.

Thus, entertainment should be so designed as to be educative. This education should be in the values, inter-personal relations, social good, work culture, etc.

To Mint Money

Mass media (including press) in the present materialistic world, is increasingly becoming a good business proposition. Press, cinema, documentaries, radio, TV, V.C.R. -- all have become commercialised. When the primary aim is to earn money, then patriotism, human and social values, physical efficiency, work culture, good entertainment etc., will naturally have to take a back seat or even vacate them and go. This is bad. It must stop. There must be a proper marriage between commercial proposition and national character. After all money is not everything.

To Build Image

Political leaders in government exploit the tools of radio, T.V. and video films for image building. This influences the voters and help them to capture power. Unfortunately, today this image is being built up of those politicians who normally do not deserve to be called ideal. This must stop. In the place of image building of political leaders the image of national heroes be projected so that it may inspire viewers and listeners.

To Give Information

The modern educationists feel that these tools should be harnessed

(a) to give all types of information to different types of people – educated and illiterate, intelligent and not so intelligent etc. – so that they may get better equipped to face the problems of life and have a rational judgement.
(b) to give latest classified information on various subjects to those who are at different levels of education so that they may know the latest developments in their respective fields.
(c) to give information with a view to improving skills, in agriculture, horticulture, animal husbandry, various crafts etc. so that quality, quantity and variety of production may improve.
(d) to give information to people engaged in different occupations so that their efficiency may improve.

The modern educators feel that these tools can help in creating a scientific temper. But is scientific temper more important than wordly wisdom? Life is not all science. There are situations where scientific decision may not be a desirable one. So, the aim of informal education should be to provide information to develop a mix of scientific and worldly outlook. If possible, efforts be also made to educate people more and more of subconscious and unconscious mind and of soul.

To Develop Physical Efficiency

Modern times are times of ailments and diseases. Not a day passes when a new disease is not known. Mass media can educate people about sanitation, pollution, diet habits, entertainment habits, etc. and make them exercise — conscious. In India TV is popularising *Yoga*, which, it is increasingly realised, is key to physical fitness, increased stamina and efficiency.

Physical fitness seems to be closely related with food habits, work habits, entertainment habits etc. These should be given proper exposure.

To Develop Work-culture

The modern educationists have yet to harness mass media to inculcate a work-culture amongst workers. In India, unfortunately, work-culture is almost missing. Here the workers waste most of their time in smoking, drinking tea at quick intervals, gossiping and going slow. They are extremely careless. By a proper education, this mentality can be changed. For example, in Japan, even an illiterate worker is serious and sincere to his work. He does not consider himself simply an employee but takes pride that he is working for the nation with the result that an average Japanese worker is the most efficient worker of the world and the strikes are rare. This attitude can also be developed in a worker of any country through proper utilisation of mass media.

To Develop Patriotism

Patriotism is one of the social values but it is one of the most important values. Hence, special mention is necessary.

Patriotism means loving and developing a sense of belonging for the territory of the country and also its greatmen, its culture, its value system, language etc. Just as loving a foreign country and having extra-territorial loyalties is considered as being a traitor, similarly, denouncing ones own greatmen, culture, way of life, value system etc. and blindly loving and respecting foreign country's culture, way of life, value system, language etc. and praising foreign rulers is a sure sign of slave mentality and treachery.

Patriotism is an easy solution even of knotty problems. It gives a goal, a direction and develops consciousness amongst people. Japan and Germany can be cited as burning examples. Due to their patriotism par excellence, Japan and Germany, which were completely ruined in the Second World War, have become economic and military giants in a very short period.

To Strengthen Democracy, Secularism and Socialism

India has given to itself, out of its own sweet will, democracy, secularism and socialism. So, the aim of mass media should be to explain the meaning of these terms to the countrymen and try to strengthen the foundation of democracy, secularism and socialism in people.

Mass media, while explaining the meaning of these terms and popularising these ideas should give the Indian version of these terms and draw inspiration from India's past. For example, socialism of the Indian brand means, out of one's own sweet will, not to have too much love for materialism, believe in detachment and ultimately practise renunciation. It also means greatest love for others and to help them to one's utmost capacity. Certainly, this socialism is much higher than the socialism forced by the State which has almost broken down in U.S.S.R. Again, secularism of the Indian brand does not mean becoming irreligious. Indian seers preached *Dharma*, which is a way of life, rather than a religion, a mode of prayer and rituals. *Rishi* Manu talks of ten characteristics of Hindu *Dharma* which are nothing but ten values and no religion of the world can have a quarrel with them. So, mass media should explain, through the scriptures of the various religions and *Dharma*, the important human, social and spiritual values of each religion and the characteristics a man should possess to become a good man. This will remove misunderstandings and confusion prevailing in religions and *Dharma* and bring people closer. To think and say that the state has no responsibility in doing this great job, because of secularism, is certainly a misplaced belief. The state should play an active role in it and try to evolve a composite culture without the fear and favour of any sect.

To Build and Strengthen Moral Fibre, i.e. Human and Social Values

There are two distinct philosophies. One says that 'Ends justify Means'. Here the set aims get priority and means lose all importance. So, morality has no place in this philosophy and it is termed as a luxury and *Dharma* or Religion as opium. The other view, let us call it the Indian view, says that "Means justify Ends". Here means, and that too, the noble and moral ones, are given the greatest importance. It is argued that ends depend upon a number of variables, known and unknown, and so cannot be controlled. There is also a close relationship between input and output. When you sow trees which do not bear fruits, how can you get harvest of juicy fruits? One has a control over means only.

Mass media should work in unison to create a healthy environment in which insistence is on moral means. This can be done by

(a) Explaining the meaning and importance of human values, social values and spiritual values.
(b) Teaching the methods to imbibe these values.
(c) Strengthening conviction in these values.

To sum up, man's personality has several dimensions – physical, mental, emotional, moral, social and spiritual. All these facets should be developed. But the development of each one of them must complement and supplement one another and should form one single whole. Moreover, it should also be a balanced one. This alone will give optimal personality development. This development of optimal personality should be the aim of mass media.

One thing more like the individual, the nation has also a personality. It has distinct social, political, economic and religious aspects. They should also be developed as an integrated and balanced whole. This, again will depend upon the personality of the people of that country. A co-relation exists between individual's personality and nation's personality. This co-relationship should be strengthened and developed. This should also be the function of mass media.

7

SOME OTHER TOOLS

In the ancient past, formal education was not available to the majority of population. The present day mass media was also not known. But ancient *Rishis* had invented some effective tools to sow the seeds of human and social values amongst the people. Some of the important tools were:

1. Places of worship and pilgrimage.
2. Family rituals, functions etc.
3. Social festivals and national functions.
4. Cultural functions – music, dance, drama, puppet shows, poetry and so on.

A brief description of these tools will be beneficial to assess their utility in the modern times.

I
PLACES OF WORSHIP AND PILGRIMAGE

There seems to be no dispute in the proposition that temples and pilgrimages played a vital role in finalising the desired human values and then cultivating them amongst the masses, most of whom were illiterate.

It is a truism that India is a vast country with diversity of geographical features, agricultural production, industrial production, languages, social functions, ways of life, etc. and yet the whole of the country had almost the same human values, aspirations and thinking. This miracle was probably achieved through, in modern terminology, temple culture and pilgrimage culture.

A historical review of gods will show that at the beginning of life, the ignorant man felt dazed at seeing the natural phenomena – the Sun, Moon, stars, wind, fire, water etc. He started worshipping them as gods because they were source of life and their anger, as they felt, could cause disaster. These natural phenomena were given a name and a shape. Thus, the statues of various gods sprang up. With advancement of civilisation, tastes got refined and with them the statues became more artistic.

With passage of time, the number of gods increased. It was 33 in Vedic period and became innumerable later.

The ancient *Rishis* found out that the nature, likes, dislikes, tastes etc. of people differ. They also discovered that the members of a family, being blood relations, have usually common genes and so their nature, likes, dislikes, tastes etc. are normally common. Based on these two observations, they invented a number of gods giving them different natures and qualities. They felt that every family and its every member should select a god, more akin to his own nature. This affinity is likely to command respect, devotion and submission to the god. So, every family had a god of its own liking. The members were given freedom to worship another god if they liked, who inspired them better.

Normally every temple had one main deity. So, people worshipped that deity in that temple. For example, temples of Rama, Krishna, Shiva, Hanuman, Durga etc. are different. But with increase in population and shortage of space, more deities were accommodated in each temple. They became multi-deities.

The temples of the different parts of the country had different architecture, different gods, different methods of worship and practically everything different and yet they aimed at common human values and successfully achieved them. It is for the modern sociologists, psychologists, philosophers and scientists to find out the secrets and the methods of this miracle.

A temple was a place where people assembled daily out of their devotional zeal to get spiritual contentment. It had beautiful surroundings with a garden attached to it. It had an atmosphere of love, humility, prayer, confidence, dedication etc. The religious prayers, discourses, rituals all had one common aim – to inculcate human values round a god. This was a psychological approach par excellence. The temple priest, a person with proven qualities, was the central point around whom temple culture rotated.

In India, a number of religious places, scattered all over the country, were established by our *Rishis* (i.e. social scientists). Each one of these places of pilgrimage has its own background with which it acquired this status. These religious places are normally located in beautiful natural surroundings giving an immediate effect of peace and beauty to the visitor. These were the places where scholars of religion, who were not only theoreticians but also practical men, assembled. There were religious discourses based on the principles of philosophy (i.e. *Darshan*) to which the masses listened and a few participated. Hindu saints have, in course of time, developed a number of *Darshans* but six of them are most authentic. Nothing was accepted which was not based on sound logic and also passed the test of practicability. So, the pilgrims, who assembled from the different parts of the country, heard these discourses, benefited from them and went back to their respective homes with re-strengthened belief that whatever was told to them by the home priests or temple priests was correct and beneficial for the individual as well as the society. Thus human values taught at home got restrengthened and at the same time national integration automatically took solid roots.

II
FAMILY RITUALS AND FUNCTIONS

Family functions and rituals are inter-changeable words.

The concept of family developed gradually in a natural way. From clan it became a joint family and now it has become a nuclear family in the West. This nuclear family is also on the verge of disintegration, with no love left amongst its members.

Indian *Rishis*, in their wisdom, used family as an effective tool to produce value-oriented men and women. They admirably succeeded in their mission.

Indian sociologists harnessed the technique of family functions and rituals to produce value-oriented end-products.

These family functions can be grouped under three broad categories:

1. The functions based on original religious scriptures such as *Vedas*.
2. The functions based on *Puran* and *Smriti*. *Smritis* were an effort to codify the way of life. Naturally, with passage of time, old *Smriti* and its associated codes gave way to new *Smriti* and new codes.
3. The functions based on, what is called in common parley,

Budhia Pujan, i.e. old knowledgeable ladies guidance. With passage of time, the old ladies went on editing the functions and rituals keeping them useful. This was dynamism par excellence.

Some of the important family functions were sixteen *Yagya Sanskars*, which started with conception and ended at death. All families observed them. Then the *Smritis* while codifying the Hindu society, provided different *Varnas*. Some functions were closely related with *Varna*. Again the ancient sociologists realised that each person has his own nature, taste, temperament etc. It was observed that most of the members of a family, being blood relations, must have common genes. Based on this observation, each family was given a god, akin to family member's nature. Some worshipped Rama, others Krishna and yet others Shiva or Hanuman. The family functions differed with the family god. Lastly, as per principle of convenience, family functions were modified by the elderly ladies.

These family functions had only one central idea. It was a well known fact that the family members, being blood relations, must have common genes. So, the family functions should be so designed as to maintain the family values or human values of the family and to try to further develop them. The whole approach was goal-oriented.

It is unfortunate that with passage of time, due to several factors – slave mentality, efforts of our rulers to brainwash us and convince us that there is no rationality in our functions and rituals and they are only a sign of our conservatism and backwardness, our losing insight into the brilliant ideas behind these functions, loss of dynamism of functions etc. – these value-oriented family functions are now being observed more or less as social compulsions.

III
SOCIAL FESTIVALS AND NATIONAL FUNCTIONS

In Indian context, we can differentiate between festivals and functions. After Independence, Government of India, has announced several National Functions such as Independence Day, Republic Day, Gandhi Jayanti, Teachers' Day, Childrens' Day, etc. unfortunately, these important national functions are becoming official functions with decreasing peoples' participation. They are becoming par rituals.

Social festivals, on the other hand are those which we got from our ancient past and we, even today, observe them with gusto.

India is a vast country with different geographical features, climate, rainfall, soils, crops, languages etc. In ancient India, the means of transportation and communication were not fast. Hence, it was not possible to have common social festivals throughout the length and breadth of the country. But in spite of this diversity the purpose appears to be common, viz. to strengthen value system and love for country through *Dharma*.

Some of the important social festivals are:

Holi	-	North India
Deepawali	-	Northern and Western India
Rama Naumi	-	North India
Krishna Janmaashtmi	-	North India
Shiv Ratri	-	North and South India
Onam	-	South India
Ganesh Chauth	-	West India
Durga Puja	-	East India

These functions remind of some greatmen or some great event and thereby the important value for which they stood. They also keep the history and culture alive.

With slavery, and consequently slave mentality, we were taught to forget our past and raise doubts about its utility. We readily did it. So, at present, the educated people having 'scientific temper', have no faith left in these Social Festivals. However, the socalled uneducated, conservative mass of India's people, have still faith in them and so they are surviving. But the objectives have become dim.

IV
CULTURAL FUNCTIONS

Cultural functions – music and dance, poetry, drama and puppet shows etc. – were unique inventions made by our ancestors. It will be beneficial to have a glance at them.

Music and Dance

Indian music and dance have a very old past. Hindu *Dharma* claims its origin from the *Vedas*. Music and dance also claim their origin from one of these *Vedas* i.e. the *Sam Veda*.

The *Vedas* taught Hindus to worship the natural phenomena — the Sun, the Moon, the stars, wind, water, fire, earth etc. So, in music and dance also they taught us to follow the principles of Nature and sing and dance to please the natural phenomena.

Indian music and dance are full of rhythm. These rhythms, we are told, have been taken from the mother nature. The roaring of the ocean, the sound of the flowing water of rivers, the sound of the wind – all have a rhythm. The earth, the sun, the stars – all move at a set pace and order. This has provided rhythm to our music and dance also.

The *Vedas* gave nine *Rasas*, viz.,

1. Romance or Libido (*Shringar*) between husband and wife.
2. Love for children (*Vatsalya*).
3. Devotion for supernatural phenomena (*Bhakti*).
4. Anger (*Raudra*).
5. Hate (*Vibhatsa*).
6. Pathos (*Karuna*).
7. Bravery (*Veer*).
8. Humour (*Hasya*).
9. Detachment (*Shanti*).

Indian music and dance are based on these nine *Rasas*. Exponents of various *Ragas* have prescribed what *Raga* is more effective at a time. These *Ragas* are also based on seasons. So, what *Raga* is to be sung or danced at a time of the day and of the year has been spelt out.

Indian music and dance are a good physical exercise. Thus, on one side, they increase vitality and on the other hand, and more important, stamina. They also provide good control over voice and body and nothing, which is not in rhythm, is acceptable.

Neither Indian music nor dance can be performed without full concentration. So, they develop the powers of concentration.

Mental power is developed because one has to understand and differentiate between different notes, *Ragas*, etc.

Indian music and dance, based on nine *Rasas* invigorate *manas* and elevate a person to spiritual heights.

It can, therefore, be said that Indian music and dance integrate body, mind and *manas* and so help in development of an integrated personality.

The effects of Indian music and dance are the same on listeners or viewers as on performers. They also got elevated.

With passage of time, classical music and dance were given a new dimension. They were popularised. This was known as folk music and folk dance. While keeping the principles intact, to popularise them, they were interwoven round a story of real life and a real situation.

Poetry

Sanskrit poetry, in its turn, is indebted to scriptures which were, as a rule, written in Sanskrit. The four *Vedas* are in verse, *Puran*, *Valmiki Ramayana, Mahabharat, Geeta* – all are in verse.

Sanskrit poetry has its own characteristics. It is in rhythm. It can be sung. It is lyrical. The language and style are effective. It has high ideals. The similies and metaphors are appropriate and effective. It invokes different *Rasa* – libido, love for children, devotion, anger, hate, pathos, bravery, humour and detachment. So, it takes both the composer and the listener to higher and nobler emotional planes.

Sanskrit poetry integrates mind, *manas* and soul. It ennobles.

Hindi poetry has borrowed everything from Sanskrit poetry – language, style, metre, rhythm, *Alankars*, *Rasa* etc. So, Hindi poetry also integrates human personality, gives high ideals and motivates people to nobler and better ends.

Hindi poetry has taken note of the real life situations and tried to give a direction to people. For example, during the Mugal rule the depressed Hindu masses were consoled, encouraged and given a goal through devotional poetry. Similarly, in British period Hindi poetry popularised patriotism, Gandhism, non-violent struggle etc.

Today *Kavi Sammelans* and *Mushairas* (Recital of poetry by the assembled poets) are extremely popular. They can develop taste of people, give them ideas and direct them to a set goal.

Drama and Puppet-shows

Sanskrit literature has given one of the finest dramas and monologues to the world. The beauty of these dramas and monologues was that besides being literary master-pieces, they could be staged. They were not only a source of recreation but moulders of ideas and also pace-setters. *Ramayana* was staged every year and the practice successfully continues to survive even today. Thus, these dramas kept us alive to our cultural heritage, value system and history.

Hindi also produced some good dramas but by then cinema had acquired predominance over the theatre and hence the Hindi plays were staged less and less. So their effectiveness to awaken the masses and to encourage them towards set goals became minimum.

Puppet shows tended to imitate the drama but could not succeed much either as a big source of entertainment or character builder. Afterall puppets are puppets, incapable of conveying emotions so necessary in successful and effective staging of drama.

PART THREE

THE STRATEGIES

8

THE SOCIAL ANGLE

India is a country of multi-religions. The idea of the importance of various religions can be had from Table 8.1:

TABLE 8.1: Population of major religions

Sl. No.	Religions	1971		1981	
		Population	Percentage to total population	Population	Percentage to total population
1.	Muslims	6.14 crores	11.20	7.55 crores	11.36
2.	Christians	1.42 "	2.59	1.61 "	2.43
3.	Sikhs	1.03 "	1.89	1.30 "	1.96
4.	Hindus	45.34 "	82.72	54.97 "	82.63
5.	Buddhists	0.38 "	0.71	0.47 "	0.71
6.	Jains	0.26 "	0.48	0.31 "	0.48
7.	Other religions	0.21 "	0.40	0.27 "	0.42
8.	Religions not stated	0.36 "	0.01	0.60 "	0.01

In Table 8.1 Hindu has been shown as a religion which it is not. It is a *Dharma*, a code of conduct, a way of life. It is a combination of religions such as Arya Samaj, Sanatani, Radha Swami, etc. Again, Sikhs, Buddhists, Jains are as much a part of Hindu *Dharma* as other religions are. To show them separately is not justified.

If we take a bird's eye view of these different religious societies of India, we will find that in course of time, certain social evils crept in each one of them. It will be advisable to take a stock of them before suggesting social strategy.

I
HINDU SOCIETY
(Sikhs, Jains, Arya Samaji, Sanatani, etc.)

The Hindu society is a very old society. When several less old civilisations and societies have perished, the Hindu civilisation and society is still alive. It shows that it had something special. But it too developed, in course of time, certain deformities and vices. Probably, these vices were necessary to meet the challenges of time. For example, *purdah* system was introduced to protect the ladies from the greedy eyes of Mughal rulers and Mughal soldiers. But once it was introduced, it took roots and was not discarded with the end of Mughal rule. Today, Hindu Society is discredited with several evils such as:

(a) Caste system – untouchability, hypocrisy, egoism etc.
(b) Women – Marriages, Dowry and *Purdah*.
(c) Indiscipline – dishonesty and hypocrisy.

It will be profitable to have some idea of these evils.

Caste System : Untouchability, Hypocrisy, Egoism etc.

In the Vedic period, society got divided into four *Varnas – Brahmins, Kshatriyas, Vaishyas* and *Daas* now known as scheduled castes.

At the very outset it may be stated that *Varna Vyavastha* was neither divine nor all the *Varnas* were born simultaneously. They were born as per needs of the time. It is also a myth that *Varnas* were determined on the basis of birth. In its developed form, a *Varna* was given after careful study of a man's nature, temperament, aptitude, skill, etc. and it was possible to change one's *Varna*. There was no question of higher and lower or an untouchable in *Varnas*. This was an original and excellent social technique to make people quality-oriented. But this *Varna Vyavastha* died a natural death when society progressed beyond a point (both in number and dimension) and *Varna Vyavastha* could not hold the ground and lost all its utility.

The place of *Varna Vyavastha* was taken by castes, which were not *Varnas*. When castes also could not meet the demand of society, sub-castes were born. Today a situation has developed where the two have lost all utility. It is unfortunate that due to orthodoxy and loss of dynamism, the Hindu society has not been able to throw them out and they have added to it, in course of time, the evils of untouchability, hypocrisy, egoism etc.

Mention of *Varna Vyavastha* is found in the *Rig Veda* (X.90.12). So this *Vyavastha* must be quite old, say 5000 B.C. In this verse, it is said that four *Varnas* – *Brahamins, Kshatriyas, Vaishyas* and *Shudras* were born from mouth, arms, thighs and feet respectively of *Virat Purush*.

In another verse of the *Rig Veda* (10.90.13), it is said that Moon was born from *Mann*, Sun from eyes, Indra and Fire from mouth and Air from *prana* of this very *Virat Purush*. Again, from this very *Virat Purush*, sky, heaven, earth and directions were born (*Riga Veda*, 10.70.14).

In the *Mahabharata* period (1000-1500 BC), Lord Krishna showed his *Virat Roop*.

This means that the myth of *Virat Purush* was used first to show the creation of universe, then the creation of social institutions and thereafter, the powers of Lord Krishna. Obviously, there is nothing divine in it. It is merely a style of presentation.

The above conclusion gets strengthened when we study the scriptures in a correct way and find similar division of societies in other civilisations also. For example:

(a) In *Iran* there is the myth that from the head of *Yim* came priests, from arms, soldiers, from stomach, agriculturists, and from feet, artisans.
(b) In *China*, the society was divided into four classes – Nobles Agriculturists, artisans and businessmen.
(c) In *Egypt*, the society was divided into land-owners, agricultural labourers and slaves.
(d) In the *Sumerian Society*, the society had four classes – Aristocracy (Nobles, Bishops etc.), ordinary citizens, agricultural workers and slaves.

It will be fair to say that in India, as at other places, society got divided into broad groups on the basis of work. It was a sort of broad functional division. There was nothing divine about it. Had the *Varnas* been born from the same *Virat Purush*, they would have been close relations. The question of higher or lower should not have arisen.

This functional division of society should have taken place gradually, as per need of time. Obviously, it could not be simultaneous. For example, in the early days of life, man lived alone. Then he started living in a clan. But even then the concept of a family life had not developed and clan led a nomadic life. This might have necessitated a division of work. The strong, fearless and brave might have been required to kill or capture wild animals and defend the clan from the attack of other clans. The other set might have, as per their skill, tried to tame these animals and look after them. The third set might have been assigned the duty of milking the animals, preparing the food and distributing it. In this clan life, all lived together. Obviously, in this system woman was a common property. In several cases, we know the names of mother but not of father. For example, Satya Kam did not know the name of his father. Again, the father of *Agasth Rishi* was not known. Illustrations can be multiplied. Probably, then the Hindu society had a matriarchal system. Head of the family who was a mother was called *Matri*, which meant one who distributed things as per a measurement *(Ma)*. In the *Ramayana* period, Queen Kaikai's parents belonged to the matriarchal system. The sculptures of *Nav-Durga* found in Mohan-jo-daro also lend support to it.

At this time productivity of a person was just sufficient to meet his bare requirements. So, when one clan attacked the other, they took away the young ladies and cattle and killed the rest. They enjoyed a feast. The arrested young ladies were called *Daasis* and not *Shudra*. They were taken as part of a clan and shared in work (*Atharva Veda*, 12.3.13; 12.4.9 and 5.13.8) and slowly lost their identity.

With the progress of society, man learnt the art of cultivation. This increased the productivity of man. So, now even the males were arrested and called *Daas*. These *Daas* were to help members of the clan in all types of work. These *Daas* were not slaves. At worst they were labourers. They were mainly involved in animal husbandry (*Maitryani Samhita*, 4.27 and 10 and *Panchwinsh Brahamin*, 6.1.11), agriculture, they were called *Krishi Daas*, *Pushan* or *Paushak* (*Vrahad-Aranyak Upanishad*, 14.13) or *Flam* (Vedic Index II, p. 389, *Vassayana Samhita* 10.10.13) and crafts.

Gautam Smriti says that everyone is born *Shudra*. Thus, *Varna* was not determined by birth. It was fixed by the family priest on the basis of close study of a child's nature, traits, virtues and actions at the time of *Upnain Sanskar*.

There are innumerable instances to show that *Varna* could be changed. Man is not static. His nature, temperament, taste, etc. can change. Moreover, *Varna* was even changed as per demand of the situation. For example.

(i) Vishwamitra was a Kshatriya. He was later known as *Rishi*, i.e., Brahamin.
(ii) Valmiki was a *Shudra* but later became a *Rishi*.
(iii) Sumitra, the wife of king Dashratha, was a Shudra. After marriage she became a Kshatriya.
(iv) Satyavati was a *Shudra* but after her marriage with King Shantanu she became a *Kshatrani*, grand-mother of the famous Kauravas and the Pandavas of the *Mahabharata*.
(v) People of Mongolian race migrated to India and settled down on the bank of the Brahamaputra river. *Shankh Smriti* (13 century) helped in their absorption in *Hindu Dharma*.
(vi) Hoona, Kushan, Tukhar, Yuchi, Kuchi etc., came to India and all became Hindus.
(vii) Mohd. Bin Kasim attacked India in A.D. 713. He went back leaving thousands of followers. They were all given different *Varna* as per *Deval Smriti*.

In Vedic literature, the word '*Shudra*' has been used only in a few verses. This shows that it came in currency quite late and was interpolated thereafter. Slowly, it replaced the original word *Daas* or *Daasi*. R.S. Sharma informs us that there was a tribe in Greece known as *Kudra*. A part of this tribe came to India and settled down in Sindh. This *Kudra* became *Shudra via Saudrai* in India. Alexander attached a tribe of Sindh which was known as *Saudrai*.

Daas, or *Daasi* or *Shudra* were never considered inferior or untouchables. On the other hand, they were respectable people of the society. For example.

1. King Sudas and King Paijvan were *Shudras*.
2. There were armies of *Shudras* (*Mahabharata* 7.66 and 19.7).
3. A *Shudra* soldier accompanied the sacred horse of *Asvamedh Yagya* (*Strot Sootra*, XX.5.13; XX.50; XIV.1.46).
4. *Shudras*, who were able craft men were given high offices in the court. They were called *Ratnin*.
5. Vyas, Parashar, Vashishtha and Valmiki are known as great *Rishis*. They were all *Shudras* to begin with.
6. There are many number of instances where *Shudra* women were married to people of other *Varnas*. Sumitra, the wife of Dashrath, was a *Shudra*. Satyavati, wife of King Shantnu, was a *Shudra*.

It can be concluded that in the Vedic period, *Varnas* were functional divisions of society with no complexes attached to them. Is it not surprising that all the incarnations of God – Rama, Krishna, Buddha, Mahavira – were born in Kshatriya families but were even worshipped by Brahamins.

It may also be added that once these few functional groups, viz., *Varnas* got firmly established, efforts were made to provide a goal to all of them which would encourage individuals to improve qualitatively and at the same time, would be in the interest of society and the nation. By this time, it was realised that neither materialism alone nor mere spiritualism is good. A proper admixture of the two was ideal. Hence, those enlightened persons who were not interested in self-engenderisation and spent all their time and energy in the service of society and moulding the lives of the people, were given great respect and called Brahamins. On the other hand, those who were active, materialistic and excelled in various crafts, i.e., were producers, were called *Shudra*.

Geeta, tried to remove deformities of *Varna Vyavastha* that had crept in it. It prescribes the qualities of different *Varnas* (Chapter 18, Verses 42, 43 and 44). Not satisfied it propounds the theory of *Nishkam Karma* (unattached actions) and says that every human being through his sustained *Nishkam Karma* can achieve the ultimate goal of life, i.e., *Moksha*, freedom from the cycle of birth and death. The complexes, if any, attached with *Varna* vanish. Everyone gets equal rights to progress and achieve *Moksha*.

With passage of time new deformities crept in and new problems cropped up. For example, due to inter-caste marriages *Anulom* and *Pratilom* – which were not uncommon, the new born got traits of both the *Varnas*. In which *Varna* to keep him, became difficult. The problem became more acute when two different hybrids married and the child got traits of four *Varnas*. Again, with progress, one profession got split up in a number of sub-professions. For example, the profession of reading and teaching required books. To produce books, writers, paper manufacturers, printers, binders etc. were required. Obviously, all of them could not be called Brahamins. What *Varna* to allot to them? These difficulties became unsurmountable and so *Varna Vyavastha* was allowed to die a natural death.

Recently some scholars have given a new angle to how the *Varna Vyavastha* developed and what was the place of *Shudras* in society. The gist of what these scholars say is as below.

In the ancient period, when population was very little, greed overtook people. This greed gave birth to several vices – over eating, lethargy, laziness, accumulative mentality, illegal and immoral actions, etc. (*Vau Puran*, 8/37-40; *Mahabharata*, *Shanti Parva*, 59/17-21).

To set things right, it was thought necessary to spread education for good conduct. (*Yoga Vasishtha*, 2/11/5-12). So, society got split up into two – *Sadachari* and *Durachari*. *Sadachari* people were called *Dev*, who had given up vices of greed etc. and *Durachari* were called *Danav* or *Asur* or *Malech*, who could not improve their conduct (*Shukra Niti*, 1/44).

Sadachari or *Dev* society was classified in four *Varnas* on the basis of education, including spiritual education:

(i) *Brahamin* who excelled in education, both literary and spiritual. It is said that all are born *Shudra* but become *Vipra* only after studies *(Gautam Smriti)*.

(ii) *Shudra*, who did not go for education but excelled in work (*Tap*) (*Yajur Veda*, 30/5), *Shudra* kills laziness through his hard work (*Yajur Veda* 26/15). Hard work (*tap*) gives mobility and activity. So, *Rig Veda* (10.12.90) says that *Shudra* was born from feet which indicates activity, mobility and hard work. *Vrahada Aryanekopnishad* (1/4/11-13) calls earth *Shudra* (because of its activity) and *Rig Veda* (10/90/14), *Yajur Veda* (31/13) and *Atharv Veda* (19/3/8) opine that earth was born from feet. *Vadrayan* split up the word *Shudra* into two – *Shuk* (i.e., sorrow) + *Dra* (i.e., to run). It means that one who helps in removal of other's sorrows through his activities is *Shudra*.

Society thus had an ideal combination in *Brahamin* and *Shudra*. *Brahamin* through his learning (which included spiritual learning also) and *Shudra*, through his hard work and knowledge of craft (arts), kept society healthy and happy. *Manusmriti* (5/129) has said that the hand of a craftsman is *Shudra*.

Shudra, according to Hindu scriptures, were never considered untouchables. *Manusmriti* (4/253) orders that one should take food at the house of *Shudras* – agriculturists, barber, *Daas*, people engaged in crafts etc. This concept of untouchability is a gift of Mughal Kings which was perpetuated by British rulers in their own selfish interest.

It is an indisputable fact that Hindu society mainly lived in villages. In villages and cities too, there was no provision of latrines. People went to answer to the call of nature in open fields. So, the question of cleaning latrines or taking away refuse did not arise. *Manusmriti* (4/49-51) and *Ayur Veda* advise that a pit be dug before replying to the call of nature. It was the Mughals, who constructed latrines for their *Purdah Nashin* ladies. They forced a section of society to clean the latrines and cart away the refuse. They naturally were segregated and became untouchables because of unhygienic conditions. The Britishers in accordance with their policy of "Divide and Rule", widened this gap. We, in our slave mentality, accepted this division.

It can, therefore, be concluded that *Shudra* was never an untouchable or less respected.

With the death of *Varna Vyavastha*, the institution of castes was developed by persons interested in self-preservation. It will be a serious mistake to equate it with *Varna Vyavastha*. For example, castes or *Gotra* show sometimes the place of residence, sometimes the *Guru* (teacher) and sometimes the profession. Gaur are the original habitants of Bengal, Saraswat of Punjab and Misra of Mithila. Gaur are both Brahamins and Kayasthas. Similarly, Misras are both Brahamins and Carpenters. The students of a *Rishi*, says Parashar, can be of any Caste.

Today castes and sub-castes have become innumerable. They have also lost the relationship with the qualities expected of a *Varna* or caste. Today, lakhs of *Brahamins* are illiterate. Thousands are doing business and any number of them are employed in all types of services, from shoe factories to textile industries. So, what is the sanctity of these castes now? Sooner we get rid of them the better.

Today there seems to be no advantage – social, political or economic – which these castes and sub-castes were supposed to give to the Hindu society. Today, they are the fountain-head of several disadvantages, namely.

1. *Political Disadvantages*

(a) In free India now elections are mainly fought on the basis of castes. Almost all parties select a candidate of the caste of the majority of voters. This caste consciousness has increased after independence. Certainly, it is not conducive to good government as best men are not selected as our representatives.

(b) With castes, the concept of hierarchy got tagged up. This acts as an hindrance to national unity.

2. *Social Disadvantages*

(a) It is a historical fact that upper castes have badly treated the lower castes and exploited them badly. They have been subjected to several types of tyrannies. Today, socially, they have become a backward lot. Probably because of tyrannies, the conversion to other religions became easier. This also gave encouragement to untouchability.

(b) The successful exploitation and ill-treatment encouraged male population to badly treat their women folk. A host of social evils, e.g. to deprive them of education, use them as domestic servants, and treat them as a source of recreation etc., developed.

(c) The caste system encourages rigidities and is a hindrance to progressive outlook.

3. *Economic Disadvantages*

Caste rigidities, adversely affected mobility of labour. This was neither in the interest of workers nor of enterprises and ultimately of economic growth.

Seeing to the defects of the caste system, Dr. S. Radhakrishnan said:

"Unfortunately this device to prevent the social organisation from decay ultimately prevented it from growing."

Hindu Women : Marriage, Dowry and Purdah

Today, in spite of repeated efforts of social reformers, Hindu women are suffering from three ailments – Marriage, Dowry and *Purdah*.

Marriage

Marriages in the Hindu society even today, are mainly arranged. When we talk of marriages we have three aspects in mind:

1. *Child Marriage:* Legally, the marriage age of a Hindu woman is 18 years but in practice, marriages, specially in villages, at the age of 14 years or even below are not uncommon. The early marriage adversely affects health and birth rate. It leads to higher infant mortality also.
2. *Widow Remarriage:* Legally now a widow is free to remarry. But society, even today, does not look at it with favour. So, widow-remarriages are not very common. In case of death of husband at an early age, widowhood becomes a curse. The lady is not wanted, barring exceptions, at the home of her husband. She is not even welcomed at her parent's house. It is natural that the sex-hunger and desire to dress nicely and enjoy life will not automatically die with the death of husband. So, this unwilling suppression is likely to lead to psychological upsettings and sexual laxities. All this is not desirable from a social point of view.
3. *Inter-caste Marriage:* In India, castes and sub-castes are still having a strong hold over masses though they have lost all their utility. So, inter-caste marriages and more so, inter-religion marriages, are not common and are looked down upon as an undesirable thing.

Divorce

Divorce appears to be a corollary of marriage.

Among Hindus, marriage is not a contract but a sacrament. It is said that marriages are made in heaven and so they cannot be broken. So, the question of divorce hardly arises.

When the two strangers are wedlocked then some adjustment to make a happy life is necessary. But this elasticity, the will to adjust must be on both the sides. And the basis of this can only be love. In India, due to socio-politico-economic changes, specially the impact of materialism and western way of life, this love, this spirit to give and take has been minimised. It has resulted in growing number of unhappy marriages. Normally a lady, being of the weaker sex, suffers.

Recently, legal provisions have been made where divorce has become possible.

Dowry

In Hindu society dowry is a very old institution. The parents of a girl thought it their moral and religious duty to give dowry to the parents of the bridegroom. There was no demand and no compulsion. Law did not provide a share to the girl in the parental property so it was probably a way to compensate the daughter. Moreover, it was a technique to keep cohesion between two families joined in marriage bond.

With the diminished hold of *Dharma*, people with materialistic outlook, thought it prudent to demand money before settling a marriage. This was a pre-condition of marriage, a compulsory tax. In real terms, it was not dowry but a price of the bridegroom.

In the post-Independence period, Hindu Inheritance Act was amended which gave a share to the daughter in the parent's property. But in spite of it, the demand for dowry is on the increase. This is because of the increased materialistic outlook.

This love for dowry is resulting in unequal marriages, tortures of brides, bride burning, tension in families and broken families.

Purdah

In ancient India, *Purdah* was unknown. When the Muslim rulers established themselves in India, they started forcibly taking away young beautiful girls. So, *Purdah* was invented. Thereafter, it became a social custom. In the post-Independence period, it has almost vanished from the middle and upper classes of the towns. It is also, it appears, under marching orders, in the rest of the classes, both in towns and villages.

Purdah leads to conservatism. It makes girl's education difficult. It robs self-confidence.

Indiscipline : Dishonesty and Hypocrisy

Hindu society, to begin with, was a disciplined society. Prof. D.P. Mukherji used to say that there was a beautiful regimentation in the Hindu society and the fun was that the target was unaware of his real fate. With the impact of western culture, western education and western way of life, the hold of *Dharma* decreased and so "freedom" came to the Hindu society. Political freedom converted this "freedom" into licence and today, indiscipline has become a birth-right of everyone. This indiscipline is now encouraging illegal activities such as violence without provocation, thefts, robberies, dacoities, kidnappings etc. The whole social fabric is in danger. Chaotic conditions are overtaking us.

Before Independence, the poverty stricken villagers were a picture of honesty. They will habitually not even speak a lie. And if you ask them to face the river Ganges and then make a statement, in ninety per cent cases, they will speak the truth. Unfortunately, after independence secularism, socialism, democracy, progress and love of goddess *Lakshmi* has made us a rank dishonest people. It needs no proof that this is a sure road to economic ruin and social degeneration.

Hypocrisy and egoism were probably the traits of the Hindu society. When and how it started manifesting itself is difficult to spell. Probably, unknowingly we started bragging of our past glory, past heroes, past philosophy, and even our own parents, without bothering about our present. This soon became a habit and a second nature. Caste system (not *Varna Vyavastha*) encouraged it. Admittedly, this is a great weakness of man.

In short, the need of the hour is to rejuvenate the Hindu society and make it a dynamic one. But while doing so, we should not forget our culture, the great depository of virtues. We have to modernise it to make it more purposeful.

II
THE MUSLIM SOCIETY

The muslim religion orders the believers not to doubt or question the *Holy Quran*, the Prophet and Hadis. One is expected to have full faith in them. So, whatever is written and whatever interpretation is given to it is accepted silently. Even if there is some doubt, one has not the courage to speak it out. So, the Muslim society had not its share of social reformers. It is primarily a conservative society. But the worst is that very few authentic works, written by Muslim scholars, specially social scientists could be found out. The non-muslim social scientists probably have attempted even less than Muslims.

The author was not prepared to believe that the Indian Muslim Society has no social evils. So, efforts were made to supplement the meagre literature available by collecting information through indirect sources and discreet enquiries from friends. The following lines are the result of this half baked information.

Most of the Indian Muslims are converts from Hindus. So, they have taken with them the customs, traditions and even social evils from their original faith. Add to it, the evils which they might have inherited from the Muslim societies which invaded India ,and established their rule, i.e., mainly Iranian and Turkish.

Child Marriage

In Muslims, child marriages, specially of girls, are not uncommon. This vice is more prevalent in villages than cities. The fixing of marriage age by law has hardly made any difference. For example, among Meos, normally people below 15 years get married.

Purdah

Purdah is very common in Muslims. Soon after Independence, some relaxation was allowed, specially amongst educated families, whose percentage is quite low. Recently, the wave of fundamentalism or 'back to *Shariat*' is again forcing even educated ladies to observe *Purdah*.

Marriage, Divorce and Maintenance

Among Muslims, marriage is a contract. And as a contract, it can easily be broken. Muslim religion grants this right only to the male. It is very difficult for a lady to get a divorce. Even the Muslim Law of Marriages made by Britishers did not make much change in the situation. The laws amended during the post-Independence period have also not given any relief to the married muslim lady.

In Muslim law, a divorced lady is not entitled to any maintenance allowance. The Indian law permitted maintenance. In the famous *Shah Bano*'s case the Supreme Court allowed this maintenance. But then there was a hue and cry and under the threats of Muslim religious bodies, Prime Minister Rajiv Gandhi amended the law. So now a poor divorced lady has been robbed of her due right.

Dowry

Dowry, in another form, is prevalent in the Muslim society also. Here, the marriage proposal is sent from the boy's side. But this proposal is sent to those families only from which one can expect handsome gifts. And once the marriage is settled, it is not difficult to send signals under the plea of avoiding waste. More westernised muslim families are coming forward to have a direct settlement. Among Meos, dowry is demanded and paid.

As per Muslim religion, the husband has to promise a *Mehar* to the bride. This is not given at the time of marriage. This was a promise made before the *Kazi* (Priest). In earlier days, *Mehar* was promised as an attraction to the girl's parents to accept the matrimonial relationship because probably the number of ladies was much less than male population, specially when four marriages were permitted. This ritual continues even today though there is not much sense in it. But the lure of *Mehar* encourages unmatched marriages.

Polygamy

Muslim religion permits a male to keep up to four wives at a time subject to certain conditions. Today, these conditions have lost all meaning. They are honoured more in breach rather than observance. This adds to the miseries of womenfolk.

Re-marriage

A Muslim lady, whose husband has died or who has been divorced is entitled to remarry subject to certain conditions. But women re-marriage is not encouraged by the society.

Sub-groups

Without entering into the academic debate whether caste is a cultural or a structural phenomenon, one wishes to take up the issue whether the Muslim society has its sub-groups? If yes, whether the membership is determined by birth? Whether the sub-group and occupation have any relation? Are there free inter-group marriages? Is there free inter-group dining? Is there any hierarchical order? The purpose is to find out whether Muslim society is a groupless (or caste-less) society as made out.

At the very outset, it may be stated that normally Muslims have common prayer places and common burial grounds though even here, the differences are visible. For example, among Moplahs of the South-West coast, the "sections even have separate mosques, separate religious organisations and separate burial grounds". (vide Victor S. D'Souza). Same is true of Muslim Tamils (vide Mattisan Mines) and Ahmadias or Quadianese. They have their religious places in Pakistan.

Muslim society can be divided into two main groups, each having further sub-groups. They are:

1. *Ashrafs*: This includes Sayyad, Sheikh, Mughal and Pathan. They can be compared with the upper-classes of Hindus. In these four also, there is a hierarchical order. Sayyads are considered highest followed by Sheikhs, Mughals and Pathans in that order.
2. *Non-Ashrafs*: Their number varies from state to state but on the basis of U.P. survey eighteen groups have been identified (vide Zarina Bhatty). They are: *Julahas* (weavers), *Mirasis* (singers), *Darzis* (tailors), *Halwais* (sweet-makers), *Manihar* (bangle sellers), *Nais* (barbers), *Bakar-kasabs, Kasab* (butchers), *Behnas* (cotton traders), *Behen-Kasabs* (a mixed caste with butchers and cotton traders), *Telis* (oil extractors), *Kabariyas* (vegetable sellers), *Gujars* (dairy men), *Kasgars* (potters), *Dhobis* (washermen), *Fakirs* (landless labourers who also watch grave-yards and beg for food), *Nats* (who perform acrobatics) and *Banjaras* (gypsies). These eighteen groups have also been arranged in a hierarchical order.

Among Moplahs of Kerala, Thangals are the highest followed by Arabias, Malabaris, Pusalors and Ossans.

Scholars' opine that the idea of superiority and inferiority is based on two factors:

1. *Foreign Blood*: Those who claim descent from the Prophet's daughter, Fatima, are esteemed the highest. Thereafter, the children from the Arab father are placed. Among Moplahs Arabias claim that their father was an Arab sailor while mother was a local. They are placed next to Thangals. Similarly any one claiming relationship with foreign Muslims – Persian, Turkish etc. are placed in order of hierarchy.
2. *Occupation*: Those who have a cleaner and respectable occupation like *Julahas, Darzis, Halwais* are placed higher and those whose job is unclean or dirty or less respectable like

Banjaras, Nats, Fakirs, are placed the lowest.

It is accepted that the sub-group of *Jaat* (another name for caste) is primarily determined by birth and it cannot be easily changed.

Normally, the inter-group marriages do not take place. For example, there cannot be a marriage between an ASHRAF and a NON-ASHRAF. Even among Ashrafs, marriage between a Sayyad and a Sheikh or that between a Mughal and a Pathan may be possible, but a marriage between a Sayyad and a Pathan does not take place. Similarly, among Meo of Rajasthan, there are 13 Pals groups and 67 *Gotras*. There are restrictions in matter of marriages – some are permissible and some are not. P.C. Agrawal holds that Meos practise endogamy. Again, among Moplahs marriages between different groups — Thangals and Ossans (Barbers), Arabias or Pusalors (new Muslims) are prohibited (Victor S. D'Souza). Similarly, in West Bengal, inter-group marriages between Sayyad and Shah or Shah Fakir, or Pathan and Momins or *Julahas* or Mughal and Patuas or Potos (Painter of Hindu idols) are rare (Ranjit K. Bhattacharya).

Normally their is common dining. But sometime segregation is also practised. For example, in Bengal, a Sheikh will dine with Pathan, or Mughal but will not dine with Shah Fakirs, Patuas or Momins. Same is the case in U.P. Among Tamils, Muslims belonging to *Hanafi* School of *Sunni* (Rawther and Labbai) would not commensal with the Muslims of *Shafi* School of *Sunnis* (Marakayar and Kayalar).

Thus, it can be concluded that the Muslim society is not a casteless or groupless society.

Sects

The Muslim society is also ridden with sects. They have *Sunni, Shia, Khoja, Bohra, Ahmadias* etc. Each sect has its own religious leaders, own rituals and own way of life. The intermingling among different religious sects is almost formal. Often they fight amongst themselves. The riots between *Shias* and *Sunnis* in India over *Tazias* are very common. Some have even different places of pilgrimage. A *Khoja* goes to pilgrimage to Iran, where his religious head might be residing and not to Mecca or Madina. Similarly, a *Quadiani* or *Ahmadia* goes for pilgrimage to Quadian, a place in Pakistan. *Sunnis* and

Quadianese often have violent clashes.

Rituals

The Muslim society has its full share of rituals. Birth, death, prayers, *Ramzan, Id* and even pilgrimage to Mecca and Madina – everything has its own rituals. None can afford to break them because even today Muslim society in India is not sufficiently forward looking. Illiteracy and hold of *Mullahs* and *Maulvis* keep them under constant subjugation.

Normally, every sub-group has its rituals. For example, not obeying customs and rules result in ex-communication among *Khojas*. Again, in West Bengal, ablution after urination, offering of *Namaz* etc. are insisted upon. Not doing so may mean placing one in a lower group (i.e., a type of ex-communication). In various groups of Meos, monogamy is a rule. Among Moplahs, *Mehar* is determined by customs.

This, in short, is the condition of the Muslim Society in India.

III
THE CHRISTIAN SOCIETY

It was surprising to know that most of the books on social studies of India confine themselves to mainly the studies of the Hindu society and hardly any book gives details about the Indian Christian society. So, the following pages are mainly based on the information collected from friends.

Indian Christians consist of :

1. *Anglo-Indian Christians*: If one of the forefathers was a Britisher and he married an Indian, then the off-springs are known as Anglo-Indian Christians. Now their number is almost negligible. They are mainly in South India, Goa and round about Ajmer.
2. *French Indian Christians:* If one of the forefathers was a French and he married a local, then the children are known as French Indian Christians. Their number is very small.
3. *Portugese Indian Christians:* If one of the forefathers was a Portugese and he married an Indian then the children are known as Portugese Indian Christians. Their number is also very small.

4. *Muslim Christians:* Those Christians who are converts from Muslims are known as Muslim Christians.
5. *Hindu Christians:* Those Hindus who embraced Christianity are known as Hindu Christians.

There are many number of churches that are functioning in India. Some of the important churches are: Catholic, Protestant, Anglican, Methodist, Evangelist etc. Each church takes inspiration from the Prophet, Lord Christ, but is different in philosophy, rituals, etc. For example, Catholic Church insists on simplicity and disciplined life for the sake of enjoyment in heaven after death. On the other hand, Protestant Church is less rigid. It does not worry about life after death. Thus, these churches can be compared with the different sects or religions of Hinduism, like, Buddhism, Jainism, Radhaswami, Arya Samaj etc.

These churches have a strong temptation to convert people of different faiths to Christianity. These conversions, earlier, were done on the basis of fear. Since Christianity has spread under the patronage of the state, the fear of the state authority was always there. Non-believers were even persecuted. But thereafter, the net of mission work was spread mainly in those areas which were backward, difficult to approach and sensitive. People worked with the missionary zeal. This, with temptation of free medical treatment, education, service, a wife, worked wonders. Today most of the North-West and backward areas of Madhya Pradesh comprising mainly Scheduled Tribes are Christians. Similarly, South, specially Kerala, is predominantly Christian.

Indian Christians, due to inter-church rivalry, try to maintain their individuality.

Indian Christians, on the basis of their original faith before conversion, are also maintaining their individuality.

These two things taken together, result in the division of Indian Christians on the basis of churches and original castes. They too suffer from the complexes of superiority. For example, a Christian converted from Brahamin caste will never marry his children to a Christian converted from scheduled caste. They do not like to have social contacts with each other even. So, change of religion has not made much of a difference.

Among Christians, a marriage proposal is made from the boy's side. But this does not mean that there is no dowry. Earlier, people did not demand a dowry but sent a proposal to a family from which they could expect handsome dowry. In talks, on the plea of avoiding waste, sensible hints about dowry were given. Now, with the old values being discarded (in the name of modernisation) direct negotiations of dowry are made.

Indian Christians have their share of rituals. The rituals connected with church are strictly observed. Besides this, the rituals of original religion (before conversion) are also followed. These rituals concern birth, death, marriage, birth-anniversaries, prayers etc. On the whole, the Christian society is in no way a less ritualistic society than a Hindu society. It is another thing that being a small society, these things are not widely known outside the community. Even a glance on the life style of Scheduled Tribes, which are mostly Christians, will confirm it.

Indian Christian society is more of a materialistic society. This has adversely affected the mutual relations within the family and also outside the family. This materialistic outlook mixed with western outlook has made family life quite formal where small issues generate tensions. Since marriage is not a sacrament but a contract and divorce is easily available, broken marriages are increasingly becoming common.

This, in short, is the story of Indian Christian society.

Summing Up

The above narration clearly demonstrates that the Indian society, in spite of its respective religious denominations, has by and large, similar social evils. The difference, if any, is of degree only. The reason for this commonness is that almost all belong to the stock of Hindus and even now are governed by almost the same culture, traditions, customs etc. It can, therefore, be concluded that the Indian Society can be rejuvenated on the basis of some principles.

Social Strategy

During the past forty years, Indian leaders tried to achieve political unity through the doctrine of secularism. It appears that they have failed miserably. It is apparent that in this land of multi-religions, political unity can be achieved only through social unity and not *vice versa*. It is time that efforts be made to develop principles on the basis of which a new united Indian social order may be constructed.

Man is a social animal. He has the herd instinct, he wants to live in a group. So, to satisfy this instinct and also to refine man, gradually society with its network of social institutions – family, marriage, religion, educational institutions etc. – came into existence. With scientific advancement followed by industrialisation, the real aim of life got blurred and materialism was allowed to take over the reins under the impression that materialism and happiness are interchangeable terms. In this mad race for materialism, man became hard pressed for time. Further, new thinking also raised doubts on the utility of the society and its institutions. So, knowingly or unknowingly, functions of the social institutions were transferred to the new hired institutions. For example, the function of the family to rear a child was transferred to baby sitters, child-minders, creche and residential schools, and of recreation, which was also a family function, to TV, V.C.R., toys, etc. and marriage became mainly a luxury to satisfy sex hunger and soon the new ways were found and the old concepts of celibacy and faith, love for partner were given a silent burial. Religion was called a disease and an opium and was slowly made untouchable. Its place was given to secularism, atheism and Marxism.

If we want to change the goal from maximum satisfaction of wants to *Anand*, i.e., where none lives in either misery or excessive luxury and all have the opportunities of optimum development of their respective personalities in an integrated and balanced way so that they may have an enduring happiness, we will have to revive the old social institutions, keeping their basic characteristics intact while changing their forms as per needs of time. This is essential for continuity sake. In doing so, we will have to remember:

(a) That life is one. Society and its social institutions are an essential part of life. They are as important as the other parts – political, economic etc. – are.

(b) That all the segments of life, which go to make the whole life, should be so designed as to work in perfect unison with each other. All should supplement and complement each other and also compete with each other to achieve the goal of *Anand*.

(c) That all the segments of life — social, political, economic etc. — can play a frictionless role only when they are built on common foundations.

(d) That society and its institutions are not an end in themselves. They are means to an end, and the end is the goal of *Anand*. So, the modern concept that society or the state is supreme and the individual is unimportant will have to be changed. Both will have to co-exist on equal and respectable terms.

To re-construct society on healthy lines, the pages of Indian history have to be turned over to draw some lessons.

Society in Harmony with Nature

The Indian seers observed the following characteristics of nature:

1. Nature moves onward in a gradual and systematic manner. It evolves. It is dynamic.
2. Nature is moving in a set direction probably to reach a particular destination.
3. Nature's onward movements are cyclic.
4. Nature in India, is never extreme. It takes a moderate course.
5. Nature affects man in a number of ways.

The history of nature, as told by the modern scientists, is that first came lifeless matter. More than 128 basic elements have been discovered so far. Ancient seers talked of five elements of nature – earth, fire, air, water and ether and said that they made life. The modern scientist agrees and says that permutations and combinations of these lifeless elements produce life. Probably, first came moss. With the gradual evolution, then came flora. Small plants came first followed by bigger plants. Modern botanists admit that plants have not only life, they have even power to feel, think and react. In the process of evolution, then came fauna. First came small insects, followed by the bigger ones, birds and then animals. And thereafter, appeared man. It appears, in this process of evolution, a better man or a super-man is to come. So, nature is slowly moving towards a set goal. Man and his institutions – social, political and economic – should help nature.

Modern scientists have also discovered that nature, specially cosmic, has cyclic movements. Earth rotates in a cyclic motion on a cyclic path. This gives the cycle of day and night and the cycle of various seasons which have a profound effect on man. The moon also rotates in a cyclic motion giving a fifteen day cycle. Modern zoologists have discovered a close co-relationship between cyclic movement of the moon and reproduction of animal world. And the doctors have discovered a co-relation between the mad man's madness and the moon's fifteen day cycle, the movements of stars and planets are also cyclic. Thus, it appears, all move onward in a systematic manner, on a cyclic path and in a cyclic motion. It means that while moving onward, they have ups and downs. After achieving optimum height, downward trend starts and when a maximum downfall has been achieved, the upward trend starts. And this goes on.

Nature, specially in India, takes a moderate course. There is neither extreme heat nor extreme cold. There is neither too much rainfall nor scanty rainfall. There are neither too long days nor too long nights.

It is apparent that mother nature has a profound effect on man. For example, man was born because of nature (matter) and his physical existence also depends on nature. Not only this. His intellect, his psychology, his way of thinking and action – all are governed by nature. So, modern science is trying to conquer nature. Indian seers differed. They, instead of conquering nature, wanted to work in harmony with nature.

Indian seers-*cum*-sociologists tried to build up a society in harmony with nature. So, Indian society, has the following foundations:

1. Matter is lifeless and also not permanent, *Atma*, the soul, which is a part of *Parmatma*, the super-conscious, is permanent. It never dies. So, society was built on the love of *Atma* and not matter.
2. Death means that *Atma*, the soul, leaves the body. This soul, after a time-interval, reappears in another body. Thus, a cycle of birth and death goes on. Modern science is inclined to accept it.
3. The Indian seers tried to make Indian society a living society, a dynamic one in which conscious efforts were made to make man a better man till he achieves the goal. And the goal or aim of life was to achieve salvation from the bondage of birth and death and not the temporary enjoyment of the worldly things or temporary abode in heaven or hell.
4. Man can travel towards the ultimate goal through his good

deeds only. He has control over his deeds and not on the results. Results are the resultants of a number of variables, known and unknown, controllable and uncontrollable. Hence, man must insist on good deeds without bothering about their results. Insistence on good acts, without worrying about results, was termed as unattached action (*Nishkam Karma*).

5. On this onward journey towards a goal, it's likely that society should go astray and downfall may start. But this downfall will be short-lived only. When the maximum downfall has taken place, with or without the help of a great man, upward trend will start. Indian seers had hinted that God Himself, in the form of a great man, takes birth to help man. They had counted more than 24 such incarnations of God meaning thereby that already 24 cycles of ups and downs have taken place. In other religions Prophets have done the same thing.
6. Extreme stands are prohibited in the Indian society. Moderate or a balanced view is always preferred. Here a middle course between attachment and detachment, between fame and love, between *Vidya* (knowledge of soul) and *Dhi* (knowledge of matter), etc. are advocated. Hence, to speak truth is recommended but, at the same time, this truth should not be bitter, it should be sweet. Similarly, in medicine, for health, a balance between three ingredients *Kafa* (phlegm) *Bata* (wind or gas) and *Pitt* (bile), is to be achieved.
7. The Indian seers felt that society should function in accordance with *Dharma* (not religion). And what this *Dharma* is? It has two meanings:

A. *DHARMA* means as per one's nature. Water has a nature to flow, fire has a nature to burn, wind has a nature to blow. Similarly, every man is born with a nature, some basic characteristics, traits, likes and dislikes etc. Indian seers wanted to develop man in accordance with his nature i.e., genes. It was called to follow *Dharma*. In this, two basic postulates were discovered.

(i) *Karma*, i.e., actions are in the hands of a person but not their results. Results depend upon a number of factors, known and unknown, visible and invisible. But one thing is certain. Good acts will give good results and bad acts will give bad results. Just as the flowery trees will give flowers, fruit trees will give fruits and thorny trees will give thorns, similarly good deeds will give good results and bad deeds, bad results. The time lag, however, between action and result, may vary, depending upon a number of factors.

(ii) Soul is immortal. After death, soul changes the body but takes along the *Sanskars* of previous life which become nature in the new life. This cycle of birth and death goes on till the ultimate goal of *Moksha* is achieved.

On the basis of these two cardinal principles, it should not be difficult to conclude that a child is born with some characteristics which are the result of his previous life's actions. In life, he is bombarded by environment – good, bad or indifferent. Conscious efforts must be made to weed out the bad things and imbibe more and more of good things so that quality of life, in accordance with the basic traits, or nature may slowly improve and take him towards the attainment of salvation, if possible in this life or, in the next life or lives. But the progress must continue.

Indian seers classified, in the broadest sense, human nature in order of gradation, into three categories:

(a) *Satvik* – One that is not at all self-centred and that believes in living for others only.

(b) *Rajsik* – One that is basically self-centred but also believes in the philosophy of live and let live. It is given to passions.

(c) *Tamsik* – One that is only self-centred and believes in the philosophy of eat, drink and be merry. It does not believe in right or wrong. For it, end justifies the means.

Similarly, they classified human actions into three – *Satvik*, *Rajsik* and *Tamsik* which follow the aforementioned three basic natures. Indian seers wanted people to move consciously from *Tamsik* to *Satvik via Rajsik*. Thus, an integration of nature and actions was attempted so that desired results may be achieved.

B. *DHARMA* also means, to observe some fundamental principles of life whose importance have been repeatedly tested in different countries, at different times, by different religious persons. These principles of life, i.e., values, may change in importance as per need of time and place and even healthy additions and subtractions be made. Some of these values are truth, simplicity, love, self-control, non-stealing, non-anger, renunciation of worldly things, non-violence, discipline, patriotism etc. It is the duty or *Dharma* of every man to imbibe more and more of these values – human, social and spiritual – so that his own life may become better and happier, and ultimately he may attain salvation and may have helpful effect on others. These values will certainly improve the quality of society as a whole.

Dharma, in both these senses, has a cyclic effect.

A FEW SUGGESTIONS

On the basis of the above, the following steps for evolving a new Indian social order can be recommended:

1. Values

The scholars of three religions – Hindu, Muslim and Christian – opine that all the religions preach almost similar values of life. We must, therefore, find out these common values. For example, Hindus give maximum importance to the values (human, social and spiritual) of purity, non-stealing, knowledge confined to matter, knowledge of soul, truth, self-control, patience, forgiveness, control of *manas*, non-anger, non-violence, fearlessness, discipline, patriotism, renunciation of worldly things.[1] I think Muslim and Christian scholars will not dispute the importance of most of these values. So, after finalising the desirable social values, through modern mass media, the meaning of these values and how to imbibe them more and more in life, be propagated. Let the Indian society be a value-oriented society where materialism takes its proper back seat.

The value of Patriotism, i.e., to develop a sense of belonging to the country, to be proud of its culture, value system and greatmen and to be prepared to lay down even one's life to protect the territorial integrity and culture of the country, should be used as the greatest unifying force. Our experience tells us that at the time of national calamities – an attack from China or Pakistan, or restoration of *Rama Janma Bhoomi* Temple at Ayodhya, for example, generated a tremendous response from all sections of people. People forget their religion, their caste and even their mutual likes and dislikes. The whole nation stood as one man. We should take lesson from this experience and think out national issues which may unite people and force them to act collectively. This flame of patriotism should be kept continuously burning.

Today law and order has been made a casualty by the self-seeking politicians. Crime and greater heinous crime has become order of the day. Use of firearms and now electronic devices is increasing. Politicians in office, bureaucrats and criminals have formed a party to rob the people. People ask, was this the freedom for which they had sacrificed a lot? The funniest story is that a law abiding person applies for a licence of a fire arm and gets it for personal safety and not as a status symbol. When violence erupts and he needs his arms most, he is asked to surrender them, for obtaining which he has spent a fortune. On the other hand, persons in possession of illegal arms and ammunitions and those who commit crimes go scot free. So, can a war against criminals, the politicians who patronise criminals and the officers and other people who protect and encourage them, be not waged in the name of patriotism? Mass patriotic awakening can end this anti-national tag-up and enforce law and order.

Wasteful government expenditure for petty personal gains has taken an ugly form. Politicians in office and bureaucrats are specialising in it. The crumbs are thrown to the henchmen and business men. So, a team work to rob the nation of the benefits of freedom and development expenditure and make it bankrupt is in operation. Patriotism demands that the people be awakened and made to oppose politicians, officers and their henchmen who indulge in wasteful expenditure. The loans, both internal and international, can be liquidated and the nation be saved of its hard earned freedom only when such anti-national people are exposed and liquidated. Let it be called a patriotic deed to expose and obstruct such anti-national persons.

Corruption is another mighty evil which is eating away the root of freedom. It is the bounden duty of every patriot to expose and oppose the guilty. Even the tiniest corruption should not be ignored.

2. Samrasta (Integral Humanism)

The late Pandit Deen Dayal Upadhyay, President of Jan Sangh, was an humble man. He was a great visionary but a down-to-earth practical man. On the basis of his long association with the movement to rejuvenate the Hindu society, he propounded ideas which he called *Samrasta* (Integral Humanism). Greatmen like Lord

Rama, Lord Krishna, Swami Vivekananda, Swami Ramtirth, Rama Krishna Deva, Chaitanya Maha Prabhu, Baba Hari Das, Narayan Guru and others subscribed to this concept. To understand it we should be clear about the following:

a. "Diversity" means different things having different nature or families. Diversified things, as such, can be united but they cannot be made equal. This is the Law of Nature.
b. "Inequality" or "Equality" refer to different parts or pieces of one thing. Nature, it appears, does not believe in equality. For example, fertility of land is not the same everywhere. Rainfall in every part of the world or even different parts of a country is not the same. Mineral wealth provided to different countries by Mother Nature is not equal. Similarly, all people are not endowed with equal height, colour, intelligence, health, talents, etc.

Similarly, no system can ensure equality. In democracy, each and every person cannot become a Prime Minister or Chief Minister, or M.L.A. Even in a communist country, all people could not become equal, even economically. Mao of China admits that after a bloody revolution and establishment of Dictatorship of the Proletariat, those who came in power became greater equals amongst equals. So, he talks of repeated revolutions. Inequality appears to be in-built in a system.

Lord Buddha saw disparities and consequent sufferings of humanity. He wanted to remove them, through *Karuna* (mercy). He pleaded that the people should have mercy for the needy, the suffering, the unhappy, in grief, in fear, in scarcity and thus help them. *Karuna* or mercy is good but immediately it divides the society into two, one who gives mercy and the other who receives it – the giver and the taker. Obviously, it could not unite the diverse or unequal sections of society. In return, it degenerated a man. It created complexes.

Gandhi almost committed the same mistake when he called "untouchables", *Harijans*. He created a new class. Instead of uniting people or making them equal, he made them class conscious. On the one hand, people were called upon to pity them and help them. Reservations in education and services were made. On the other hand, the scheduled castes became conscious of their number and considered it their right to get patronage. Unity and equality became a farther dream.

Dr. Ambedkar, who was a great scholar and a patriot got swayed by a feeling of revenge. He organised scheduled castes and brought them to fight for their rights. When the calls for rights and duties and of class conflict start, the first casualty is unity and equality.

When we ask our countrymen to have pity on the scheduled castes, scheduled tribes and backward classes; when we talk of reservations for them; when we organise weeks to remove untouchability and we pay similar other lip sympathies, the effect is exactly opposite to that we contemplate. Separatist tendencies, complexes, etc. become more pronounced. Deen Dayal seems to ask: has anybody seen a mother to have a pity on her invalid child? She loves and the child responds and a new world is created.

India is a multi-religious country. Here Hindus are in a majority and the largest minority is of Muslims. Muslims were taught to organise themselves as a separate identity and fight for their rights. They were taught not to consider this country as their own. They were made to fear Hindus. By implication it meant to be ready to retaliate. This preparedness, this fear complex and this separatist tendency resulted in the division of the country. Not satisfied, the history is being repeated. The appeasement policies pursued by the different political parties seem to have opposite results. Unity is evading us. Communal riots are increasing. We are unable to solve the problem. It confirms the hypothesis that Muslims are being discriminated against, it is in the interest of muslims to remain united and attack whenever the need be. This mentality is now being increasingly disliked by Hindus, who are, in reaction, getting organised. All this is not providing unity or solving the problem of economic, social and political inequalities. Suspicion, violence, claims for rights etc. act in opposite directions.

Deen Dayal Upadhyaya revived the old philosophy of *Samrasta* (Integral Humanism). When milk and water are mixed, they get integrated and it becomes difficult to differentiate between the two. In spite of this integration they do not become equal. Deen Dayal, therefore, decided not to bother about making all segments of the Indian society equal – economically, socially or politically. He thought that neither nature nor any system favours it or can assure it. So, he wanted to integrate different sections of society so that they may even lose their individual identity and become a united and healthy society.

How does he integrate different sections of the Indian society?

Karuna (mercy), *Daya* (pity), reservations, demand for rights etc. cannot do it. Experience proves it. It is only the magic of *Mamta*, i.e., **love** which can integrate the society. So, *Samrasta* (Integral Humanism) means to unite or integrate through *Mamta* (Love). Love alone can help in social, political and economic rejuvenation of each section of the society.

For love, there must be a common ground. A mother loves her children because they are a part of her body and soul. What is the commonness in the different sections of society? Hindus believe in soul and its immortality. Other religions also believe in soul though they do not subscribe to the cycle of birth and death. Modern science appears to be accepting the existence of this soul hesitatingly. Deen Dayal Upadhyaya tried to make this soul the common linkage. He said that our soul is the tiny part of the super-conscious, i.e., *Parmatma*. So, we are children of the same super-conscious. This concept should generate mutual love and regard. This love will automatically encourage willing sacrifice without drum-beating. This will not only unite but help in speedy removal of deficiencies and weaknesses and grant of equal opportunities to all.

This is the magic of *Samrasta* (Integral Humanism).

3. Family Life

Family is the basic school where the deep rooted impressions are created and the seeds of future life are sown in the child. The family atmosphere, full of respect for elders, sacrifice by elders, discipline, sharing sorrows and happiness together, etc. should be revived in India. This is the most important single unit from where the rays of a good social order may emanate.[2]

4. Ashram Vyavastha

Indian seers turned sociologists, with a view to working in unison with nature, invented a strategy to produce a superman out of an ordinary man who will ultimately achieve *Moksha*, salvation from the bondage of life and death, through *Anand*. This social strategy is popularly known as *Ashram Vyavastha*.

These seers, while trying to produce a superman, wanted to solve many socio-economic problems such as frustration, unhappiness and differences between generations resulting in tensions. For all this, they evolved the scheme of *Ashram Vyavastha*, which admirably succeeded.

Meaning

The normal span of life in ancient India, it appears was 100 years. This span, under *Ashram Vyavastha*, was divided into four equal parts, each part extending for 25 years. These parts, on the basis of their characteristics and functions, were called: *Brahamcharya* (student life), *Grahastha* (married life), *Vanprastha* (part time social worker) and *Sanyas* (detachment).

The Brahamcharya Ashram

The first 25 years were devoted to acquiring knowledge, character building and all round development – physical, mental and spiritual. In these 25 years a person was taught three R's and was gradually taught the basic virtues and truths of life such as truth, fearlessness, simplicity, dignity of labour, moral values, patriotism, economic progress and moral progress do not march hand in hand for long, the aim of life is salvation, i.e., eternal happiness (and not temporary pleasures) which comes not through too much attachment to things material but by slow and gradual self-renunciation, self-control of all the senses and service of God through service of His creations. A *Brahamchari* was taught the fundamentals of all these truths and efforts were made by his teachers to sow the seeds of a full life in him. He was also given practical lessons on how to imbibe these virtues. The atmosphere of the school and colleges, then known as *Gurukulas*, and exemplary effect of teachers' lives played an important role. The social atmosphere no less contributed in impressing upon the young minds the truth and practicability of these ideas.

The Grahastha Ashram (i.e., the Married and Active Life)

After completion of education and passing the tests of the *Guru* (i.e., teacher) a student was permitted to enter into the second Ashram of life i.e., the *Grahastha*. The span of *Grahastha Ashram* was also of 25 years.

The Hindu saints were well aware of the truth that mere teaching of principles of life did not carry much conviction and that when a person was able to test the validity of these principles in his own life, only then he was convinced and was keen on adopting them. Besides, they also knew that society demanded that the material needs of life should be met and life should continue and not come to an end. So, the young *Brahamcharis*, after the completion of their education and training, were asked to marry, beget and rear up children, have a house and devote all their energies to earning and spending activity. This second leg of life's journey was considered the most important one and normally none was allowed to jump it over. It was said to be the best and most important *Ashram* of life because it was only through this *Ashram* that one discharged one's duty towards the country, society and the family, and through one's own experiences got convinced of the futility of materialism and correctness of the preachings of the *Guru* (i.e., teacher) and the scriptures.

The Vanprastha Ashram (Social Worker)

During the 25 years of grinding in *Grahastha Ashram*, not only did one gracefully discharge one's duties towards one's country and family but in the process also became aware of the truth of the fundamental principles so arduously taught by the teachers during *Brahamcharya Ashram*. Realising that material pursuit did not give permanent peace and happiness but made one restless and unhappy, running after a mirage, one, by sweet will, started the journey on the third leg of life, i.e., the *Vanprastha Ashram*. Here one started slowly but steadily renouncing material things and devoting more and more time and energy to non-material pursuits. The responsibility of the family was willingly passed on to the younger generation and more and more time was devoted to transcendental meditation and social service. King Dashrath, father of Lord Rama, himself expressed a desire to abdicate throne, the symbol of material power. And this is not the solitary example. It was a common feature prevailing in the Hindu society in antiquity.

When an aging father willingly passed on the leadership of the family to his son, the scope of family tensions automatically ended and instead an atmosphere of mutual love and respect for elders grew.

When a mature, retired and self-satisfied person, on his own, took to social work, which included political work also, the material temptations did not normally sway him, since he had seen the world, had acquired maturity of mind and could dispassionately analyse things. This type of social workers did immense good to society and remained contented themselves. They earned gratitude and respect of society and their advice became law. When such social workers, who were called saints, visited the court of a king, the king used to get up and welcome them. The king, under the compulsion of circumstances and traditions, normally carried out the advice and wishes of such social workers. King Dashrath had to send his two teenage sons, Rama and Lakshmana, with Vishvamitra in spite of the fact that he did not relish the idea.

The Sanyas Ashram

Twenty-five years in *Vanprastha* made a man pretty old and mentally and physically unfit for any arduous work. So, after the age of 75 years, one had to retire even from active social work. But lest time hang heavily, the Indian seers suggested that the persons in *Sanyas* should devote their spare time to transcendental meditation and prayers. They should even leave their hearth and home and start living in comparatively lonely places, away from the noise of cities and habitation, where it might be easier to concentrate on spirit. These elderly persons, on the basis of their experience and knowledge, did educate people through their discourses, writings or any other constructive hobby which they happened to like to follow. These persons were supposed to reside away from their families so that they might not be considered as a liability by their children. Hence, these persons were expected to cut down their wants to the minimum. This kept them physically and mentally fit. And it was the duty of the society to look after these respected persons by providing them the basic necessities of life. However, there was no state compulsion to retire, nor was there any scheme of old age pension. Everything depended on one's sweetwill. The social atmosphere was such as enabled everyone to consider it as one's part of duty to contribute, as per one's resources, to the welfare of these retired persons.

NOTES

1. For details see Chapter Second.
2. See Chapter 4.

9

THE POLITICAL ANGLE

India became independent on August 15, 1947. Soon afterwards a Constituent Assembly was constituted to frame a Constitution for India. This Constituent Assembly consisted of choicest jems of political workers, who had given the very best of their lives to the freedom struggle. It had also the best available constitutional experts, jurists and lawyers. The leaders of industry, commerce, trade, agriculture and noted scholars also found a place in the Assembly. Thus, it had the cream of the country. These people laboured hard and after ransacking all the known constitutions of the world gave India a model constitution. This Constitution came in force on Janurary 26, 1950.

Since the Constituent Assembly was composed of people who were elite and mainly acquainted with the Westminster Model, two things happened. First, Indian Constitution became heavily tilted towards the British system without bothering whether it suits us or not. So, this transplantation resulted in sprouting strange mutation. Secondly, this elite was less bothered about the economic prosperity of the people but more concerned about political freedom. Indian Constitution, therefore, talks more of democratic rights.

During the past forty-one years, the Indian Constitution had to be amended 75 times. In spite of so many changes, people are not satisfied. The demands are daily being raised to change this or that basic structure of the Constitution. These demands are becoming fiercer with everyday that passes. Hence, it seems advisable to briefly summarise basic characteristics of the Indian Constitution, issues raised and alternatives given in the light of our goal of *Anand*.

I
THE STATES

When the Britishers left India, they left Governors' Provinces and

Chief Commissioners' Provinces and 601 Princely States with different types of treaty with them. Governors' Provinces were – Assam, West Bengal (East Bengal had gone to Pakistan), Orissa, Bihar, United Provinces, Punjab, (West Punjab had gone to Pakistan), Bombay, Madras and Central Provinces. And the Commissioner's Provinces were Ajmer, Coorg and Delhi.

The Britishers did not create these Provinces on any scientific basis. The history of the conquest of India will show that Provinces were created purely "by considerations of administrative convenience and by reasons of military strategy and security" to serve primarily the British imperialist interests. Even the Montford Report, 1918 and the Indian Statutory Commission Report, 1930 admit this fact. The interest of people found no place in this drawing of the map of India. A peep into the past confirms it.

Vasco da Gama discovered the sea route to India in 1498. Consequently, the sea trade with India became possible. Portugese were the first to take benefit of it. Others were tempted to follow soon.

East India Company was given Charter by Queen Elizabeth I in December 1600 "for the honour of our nation, the wealth of our people".

East India Company could not make much headway in promoting trade with India during the first one hundred years of its existence because of three types of problem – internal difficulties, foreign rivals in India and stiff opposition from Marathas, Nawab of Bengal and the Mughal Emperor himself. But once it got a foothold, there was no going back. Battle of Plassey (1757) and Battle of Buxar (1764) were the deciding wars. The enclosed maps show how the British rule expanded in India between 1772-1856, (vide pp. 210-213 for Maps).

The war of Independence called Mutiny by the Britishers, started on May 10, 1857 from Meerut. It soon spread to the other parts of the country. However, it could not succeed due to Britishers' better arms and ammunition, better strategy and better trained and larger forces. The indifferent attitude of the Princely States also contributed to it. The revolt was crushed on June 20, 1858 and the supremacy of the Britishers was once again established. However, with this came the end of the rule of East India Company. The British Crown formally took over the reigns of India on November 1, 1858.

The British crown did not re-organise the territory of India on any scientific basis but continued to pursue the old policy of serving the British interests. By the end of the nineteenth century, India was divided into three types of Provincial Governments – under the Governors, under the Lt. Governors, and under the Chief Commissioners. However, in 1935, after the passing of the Government of India Act, the Provinces were divided into two categories – Governors' Provinces and Chief Commissioners' Provinces. This continued up to the transfer of power to the Indian people.

A Constituent Assembly was elected for the undivided India. It held its first meeting on the 8th December, 1946, but thereafter it reassembled on the 14th August, 1947 as the Sovereign Constituent Assembly for the Dominion of India only.

When the Britishers were leaving India, they freed 601 Princely States to decide their future – to merge with India, or to merge with Pakistan, or to remain independent. India formed a special ministry in 1947 itself under Sardar Vallabh Bhai Patel to deal with the Princely States. It was the magic of the great Sardar that 555 Princely States signed the Instrument of Accession and became part of India. The integration was done as below:

- 70 States were incorporated as centrally-administered territories.
- 216 small States became part of neighbouring States as new districts.
- 266 were grouped together as new States such as PEPSU, Rajasthan, Madhya Bharat, Saurashtra, Travancore-Cochin etc.
- 3 States – Jammu & Kashmir, Hyderabad and Mysore were left as such.

It is a pity that two states, Junagarh and Hyderabad, whose rulers were Muslims, did not acceed to India and tried to manipulate things. There was uprising by people. On the other hand, Pakistani Tribesmen attacked the state of Jammu and Kashmir where the ruler was a Hindu but the majority of the people were Muslims. So, troops had to be sent to all the three states and ultimately they all signed the Instrument of Accession in favour of India.

The Indian Constitution was adopted on the 26th November, 1949 and it fully came in force on the 26th January, 1950.

The Indian Constitution says:

Article 1(3) The territory of India shall comprise

(a) the territories of the states;
(b) the union territories specified in the First Schedule, and
(c) such other territories as may be acquired.

The expression 'Union of India' should be distinguished from the expression 'Territory of India'. While the 'Union' includes only those States which enjoy the status of being members of the federal system and share a distribution of powers with the Union, the 'Territory of India' includes the entire territory over which the sovereignty of India, for the time being, extends. Thus, besides the States, there are two other classes of territories which are included in the 'Territory of India', viz., (I) Union territories, and (II) Such other territories as may be acquired by India. For example, the territory of Pondicherry was acquired from the French Government in 1954. Again, Sikkim, first became a Protectorate of India, then it became an 'Associate State' in 1974 and finally a state of India. Similarly, Goa was acquired from the Portugese. On the other hand, some territories were allowed to go out of India. For example: in 1951, some territories of Assam went to Bhutan and in 1960, certain territories from West Bengal and Assam were transferred to Pakistan.

Union of India was divided in the following types of states:

Part A – The Governors' Provinces were termed as Part A States. It had ten Provinces – Assam, Bihar, Bombay, Madhya Pradesh, Madras, Orissa, U.P., West Bengal, Punjab and Andhra (1953).

Part B – The new states formed by grouping of Princely States were in Part B. They were eight, viz., Hyderabad, Jammu & Kashmir, Madhya Bharat, Mysore, PEPSU, Rajasthan, Saurashtra and Travancore-Cochin.

Part C – To begin with, they were eleven, viz., Ajmer, Bhopal, Coorg, Delhi, Himachal Pradesh, Kutch, Manipur, Tripura, Vindhya Pradesh, Bilaspur and Cooch-Behar. Later on, Bilaspur was merged with Himachal Pradesh and Cooch-Behar with Bengal.

Part D – Andaman and Nicobar Islands.

This shows that re-drawing of map was not made on any long-term scientific basis. The inheritance from the British masters and ad hocism to meet the immediate problems were the sole criteria. Unfortunately, this is continuing till this date. For example:

(a) Patti Sriramalu demanded the formation of a new state of Andhra on the basis of language. He began a hunger-strike and ultimately died on Dec. 15, 1952. There was mass scale violence and the Government of India caved in. It declared the formation of a new state of Andhra on December 19, 1952 but on the same principle, other linguistic states were not formed.
(b) The persistent demand for linguistic states forced Parliament to appoint the States Reorganisation Commission in 1953. It submitted its Report in 1955. Consequently, Parliament enacted the State Reorganisation Act, 1956 in which old classification of Part A, Part B, Part C and Part D was given up. But neither the linguistic States were formed nor any long-term scientific view was taken.
(c) Due to agitation, a separate state of Gujarat was carved out from Bombay in 1960. The remainder part was renamed as Maharashtra.
(d) Due to political expediency, Punjab was split up in 1966 and a new state of Haryana and a new Union territory of Chandigarh were created.
(e) To meet the armed revolt of Nagas, Assam was bisected and a new State of Nagaland was formed in 1962.
(f) To satisfy people of the eastern border states, who were mainly Christians, new states of Meghalaya (1969), Manipur (1971), Tripura (1971), Mizoram (1986) and Arunachal Pradesh (1971) were formed.
(g) Himachal Pradesh was created in 1954 and up-graded to the status of a state in 1970.

Today, India has 18 States, 7 other States and 7 Union Territories. Table 9.1 gives their areas, population, sex ratio etc.

Encouraged by chicken heartedness of our leaders, lack of a rational long-term policy and urge to acquire power, the demands for new states in the name of language, independent ethnic identity, economic development, more power etc. are daily being raised. Belligerence and unpatriotism have reached a stage where even the threat of secession is being given. The scholars seem to be rallying round the idea of smaller states. Small, the beautiful, has become the slogan.

TABLE 9.1: States, areas, population, districts and backward districts

Sl. No.	State/Union Territories	Area 000 km² as on 31.3.1982	Population (in crores)			Percentage of population below poverty line	Female per 1000 males	No. of districts	No. of backward districts	Districts eligible for central subsidy
			Rural	Urban	Total					
1	2	3	4	5	6	7	8	9	10	11
States										
1.	Andhra Pradesh	27.5	4.10	1.25	5.35	36.4	975	23	14	11
2.	Assam	78	1.78	0.20	1.98	23.5	901	23	7	6
3.	Bihar	174	6.12	0.87	6.99	49.5	946	42	15	6
4.	Gujarat	196	2.35	1.05	3.40	24.3	942	19	10	3
5.	Haryana	44	1.01	0.28	1.29	15.6	870	12	4	10
6.	Himachal Pradesh	56	0.40	0.02	0.42	13.5	973	12	8	5
7.	Jammu & Kashmir	222	0.47	0.12	0.59	16.3	892	14	10	6
8.	Karnataka	192	2.64	1.07	3.71	35.0	963	20	13	3
9.	Kerala	39	2.07	0.48	2.54	26.8	1032	14	5	4
10.	Madhya Pradesh	443	4.16	1.05	5.21	46.2	941	45	36	22
11.	Maharashtra	308	4.07	2.20	6.27	34.9	937	30	0	3
12.	Orissa	156	2.33	0.30	2.63	42.8	981	13	8	6
13.	Punjab	50	1.21	0.46	1.67	13.8	879	12	5	3
14.	Rajasthan	342	2.71	0.71	3.42	34.3	919	27	16	16
15.	Sikkim	7	N.A	N.A	0.03	N.A	835	4	4	4
16.	Tamil Nadu	130	3.24	-1.60	4.84	39.6	977	20	9	5
17.	Uttar Pradesh	294	9.10	1.98	11.08	45.3	885	63	38	6
18.	West Bengal	89	4.01	1.44	5.45	39.2	911	17	13	3

(Contd.)

TABLE 9.1 *(Contd.)*

1	2	3	4	5	6	7	8	9	10	11
Other States										
19.	Arunachal Pradesh	84			0.06			11	N.A.	
20.	Goa	3.7			0.10			2		
21.	Manipur	22			0.14	12.3	971	8	6	6
22.	Meghalaya	22			0.13	28.0	954	5	3	3
23.	Mizoram	21			0.04			3	N.A.	
24.	Nagaland	17			0.07		863	7	3	3
25.	Tripura	10			0.20	23.0	946	3	3	3
Union Territories										
26.	Andaman & Nicobar	8			0.01			2	2	2
27.	Chandigarh	0.1			0.04			1	—	—
28.	Dadra & Nagar Haveli	0.5			0.01			1	1	1
29.	Daman & Diu	0.1	0.27	0.71	0.007	0.98		2	2	2
30.	Delhi	1.5			0.60			1	—	—
31.	Lakshdweep	0.03			0.004			1	1	1
32.	Pondicherry	0.5			0.06			4	4	4
	All India	3287	52.55	15.96	68.51	37.4	933	461	240	147

N.A. = Not Available.

Prima facie sub-division may appear to be a centrifugal move but if considered rationally, it may prove to be the best way of securing India's integrity and rapid socio-economic development. Let the proposition be examined a little more closely.

Bombay was bifurcated into Gujarat and Maharashtra. Both are happier since their separation. Maharashtra continues to flourish but Gujarat has made tremendous economic progress.

Haryana was a backward part of United Punjab. After an independent identity, Haryana has emerged as one of the granaries of India in the past 20 years. It has also remained free from the terrorist menace of Punjab.

Conversely, bigger states, even if they have a higher total GNP, have backward regions. Gujarat, in spite of industrial progress, has a woefully neglected Saurashtra-Kutch region. Again, U.P. has prosperous areas in Western U.P. but an equally backward areas in Eastern U.P. The same is true of Bihar, Madhya Pradesh and almost all other states.

It appears that the size of a state and the degree of corruption, because of greater state power, are directly related. Recently, in spite of the Election Commission's clear orders that with a view to prevent rigging in election, no transfers be made on the poll eve, five state governments – Haryana, U.P., Bihar, Rajasthan and Himachal Pradesh transferred officers on a mass scale. The Election Commission had to ask these States not to do so.

It can, therefore, be concluded that it is essential that India's map be redrawn and smaller states be created. Certainly, the smaller size of a state is likely to increase efficiency, reduce corruption, give impetus to rapid economic development and decentralise power to such an extent that the Chief Ministers, instead of trying to stick to their states, will like to migrate to centre even as an ordinary minister. India's unity will become more secure with smaller states. Even the centre-state relations are likely to improve. The only precaution to be taken is that the size of a state should not become so small as to make it a non-viable unit.

II
FEDERAL vs UNITARY

Historians tell us that India was never a united country. It had always innumerable independent kingdoms, which often fought amongst themselves. They further tell us that it was the magnanimity of the Britishers, who for the first time, united India under one single flag.

And at the same time, seeing to India's vastness artificially divided it into smaller administrative units called Governors' Provinces, Lt. Governors' Provinces and Chief Commissioners' Provinces. It promoted efficiency and established the rule of law. So, when the Britishers left, India was a unitary type of government with a very strong centre and a very well oiled administrative machinery.

Problems

India got freedom with two forces working in opposite directions. First, united India was partitioned into two parts and the truncated India lost its economic self-sufficiency in several fields like wheat, cloth, jute etc. Not only this. The partition of the country also resulted in an unprecedented violence followed by mass migration of population. So, the question arose how to keep the country united and at the same time plan a rapid economic development. This necessitated a strong centre.

Secondly, Gandhi and Congress were continuously assuring the people that the power will be decentralised. Leaders talked of *Rama Rajya* through village Republics. So, when India became free, the people expected that the Congress will fulfil these promises. It meant that at least the existing provinces and other territories shall be granted maximum autonomy.

Solution

Dr. Ambedkar, founding father of the Indian Constitution, while submitting the draft constitution stated that although the constitution may be federal in structure but the drafting committee had used the term "union" (and not Federation) because of the two advantages, viz.:

(a) That the Indian Federation is not the result of an agreement by independent, sovereign unit states as in the U.S.A. where thirteen original independent states agreed to form a federation. In India, already a unitary type of government existed. Here a federation has been formed by breaking a unitary state into a number of federating units.
(b) That in India, the federating units have not been given right as in the USSR to secede.

The experts of constitution opine that the Indian Constitution is an admixture of the best of the two, unitary and federal, and so it can be called "co-operative federalism" with strong centralising tendency. It has several essentials of a federal system such as:

1. *Dual Government* – Both at centre and in the states.
2. *Distribution of Power* – The Constitution has distributed power between the centre and states on the basis of three lists – Union List, State List and Concurrent List (Seventh Schedule).
3. *Supremacy of the Constitution*.
4. *Authority of the Courts*.

The Indian Constitution has also some equally strong unitary characteristics such as (a) the mode of formation by breaking a unitary state, that India was, into a number of federating units, (b) Position of the states in the Federation, and (c) Nature of the polity. To illustrate the point, a few illustrations are being given below:

(i) Even the name of state, or its boundaries can be changed by the Parliament (Art. 3).
(ii) There is no equality of representation of the states in the Council of States (Fourth Schedule).
(iii) There is single citizenship and that is of India. There is not dual citizenship (Arts. 5 to 11). To be a domicile of a state has not much importance.
(iv) There are All India Services under the control of the centre (Arts. 308-313). Officers of the Provincial Services are subordinate to the officers of the All India Services.
(v) The courts are common, which are headed by the Supreme Court, which administers both Central and State laws (Arts. 124 to 147 and Arts. 214 to 237).
(vi) The machinery for Elections and Accounts and Audit is under the control of the Centre.
(vii) The Emergency powers make the Centre supreme (Arts. 352 to 360).
(viii) The Constitution of States has been prescribed by the Parliament and the States have hardly any freedom in the matter (Part VI of the Constitution). An exception has been made only in the case of Jammu & Kashmir through temporary Art. 370.
(ix) Governor of a State is appointed by the President and holds

office at his pleasure. (Arts. 155, 156). The Governors' appointment and their conduct specially in dissolving state legislatures have come under severe criticism.

(x) The states have no right to secede.

(xi) The Indian Constitution had divided spheres of activity between Centre and the States on the basis of three lists given in schedule seven – Union List, State List and Concurrent List. But the Parliament has been given power to legislate with respect to a matter in the State List under the pretext of national interest (Art. 249).

Seeing to these and many more articles in the constitution which give overriding powers to the Union, experts opine that "States have been reduced to municipalities" or "centralising is defeating federalism".

The working of this Federal Constitution in spite of strong bias towards unitary characters has thrown, during the last forty years of its existence, some serious problems such as:

(a) Centre-State relations, specially in the distribution of revenues between the Union and the State. Finance Commissions have been appointed but the solution is still evading us.

(b) Inter-state disputes in matter of boundaries, sharing of river waters etc. Several principles like linguistic and cultural homogeneity have been propounded but the disputes are growing.

(c) Demands for new states and also more powers to a state.

(d) Comprehensive sweep of the Union Planning Commission with the result that regional disparities, uneven distribution of wealth, percentage of people below poverty line etc. have increased.

This and many more facts have shown that to keep India united and make it bloom, more of patriotism and more of decentralisation of power (rather than more of unitary character) is needed. Experts opine that in India, the decentralisation of power has stopped at the state level. It does not go below it. Talks of *Panchayat Raj*, *Nagar Palika Raj* and *District Board's Raj* are more of an eye wash. The recent *Panchayat Raj Act* passed by Rajiv Gandhi Government is full of faults and does not meet the demand and aspirations of the people.

III
PARLIAMENTARY vs PRESIDENTIAL FORM OF GOVERNMENT

The framers of the Indian Constitution had three models of form of Government before them. One was of England, known as Parliamentary form of Government, the other of Presidential system of America and the third of Switzerland, called Collegial form of Government. Out of these three, England's Parliamentary type of government was preferred mainly because people were accustomed to this form.

In Presidential type of government, power of the executive and the power of the legislature are separated. Here, the President, who is the executive head, is not actively associated with the legislature and his members of the cabinet are not even members of the legislature. A hostile vote in the legislature does not terminate the Presidentship. He continues to be the Head of the State.

In Parliamentary type of government both the powers of the executive and that of the legislature vest in the Prime Minister who is the leader of the House. He has a majority in the House and is answerable to the Parliament. In this system Head of the state is almost a figure head. He is bound to accept the advice of the cabinet.

In India, by and large, the British model has been accepted but unlike Britain, certain restrictions have been imposed. For example, in England, Parliament can legislate what it pleases, as it pleases, and that what it enacts is law. The courts have no power to sit on judgement over it. In India, Parliament can legislate only on the matters given in the Union List and the Concurrent List (Seventh Schedule). Again, its supremacy is limited by the Fundamental Rights given in Part III of the Constitution. Further, in matters of the Constitutional Laws, it is not that much free. It has to follow a prescribed procedure. Lastly, the courts have the power to decide whether a piece of legislation passed by the Parliament is valid or void.

A review of the last forty years of the Parliamentary work will show several unhealthy tendencies. Some of them are:

1. The Constitution has been amended seventy-five times so far. So frequent and multiple changes in the Constitution have undermined the sanctity of the Constitution. The 42nd and 44th

amendments can be cited as extreme cases. Through these amendments the scope for judicial review was narrowed down and the Fundamental Rights were jettisoned by inserting Art. 51A. This is fortunate that most of the mischief done by the 42nd and 44th amendments was set aside by the Janata Government in 1977-78. Nevertheless, the question remains that there appears to be a genuine case to review the Constitution, once for all, instead of piecemeal mutilation. The experts on Constitution feel that the following parts need codification:

(a) Whom the Head of the State should invite to form a Government in a situation where no party commands a clear majority.
(b) What Head of the state should do when it is alleged that a party in power has lost its majority due to defections etc.
(c) When the President or Governor can dismiss a Prime Minister or Chief Minister.
(d) When there is a dispute between a decision of the Supreme Court and the will of the House, which will prevail.
(e) How and when the Directive Principles of the State Policy should be implemented.
(f) The question of the privileges of the House.
(g) How to check the tendencies to erode the authority of the federating units through extra constitutional bodies like the Planning Commission, the National Development Council, the Finance Commissions etc.
(h) How to check separatist forces at work such as:

  (i) Sikh Demand
  (ii) Jammu & Kashmir Demand
  (iii) The Assamese Demand
  (iv) Demand to make Urdu official language
  (v) Demand for proportional Representation by Muslims in the legislatures and communal reservation in services like Police, Army, Public Sector Services, etc.
  (vi) Demand to be considered as Scheduled Castes even after conversion to other religions.
  (vii) Demand that Muslims be treated as Muslims first and Indians afterwards, and the "Muslim culture" be

promoted instead of the "Indian culture".

(viii) Increasing lack of patriotism.

2. Crossing of the floor has become so common that the governments are unable to run the full period for which they were elected. The Anti-Defection Act passed in 1985 through 52nd Amendment of the Constitution could not check this trend.
3. The Political parties have lost credibility to such an extent, in the eyes of people, that none is able to muster a majority. Seventh Parliament was a hung Parliament. Same is true of the Eighth Parliament. In such a case neither they are able to run for the whole period nor work confidently in the interest of the nation.
4. The experiment of minority governments and coalition governments has also repeatedly failed. V.P. Singh Government was a minority government with the support of B.J.P. When the B.J.P. withdrew its support it fell. Thereafter, another still more minority Government of Chandra Shekhar with the support of Congress (I) was installed but it also collapsed within a few months.
5. The Haryana case is a very strange example of functioning of the Constitution. The Chief Minister was forced to quit because heinous crimes committed at Meham were attributed to him. But he made a quick return. Again, he was persuaded to give up the Chief Ministership. And again he returned and thus made a hat-trick. Soon, he saw that three party M.L.A's are debarred under the Defection Act. This boomeranged and he became in minority. Hurriedly, he requested the Governor to dissolve the House and order elections. Opposition parties pleaded with the Governor that since he became in minority before recommending dissolution of the House, the President's rule should be imposed. This was done.

These illustrations and many more will show that the Parliamentary form of government is not functioning effectively in India. To think that only a change in form of Government will help seems to be wrong. The evil lies in our failure to develop healthy conventions so very necessary for the success of a Parliamentary form of government. A few illustrations will prove the point:

1. In U.K., by convention, the Speaker is a non-party man. No political party opposes his election to the House of Commons. So, he discharges his obligations boldly and honestly. In India, on the other hand, the speaker continues to be a party-man even after his election as a Speaker. All political parties put up candidates in the constituency of the Speaker. So, he is neither bold nor honest. His rulings are often coloured.
2. In England, an honorable Minister will either resign or file a suit of defamation if a charge of corruption or moral turpitude is made against him. In India, this convention has not developed. On the other hand, persons with criminal record and dozens of criminal cases pending against them in courts have become Chief Ministers. Criminality in authority breeds criminality. Gruesome murder of Rajiv Gandhi proves it.
3. In England, Ministers act as Trustees. They do not merely act honestly but look to be so. No minister can, by convention, remain a minister if he acts otherwise. In India, Ministers do not consider themselves as trustees. They consider it as their right and duty to shower favours on themselves, their relations and friends and even on political parties. For example, a Prime Minister issued verbal instructions to the army to make arrangements to provide drinking water to the audience of a meeting organised by his own political party. Use of government machinery to provide free transport by rail and road to the city where a meeting of a political party is taking place are not rare instances.
4. In England, Ministers formulate the policies and watch its faithful implementation by the civil servants. They do not interfere in the day-to-day working of the civil servants. In India, reverse seems to be the case. Here civil servants formulate the policies and the ministers simply take credit for them. Further, the ministers are least bothered about its timely and faithful implementation. They do not act as a watch dog. They think it their primary duty to interfere in the day-to-day administration for bestowing favours. Thus, a civil servant has been forced to a peculiar situation. If he wants to discharge his duties honestly and effectively, he is disliked and harassed in a number of ways. It is alleged that he is an obstacle in the great strides the country would have taken after independence. Demand for a "Committed bureaucracy" was raised by no less a person than

the Prime Minister himself. This has demoralised civil services and a class of sycophants and courtier class amongst bureaucrats has developed. Now bureaucracy mainly concerns itself in pocketing its pay packet. The whole administration is being run by the ministers. Demarcation of fields of functions of a Minister and a civil servant has vanished. This is at the root of growing corruption and inefficiency.

Under these conditions, can a change in the form of government alone will help? Probably not. But even then it is essential to give the idea a serious thought to prevent the habitual fall of the governments because of the crossing of floors by individual legislators or even by the supporting political party. The poor people are forced to bear extra expenditure of more than one hundred crores of rupees for the luxury of a fresh mandate of people. But this fresh mandate may mean nothing if the new legislators or political parties may continue the old game of horse trading. So, an alternative will have to be found out. It may be a modified form of a Presidential form of government or a mixture of Parliamentary and Presidential form of government.

IV
DEMOCRACY

Pre-requisite of a democracy is independence of the country.

After independence, the question of the form of a government arises. The experts of political science tell us that the form of an independent government can be Monarchy, Dictatorship (including Dictatorship of the Proletariat), Aristocracy or Democracy.

Democracy is a form of Government, to repeat the famous sentence, "of the people, by the people and for the people". Democracy provides a system of government under which the people exercise the governing power either directly or through representatives periodically elected by themselves. There is supremacy of the popular will on basic questions.

Essentials of a democracy are:

(a) Periodical free and fair elections so that a judgement can be passed on the working of the party in power.
(b) Equal rights to elect representatives. It implies that voters have

a minimum level of ability to take a rational judgement and they possess good character.

(c) Freedom of speech, publication and association. This means, "I detest your opinion, but I will contend to the death for your right to utter them".

(d) Tolerance. Uncompromising stands by the minority are not conducive to democracy.

(e) Good leadership and value based parties.

(f) Possibility of an alternate Government, i.e., more than one party.

Experts are of the opinion that the small size of the state, economic equality and fraternal feelings are desirable to make democracy successful.

The framers of the Indian Constitution decided to give India a democratic form of government. The original Preamble reads:

"We, the people of India, having solemnly resolved to Constitute India into a Sovereign Democratic Republic. . . ."

In 1976, through forty-second amendment "Socialist secular" words were added after the word "Sovereign".

The whole Constitution, article after article, shows that India has a democratic government. The elections are held after every five years [Arts. 56, 67, 83(2)], people have all types of freedoms as laid down in the Fundamental Rights (Part III) and there are several political parties and everyone has a chance to form a government.

The functioning of democracy during the last forty years has shown certain very unhappy tendencies:

Lack of Free and Fair Elections

Free and fair elections are the first pre-requisite of democracy. In India, it appears they are in a bad shape. Several ugly faces have come up, viz.:

(a) Majority of the voters are illiterate. They even lack a rational judgement. They are swayed by the emotions of religion, caste, etc. So, there are waves of anti-emergency, of Pro-Indira Gandhi sympathy for Rajiv Gandhi, of Mandir and Mandal and recently of Pro-Rajiv Gandhi for Congress.

(b) Less than 70 per cent voters cast their votes.[1] Add to it that normally there are 6 to 10 candidates for one seat. The result is that a candidate gets elected who secures somewhere about 30 per cent votes cast. Certainly, he does not represent the majority. And a party which comes in power, with the same logic, does not represent majority of people.

(c) The elections are not fair because caste considerations play an important role. It is not the merit of the candidate or ideology of a party, which is important. It is the caste of the candidate which is important.

(d) In most of the scheduled castes and backward classes, even today, community leaders called *Mukhias* (head) have their own importance. Their writ runs. And they are generally purchased through wealth and wine.

(e) There is block-voting by certain sections of the society. Muslims, scheduled castes and now backward classes specialise in it. The recent logic of Mandal Commission is likely to intensify this block-voting.

(f) Rigging and Booth Capturing is a new technique which has made democracy a mockery. It appears rulers are making it a perfect science now. On the eve of elections, mass transfers of government officers, specially the police officers, have its own story to tell. The poor Election Commission is protesting but with no results.

(g) It appears that most of the political parties, which are the main contestants, have no faith in democracy. It is an open secret that their membership is bogus, they have hardly a constitution, they are not registered and they do not have regular elections. It is because of this anti-democratic attitude of leaders that often, even Chief Ministers are not really elected but are thrust upon from above. And the Communist Parties of every shade have no faith in democracy. For them barrel of the gun is more important. They have accepted democracy only as a clout to come in power.

(h) Add to this one more pertinent development. There seems to be a race to establish a dynastic rule. Jawaharlal Nehru, Indira Gandhi, Sanjay Gandhi as a centre of extra-constitutional authority and Rajiv Gandhi are not the only examples. Ch. Charan Singh, Devilal and others are raising their voice against dynastic rule but are doing exactly the same. Dr. Ambedkar was right when he said:

> "*Bhakti* in religion may be a road to the salvation of the soul. But in politics, *Bhakti* or hero worship is a sure road to degeneration and eventual dictatorship."

Non-availability of a Viable Alternative

For the success of democracy, it is essential that there must be more than one All India parties, each capable of providing a viable alternative. Unfortunately, this was not in India up to recently. This time B.J.P. has tried hard to acquire that status.

For the first 15-20 years, virtually there was only one All India political party in the All India Congress Committee. Congress was credited with having waged the war of independence and ultimately winning it. So, the people almost worshipped the Congress leaders. The proverb was that even a dog, if given a congress ticket, will win. But slowly the scene changed. Most of the old and tested leaders of the pre-independence era died. Their place was taken by pseudo-leaders claiming self-sacrifices for the cause of the nation. This was not a fact. So, the veil started lifting and new political parties started appearing on the scene. Today, we find a peculiar situation. Except the Bhartiya Janata Party (Jan Sangh earlier) and Communist Parties, the bulk of leaders in the new political parties like Lok Dal, Janata Dal, Janata Dal (S) and regional parties had started their career in the Congress Party and having failed to get recognition and power there formed new parties. They all belong to Congress culture and Congress mentality. They have no separate and distinct ideology. Further, even today, there are not many All India parties capable of winning elections and forming stable government on their own. The last Lok Sabha has witnessed the drama of one minority government following another minority government and ultimately unable to run for the whole duration. So, there is neither good leadership, nor many political parties of All India level, nor value based politics.

Intolerance

To make democracy a success, tolerance and live and let live attitude are necessary. Unfortunately this tolerance seems to have left the political parties. Religious minorities, specially the Muslims, are not prepared to join the national mainstream and are insisting on their independent muslim culture. They want to call India, 'Muslim India', 'Hindu India', and 'Christian India'. They insist on formation of new districts with muslim majority. They are demanding weightage and reservation. They insist that Urdu, which has nothing to do with Muslim religion, be recognised as the second official language. They have made it impossible for the Hindus to live in Kashmir valley where they are in majority. Kashmiri Muslims want to secede to Pakistan. Communal riots have become a common feature. And it is a pity that all the political parties are competing with one another to win their favour because of their block-voting. As a reaction to it, the Hindus are also learning to become vocal and aggressive. Seeing the attitude of the Muslims and the untiring efforts of leaders of almost all political parties to woo them *via* their religious leaders, the other sections of the Indian society are trying to do the same. The Sikhs, the scheduled castes, the backward classes – all have now high ambitions and the political parties are vying with one another to woo them. How democracy can survive in such a situation?

Lack of Freedom and Dignity of the Individual

For democracy, it is essential that people may feel free to act the way they like. Unfortunately, in the post-independence period, gradually we are losing our freedom and dignity. In spite of our claiming to be a leader of the third Block, a Neutral, a rising nation and an independent nation, we are fast losing our individuality both at home and abroad. Due to heavy debts, both internal and international, we are at the door step of Debt Trap. We have to beg fresh loans to pay off interest on old loans or clear our adverse Balance of Payments. We have to bow before dictates of I.M.F. and other obliging Members. We are already closely tied down with U.S.S.R. As if, it was not sufficiently humiliating position, we started raising slogans like "Indira is India" and "India is Indira". Our sycophancy and courtier mentality went to the extent of suggesting that the wife of the Prime Minister, who is a foreign national, be made President of a Political Party. How a nation can survive and remain independent and democratic under these circumstances?

Less Decentralisation of Power

Democracy implies decentralisation of power. In India, unfortunately, decentralisation of power has stopped at the state level. It could not percolate down to the District level and the village level. We talk of District Boards and Village *Panchayats*. But a peep into their working will show that they have neither powers nor funds. And the way they are tied down to the State Government's apron has its own story to tell. Recently, Rajiv Gandhi got a *Panchayat Raj Act* passed. It appears as another example of political gimmickery.

Sycophant and Inefficient Civil Services

Democracy will thrive only when we have an independent, honest and efficient civil service.

In British days, Indian Civil Services were very strong, efficient, bold and independent because Britishers made them so. Unfortunately, in the post-independence period, they have been slowly reduced to the level of sycophants, courtiers, dishonest and inefficient persons. Now honesty and efficiency are at a discount. Political bosses take pride in insulting and humilating the good officers. Some glaring examples are:

- Vaidyanathan, Secretary Health, was reverted to his cadre because of displeasure of the Prime Minister.
- Subramanian, Secretary Agriculture, was retired.
- N.R. Reddy, a senior I.P.S. officer was reverted.
- Venkateshwaran, Foreign Secretary, resigned in utter disgust.
- C.S. Shastri, Rural Development Secretary, was disgracefully removed.
- D. Bandhopadhyaya, Special Protection Group Director, transferred.
- In 1975 there were purges of Civil Servants.
- Members of the Foreign Service (I.F.S.) expressed their resentment through a formal representation.

When the Prime Minister wants a "Committed bureaucracy" and calls them names, a class of flatterers, seeking prize postings will certainly grow. This is actually what is happening. Now the bureaucrats themselves make millions and help their political masters in making billions.

It was Sardar Vallabh Bhai Patel who insisted that provisions in the Constitution be made providing the functions of the Council of Ministers and also the rules of recruitment, placement and promotion of Civil servants and he got it done. But today, most of them have been placed in cold storage though they still stay in Statute Books.

One may conclude, in the words of great sons of the soil, that Parliamentary or Presidential form of governments and democracy will succeed only when we have good people at the helm of affairs. To quote.

> ". . . the structure has been erected by architects of consumable skill and fidelity, its foundations are solid. . . its defences are impregnable from without. It has been reared for immortality. . . . It may, nevertheless, perish in an hour by the folly, or corruption, or negligence of its only keepers, the People. . . ."
>
> – *Sachchidanand Sinha,*
> *Provisional Chairman, Constituent Assembly*

> ". . . I feel, however good a constitution may be, it is sure to turn out bad because those who are called to work it happen to be a bad lot. However bad a constitution may be, it may turn out to be good, if those who are called to work it, happen to be a good lot. . . ."
>
> – *Dr. B.R. Ambedkar*

> "If people who are elected are capable and men of character and integrity, they would be able to make the best even of a defective constitution. If they are lacking in these, the constitution cannot help the country."
>
> – *Rajendra Prasad*

How correct a prophecy!

V
SECULARISM

The word secularism was not used by the framers of the Indian Constitution. It was interpolated by Indira Gandhi in 1976 through the Forty-second Amendment. Consequently in the Preamble, in place of *Sovereign Democratic Republic* the words *Sovereign Socialist Secular Democratic Republic* were substituted.

The term "Secular" was, for the first time, used to divide Church preachings into two. One type of preachings that were based on logic and/or science, were called "Secular". The other type of preachings were called "Religious". They pertained to faith and established a relationship between a worshipper and his God. They were mainly ritualistic. From there, on its onward march, the meaning of 'Secularism' has underwent several changes. For example, in the U.S.A. it means that the state will have no religion and it will maintain itself at equi-distance from all religions. In England, it means that the state will have a religion but it will not discriminate between people on the basis of religion. In India, the Indian Constitution gives one meaning to secularism and the Nehruvian Model has attached another meaning to it. Both have miserably failed to appreciate the difference between religion and *Dharma* and so have committed the serious mistake of equating *Hindu Dharma* with Muslim Religion, or Christian Religion. So, Bhartiya Janata Party's Shri L.K. Advani is now talking of 'Hindu Secularism'.

The framers of the Indian Constitution knew that India is a multi-religious country – Hindu (it is not a religion), Muslim, Christian, Parsi, Sikh, Jain and Buddha (it is a mischief to separate Sikhs, Buddhists, and Jains from Hindus). So, they provided two safeguards. First, there shall be complete freedom, subject to public order, morality and health, to worship, profess, propogate one's religion and manage religious affairs. (Arts. 25 and 26). Secondly, the state shall not promote any religion (Arts. 27 and 28).

The Indian Constitution also provides certain safeguards to minorities, such as to conserve one's language, script or culture and not to be discriminated against *only* on the basis of religion, race, caste and language (Art. 29). It also provides a right to minorities to establish and administer educational institutions of their choice (Art. 30). These minorities may necessarily be not religious minorities. They can be minorities on the basis of language, race, caste, script, or culture.

Unfortunately, the extra zealots of secularism in India, knowingly or unknowingly, clubbed these two distinct sets of Articles into one and gave a new interpretation to Indian secularism which certainly the Indian Constitution does not mean. These politicians, in practice, made secularism of Indian brand pro-minorities, specially muslims, and anti-Hindu.

The political leaders, out to appease Muslims for vote-bank and not serious in their real betterment, failed to understand the meaning of religion and appreciate that *Dharma* is not Religion. "Religion is belief in, recognition of, or an awakened sense of a higher unseen controlling power or powers, with the emotion and morality connected therewith, rites or worship, any system of such belief or worship". Dr. Ambedkar said that "Religion is a strictly personal affair". Religion pertains to faith and tries to establish a relationship between man and his Creator. It includes rituals.

Dharma, according to Dr. Ambedkar, is a social affair. It prescribes a universal code of conduct, a charter of duties. This code of conduct and charter of duties are based on universal Laws, Truth, Justice and Betterment of living beings. This code of conduct or values (Human, Social and Spiritual) have been tested several times on the touch-stone of logic and science. Hindu *Dharma* has itself propounded six systems of logic known as *Darshan*. The validity of the code of conduct of the Hindu *Dharma* has been repeatedly tested by these different *Darshans*. Even today, no scholar of any country, has challenged the desirability or logic of this code of conduct. It is for this reason that Hindu *Dharma* has, from time to time, accommodated in its fold, any number of Religions, the only condition being that in social affairs these codes of conduct are accepted. Buddhism, Jainism, Sikhism, Arya Samaj, Radha Swami, etc. are all parts of Hindu *Dharma*. It is possible to be a Hindu in spite of being an atheist or anti-religion.

Due to these two mistakes, first, to read Arts. 25 to 28 and 29 to 30 together as one dealing with religion and secondly, not to appreciate the difference between *Dharma* and religion, Indian politicians committed serious national crimes. They indulged in filthy appeasement of Muslim leaders, specially the rabid religious leaders. Certainly, this was neither secularism nor patriotism. A few instances can be cited:

(a) It encouraged divisible tendencies. Today, Muslims and Sikhs are in revolt in Jammu & Kashmir and the Punjab respectively and refuse to flow with the national stream. They are demanding independence.

(b) Important Articles of the Indian Constitution could not be implemented such as Art. 44 (Uniform Civil Code), Art. 48 (Prohibit Cow Slaughter), Art. 343 (Hindi in Devnagri script to be the official language of the Union) and Art. 370 (Temporary provisions with respect to Jammu & Kashmir) is still continuing, and so on.

(c) In the religious dispute of *Rama Janma Bhoomi-Babari Masjid*, the Governments, both at the Centre and in the U.P. State, took a partisan attitude. They sided with Muslim religious leaders and obstructed Hindus through an undeclared emergency from performing even their religious ceremonies at Ayodhya. They went to the brutal extent of opening unprovoked firing on the unarmed Hindu mob. They even ignored the highly provocative and unpatriotic statements of the Shahi Imam of Delhi of wanting a U.N.O. force etc.

(d) The Government allowed Hindus to be driven out from the Kashmir valley by the Muslims and did not even think it proper to do any thing material to rehabilitate the Hindu refugees. On the other hand, they spend more than three hundred crores in air lifting Indians stranded at Kuwait because most of them were Muslims who had gone there to earn a fortune.

(e) In the famous *Shah Bano's case*, the epoch making decision of the Hon. Supreme Court was nullified because of the opposition of fanatic religious leaders though it was in the interest of Muslim women.

(f) During the past forty years, any number of acts have been passed concerning different aspects of Hindu Personal Law such as marriage, inheritance, divorce, dowry, etc. But in this period, not one single act was passed concerning Muslim Personal Law.

(g) Every Islamic State of the world has its own distinct culture. It takes pride in this culture and none wants to follow the culture of Saudi Arabia. For example, Iran takes pride in its own heroes and culture. Similarly, Indonesia is proud of its great men's thoughts, language and even the sanskritised names. But in India, Indian Muslims under the guidance of fundamentalists and politicians are trying to give up Indian culture and adopt foreign culture. They do not want to love and respect the greatmen of the land but want to adore foreigners who had nothing to do with Indian Muslims.

(h) The virus of communalism was not only allowed to persist at the

Aligarh Muslim University, which was responsible for the partition of the country and continues to be a seat of Muslim politics, but was given a boost by amending the A.M.U. Act and indirectly granting it a "Minority Character".

Instances can be multiplied, but it is suffice to say that in India neither the provisions of the Indian Constitution dealing with safeguards to religions (Arts. 25 to 28) were honestly followed nor the government took a non-interfering attitude in matters of religion. So, separatist tendencies were encouraged which have now assumed dangerous proportions. Now time has come, which demands immediate corrective steps.

VI
SOCIALISM

The concepts of Socialism and Communism have developed gradually in a period of time. The concepts got a fillip due to inherent defects in the capitalist system which were highlighted by too rapid industrialisation of Europe. Private ownership of property was considered responsible for the uneven distribution of wealth, grinding poverty amongst plenty, unemployment, price fluctuations etc. So, political and economic thinkers started offering alternatives to capitalism. The journey from early socialist (St. Simon, Sismondie) to scientific socialist (Karl Max) *via* utopian socialists and Associationists (Robert Owen, Charles Fourier) was not very long. It hardly took fifty years (1814 to 1867). For the first time, ideas of socialism were put to practice in Russia and it hardly took 75 years to reach a climax and also start a downward journey. It appears to be on exit in the USSR.

Socialism may be defined as "a theory and a movement aiming at the collective organisation of the community in the interest of the mass of the people through the common ownership and collective control of the means of production and exchange". According to Morrison, "its essentials are that all the great industries and the land should be publicly or collectively owned, and that they should be conducted for the common good instead of for private benefit". Thus, public ownership, public management and central planning appear to be the three pillars of socialism.

Nehru and other persons associated with the drafting of the

Indian Constitution could not be unaware of the rising wave of socialism. Nehru specially was enamoured of it. So, the framers of the Indian Constitution, in the original Preamble, have used the words Justice, Liberty, Equality and Fraternity; and added a chapter on Fundamental Rights which includes the Articles on Right to Equality and Right against Exploitation. Not satisfied, they gave Directive Principles of State Policy where they talked of establishment of a Welfare State. Thus, the goal envisaged by the Constitution is that of the establishment of a "Socialist State". Explaining this goal at the Avadi session in 1955, the Congress explained this objective as a "Socialistic Pattern of Society". The following resolution was passed:

> "In order to realise the object of Congress . . . and to further the objectives stated in the Preamble and Directive Principles of State Policy of the Constitution of India, Planning should take place with a view to the establishment of a socialistic pattern of society, where the principal means of production are under social ownership or control, production is progressively speeded up and there is equitable distribution of the national wealth."

Slowly this "socialistic pattern" was changed to a "Socialistic State". For this the following changes were made:

1. The Preamble was amended (42nd Amendment Act of 1976) and the word "Socialistic" was added after "Sovereign".
2. Article 38 was amended by inserting sub-section (2) which makes it obligatory on State to minimise the inequalities in income, inequalities in status etc.
3. Article 39 was amended by inserting sub-section 39A. which deals with equal justice and free legal aid.
4. Article 43A was added to make participation of workers in management of industries possible.

In keeping with this policy of socialism, land and industries were nationalised and gradually a powerful public sector was created, central planning was started and an extra-constitutional authority of Planning Commission was established, distribution of essential commodities was taken up by the state through Super Bazars and ration shops, purchases were quasi-monopolised through Food

Corporation of India etc. and efforts are being made to control prices and uneven distribution of wealth through Monetary and Fiscal Policies.

In spite of all this, the economic health of the country is far from satisfactory as will be evident from the following facts:

1. People below poverty line have increased. Now almost 50 per cent of population lives below poverty line.
2. Unemployment is increasing.
3. Uneven distribution of wealth has increased. The rich have become richer and their number has also increased. On the other hand, poor have become poorer and their number is fast swelling.
4. There are imbalances in regional developments and they are growing.
5. Prices are rising daily. They are increasing in two digits now.
6. Public sector has become a white elephant. In England Prime Minister got rid of major part of it by denationalising it. Even in the U.S.S.R., it has badly failed the government where it was a dictatorship.
7. Internal and External debts have rocketed high. Now we take loans to repay interest on past loans.
8. Unfavourable Balance of payment has become alarming.

To say the least, the economy is in a very bad shape.

The mirage of socialism has almost sounded our death knell. The reasons are not far to seek:

(a) Democracy and socialism do not go together. There is inherent contradiction between the two because socialism can thrive only with the crutches of regimentation.

(b) Excessive love for matter is the foundation of socialism. With this, one is expected to give up ownership of matter, i.e. private property. This is an inbuilt contradiction. Man cannot be a worshipper of Mammon as well as a saint simultaneously. Socialism takes away the sentiments of self and so man becomes an order-taking machine. Business and Industry needs on the spot decisions and capacity to take risks. No government servant will like to take them. So, losses are a natural corollary. With this is tagged inefficiency and corrupt practices.

The solution seems to be to make a new man, who, in search of *Anand*, may love matter to the minimum essential extent and by his own sweet will observe detachment followed by renunciation. This man will naturally prize values – human, social and spiritual – much more than the material values of today. This will automatically give a higher type of socialism, Socialism by Will.

VII
A PEEP INTO THE PAST

India in the *Ramayana* period or even in the *Mahabharata* period was divided into innumerable independent Kingdoms known as *Jan-pads*, such as Ayodhya, Mithila, Vaishali, Ang, Kaushambi, Magadh, Kakai, Ujjaini, Kaling, Jammuprastha, Giribrij, Mahakoshal, Dharma Vardhan etc.

The area of each one of these *Jan-pads* was almost equal to the present day Districts. For example, Ayodhya was about 12 *Yojan* long (72 miles) and 3 *Yojan* (18 miles) wide. In Plato's terms, we can call them "District States". This shows that in ancient India, political power was decentralised to the maximum point beyond which it would have ceased to be a viable unit.

Each *Jan-pad* had a king. Normally after the death of the king, his son inherited the throne. Hence, the system is called monarchy. But monarchy in India was different from the term in which it is used today in the West. Here, the king was not that all powerful. For example the qualities (qualifications) of a king were prescribed. He must be handsome and healthy. He must be well educated, lover of art and expert in armoury and logic. He must be intelligent, with good memory, brave, farsighted, practical, tactician, sweet tongued, possessing qualities of a leader, honest, well wisher of the people, having self-control, knower of *Dharma* (*Dharmagya*), follower of *Dharma* (*Dharmatma*) and ensure that people follow *Dharma*[2] (*Dharma-palak*). Naturally, a person possessing these qualities will be much better than an average man. He will prove to be an able administrator. A person, who did not possess these qualities could normally not inherit the throne.

In those days, the personal life and public life of a ruler were not separated. A ruler was judged in his entirety.

Seers of those days had probably discovered that a child inherits the good and bad qualities of the parents. They had full knowledge of genes theory. Besides this, they knew the importance of family atmosphere. Hence, they had reached the conclusion that normally the good qualities of a king will be inherited by his children and the family atmosphere and intensive training will most likely make the sons able, quality-oriented and good administrators. So one of the sons, normally the eldest, inherited the throne. But, if per chance, a son did not measure up to the qualities demanded, he was not allowed to inherit the throne. For example, King Sagar's son was not allowed to succeed his father. None of the four sons of King Kush were allowed to become king. Instances can be multiplied.

The son of a king could inherit the throne only when the people's representatives accepted the suggestion. For example, even for a person like Rama, the son of king Dashrath, who is today considered the incarnation of God and an ideal administrator, the resolution had to be passed by the people's representatives specially invited for the purpose.

After being throned, the king in those days was not that powerful as he is thought today. He had innumerable limitations. For example:

(i) The king had innumerable advisors, one for each main department. The king was expected to normally go by their advice. These advisers were very capable tested persons, wedded to welfare of the people.

(ii) The kingdom had an attached saint-priest, known as *Raja-Purohit*. It was very difficult, even for a king, to overrule this *Raja-Purohit*. He represented the voice of sanity, public-welfare and public force.

(iii) The unattached saints were known as *Rishis*. These persons had renounced the world and were highly respected social workers not confined to any *Jan-pad*. Their request were orders for a king. For example, King Dashrath, had to send his two sons, Rama and Laxman, most unwillingly, when ordered to do so by Rishi Vishwamitra, to fight and kill *Danavs*, the enemies of people, specially saintly persons.

A king, bound by these checks and controls, could not be all powerful as the modern term, monarchy, seems to convey. So, it will be better to call it "controlled Monarchy".

A reading of *Ramayana* and *Mahabharata* reveals that some kings acquired the title of *Chakravarti-King* to whom a number of independent kings owed allegiance. But this title could be acquired only at an advanced age and that too not through bloody wars. When a king by his good deeds, welfare activities, wisdom and qualities of head and heart acquired wide reputation, then he was allowed to perform a *Yagya*, known as *Ashwa-medh Yagya*. This was a procedure to have a close association amongst several independent kingdoms so that with the help and advice of *Chakravarti* king, the benefits could accrue to the other kingdoms and their people. The relationship between *Chakravarti* king and other kings was not that of a master and a servant but of equals. Further, after the death of a *Chakravarti* king, the title did not automatically pass on to the inheriting king. Each had to acquire it for self.

The duties of a king, i.e. functions of a state, were quite wide. The principle that zero government is the best government was not acceptable. Similarly, communist ideology of making the state all powerful so that ultimately the State may wither away, was not favoured with. The central idea seems to be to make the king, or the state, responsible to regulate all aspects of life – political, economic and social without directly acquiring the control, so that maximum happiness could be promoted. This they preferred to call *Anand*.

The Indian seers did not think it prudent to keep India politically united under some sort of central authority. This unity was achieved with the miracle of emotional integration.

VIII
THE STRATEGY

It is the considered opinion of the scholars and confirmed by practical day-to-day experiences that economic life and political life are inter-dependent. One influences the other and in return, gets influenced. Economics touches politics at more than one point because the production and the distribution of wealth are today largely influenced by government, and because the solution of many economic problems must come through political channels. Earlier, due to this close affinity, economics was considered as a branch of politics and was called 'Political Economy', Taxation, Tariff Law, Public Sector, State Aid to agriculture and industry, Import-Export Policy, etc. clearly show that governmental policies affect economic prosperity. USSR is a living example to demonstrate this point.

Political ideas and institutions are also influenced equally by economic conditions. Rise of feudal government in medieval Europe was because of economic factors. Again, rise of democracy owes not a little to the Industrial Revolution. And rise and seemingly imminent fall of socialism is also due to economic conditions.

It is, therefore, essential that a harmonious relationship should exist between economic and political life. Both should at least try to achieve a common goal. In India, the seers had given the goal of *Anand*. Experience has shown that it appears to be better than the goal of welfare. So, the political effect should also be to help in the achievement of the goal of *Anand*.

The continuity principle requires that efforts be made to base the political life in accordance with our culture, thought process, value system, and way of life and make necessary changes to make it dynamic and up-to-date so that it may successfully meet the demands of the modern times.

Keeping the above two ideas in mind and on the basis of the review of the forty-one years of post-independence period, the following strategy can be ventured.

1. *Federation of District States*

We have already accepted a federal type of government and artificially created a number of states. Experience has shown that this has not satisfied people. Further, the administrative efficiency is daily deteriorating and politicians are busy to exploit state apparatus for selfish ends. This is eroding morality and encouraging corruption. And in addition, respect for the rule of law is deteriorating and crime is increasing. To set our house in order, it is desirable, on the one hand, to meet the genuine aspirations of people and on the other to decentralise state power to the maximum. Both these ends can be met, to a very great extent, if the number of federating units is increased.

In ancient India, there were innumerable *Jan-pads* and the size of most of the *Jan-pads* was equal to the present day district. So why each district cannot be made a federating unit now? Of course, where the size of a district is very big, it may be bifurcated further and where the size is too small, more than one districts should be clubbed together to form one unit. The viability of a federating unit should be the sole criterion of formation of a state.

(a) Each District state, from administrative point of view, should be divided into cities, Tahsil Towns, Block Headquarters and Focal Villages. These cities, towns, headquarters, focal villages[3] must be made administrative centres for their respective areas. They must house all government and quasi-government essential departments — Administration, Police, Judiciary, Post office, Bank, P.W.D., Tube-well, Irrigation, Electricity, to name a few, on one campus. As far as possible, 'One Window Service' formula should be followed. This administrative set-up will promote real decentralisation of power.

(b) In this scheme of federating District States, the size and composition of the constituencies will have to be changed. Today we have very big constituencies. To stand for elections, one needs lot of money, workers, who include muscle power, and other resources. So, the size of the constituencies should be reduced to manageable size, area-wise and population-wise. To make it more comprehensive, the old idea of demarcating constituencies on the basis of professions and economic interests be given a trial. For example, we must have constituencies of farmers, land-less labourers, traders, transporters, industrialists, financial institutions, government servants etc. This will automatically reduce the importance of religion and caste.

2. *Presidential Form of Government*

We have designed our government on the pattern of England and made it a Parliamentary form of government. Experience has shown that this type of government is not able to deliver the goods. The disease of *Aya Ram* and *Gaya Ram* became so acute that it took no time to reduce a majority government into a minority one. So, 52nd amendment of the Constitution was made in 1985, an Anti-Defection Act was passed (Tenth Schedule) and Articles 102(2) and 191(2) were added. But this did not cure the patient. V.P. Singh's Government, which was a minority government, fell and another minority government of Chandra Shekhar was sworn in. Its life was also short. This malady should be immediately cured. It is, therefore, suggested that we should immediately switch over to the Presidential form of Government.

(a) On the pattern of the centre, District States must also have elected Governors called *State-Pradhans*. This will be in keeping with our national pride and culture. They must be Executive Heads, unaffected by the legislative majority or minority.

(b) It is essential that the qualifications of the President of India and *State-Pradhans* of the District States should be specified. For example, they should be healthy, holder of Post Graduate Degree, not below 50 years or above 65 years, no criminal record, no record of changing political parties, etc. These high offices should not be retiring places for rejected persons or career giver for the young. Social service needs maturity and experience.

3. *Democracy*

Democracy can flourish only when:

(a) There are more than one political party with clear cut different ideologies. Till recently, India had only one party, i.e., Congress. It threw a number of political parties with almost similar ideologies formed by power-hungry and disgruntled members of the Congress. So, socialist parties, Lok Dal, Swatantra Party, Janata Dal, Janata Dal (S) were formed and all are chips of the same block. They have Congress culture, Congress mentality, Congress methodology, etc. Luckily enough, now a new political party in Bhartiya Janata Party is coming up with clear cut differences in ideology. It is a good sign for democracy.

(b) There are responsible legislatures. We did two things. First, given adult franchise to the people. Right to vote requires voter's awareness to his rights. In India, less than 70 per cent voters (now 30%) exercise their right to vote. It also requires voter's rational outlook. Here religious and caste considerations sway the voter. Secondly, we have not prescribed qualifications for a legislator. Membership of a House requires, in modern times, capacity to understand

and contribute on the Bills or issues that are before the House. Today bulk of the MLAs and MPs are unable to participate in these debates. So, majority of them has no interest in these proceedings. Often the quorum is not complete. Participation of an average Parliamentarian is almost zero. So he freely indulges in non-parliamentary work such as appointments, transfers, promotion, sanction of quotas and permits, interference in police and administrative work, etc. All these activities are injurious for democracy.

(c) There is all pervading spirit of nationalism and patriotism. The Constitution should, therefore, provide:

(i) It will be a crime not to exercise one's right of vote.

(ii) Qualifications of a legislator. He should be a Post-Graduate, between the age group of 45 years to 65 years and should have no criminal record. Criminalisation of politics can be controlled only when no criminal is allowed to contest an election.

(iii) A clause in the Constitution, which will debar a legislator from membership of the House if found interfering in administrative affairs be inserted.

(iv) MP or MLAship should not enable one to lead a life of luxury. So, none (including Ministers) should be allowed to have big houses, telephones, TV and Radio sets, furniture and other equipment beyond a minimum, Air or even first class tickets for free rides, pensions etc. The constitution should provide these restrictions. Let not the tribe of new Zamindars and Princes be created. And social service should not be considered an investment to collect huge profits. It should not be a profession either.

(v) It will be ideal if in every constituency a vote is cast to a party and not a person. If the party is elected, it should be free to name any person belonging to any religion or caste subject to his fulfilling the conditions prescribed by the Constitution.

4. *Secularism and Socialism*

(a) Indian Constitution has provided article after article, to encourage secularism and socialism. The condition of Scheduled Castes, Scheduled Tribes, Backward people has remained almost unchanged in spite of reservations in education and services. Of course, a few families of a few privileged classes have pocketed most of the benefits of these constitutional provisions. So, implementation of Mandal Commission recommendations will not make much change except creating a new vote-bank and further dividing the country. Similarly, loud talks of secularism have not benefited Muslims at large except some political leaders of Muslims or some political parties who succeeded in exploiting the religious sentiments of minorities. All this has released tendencies of disintegration. It should be stopped.

It is time that we should remove the provisions of secularism and socialism from our Constitution and in their place add the provision of values – human, social and spiritual such as Simplicity, Truth, Non-anger, Self-control, Non-stealing, Patriotism etc. The propagation of values will be in tune with our past and so will easily be accepted by the people. This will help in solving several problems which secularism and socialism have failed to solve.

(b) The concept of Indian culture, in keeping with our national pride, historical facts and patriotism should be encouraged and given an honourable place in our Constitution. We must accept that Babar and his descendants, howsoever great and noble they might have been, were foreign invaders and foreign rulers. Our national pride and patriotism should forbid us to accept them as national heroes. Even the Islamic countries do not take pride in other countries' greatmen, thoughts, culture etc. For example, in Iran, the death day of the great Muslim Caliph Umar is celebrated like *Id* as a day of redemption. Indonesia, which is a Muslim country, takes pride in giving Sanskritised names to their children and enjoying *Ram's Ramlila*. Every Muslim country takes pride in its own culture. So, why can it not be accepted in India? One not accepting our heroes, our culture, our thought and value system should be deprived of the citizenship right of India.

This political strategy will assist India to march towards the goal of *Anand* and solving our multiple political problems which have been born in free India and/or assumed present magnitude. Probably, this was the picture of *Rama Rajya* of the Father of the Nation, Mahatma Gandhi.

NOTES

1. In the General Elections of May 1991, the percentage fell to 25 per cent to 33 per cent. Add to it rigging which is estimated to be 10 per cent and Booth-Capturing. So, the actual voting is 20 per cent or so.
2. *Dharma* is not religion. It is a duty, justice, well-being of people and a code of conduct covering all these aspects.
3. *See* Economic Strategy.

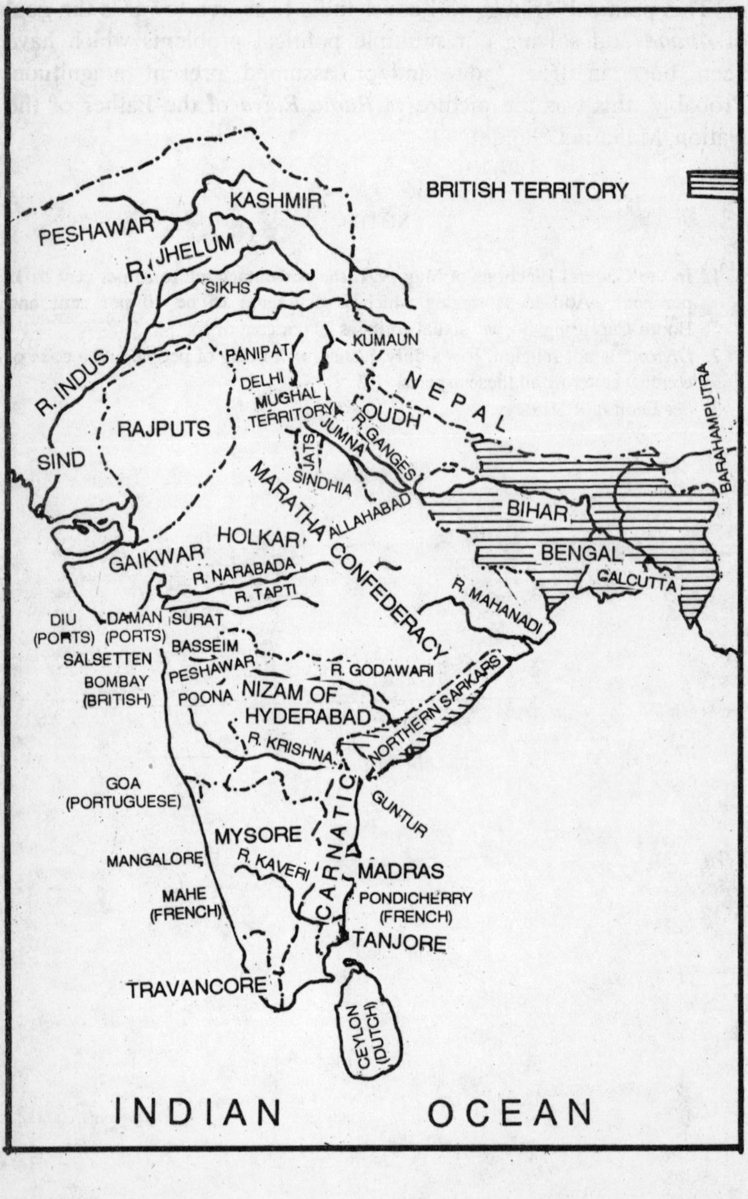

MAP 9.1: British Territory — Part A: (1772-85)

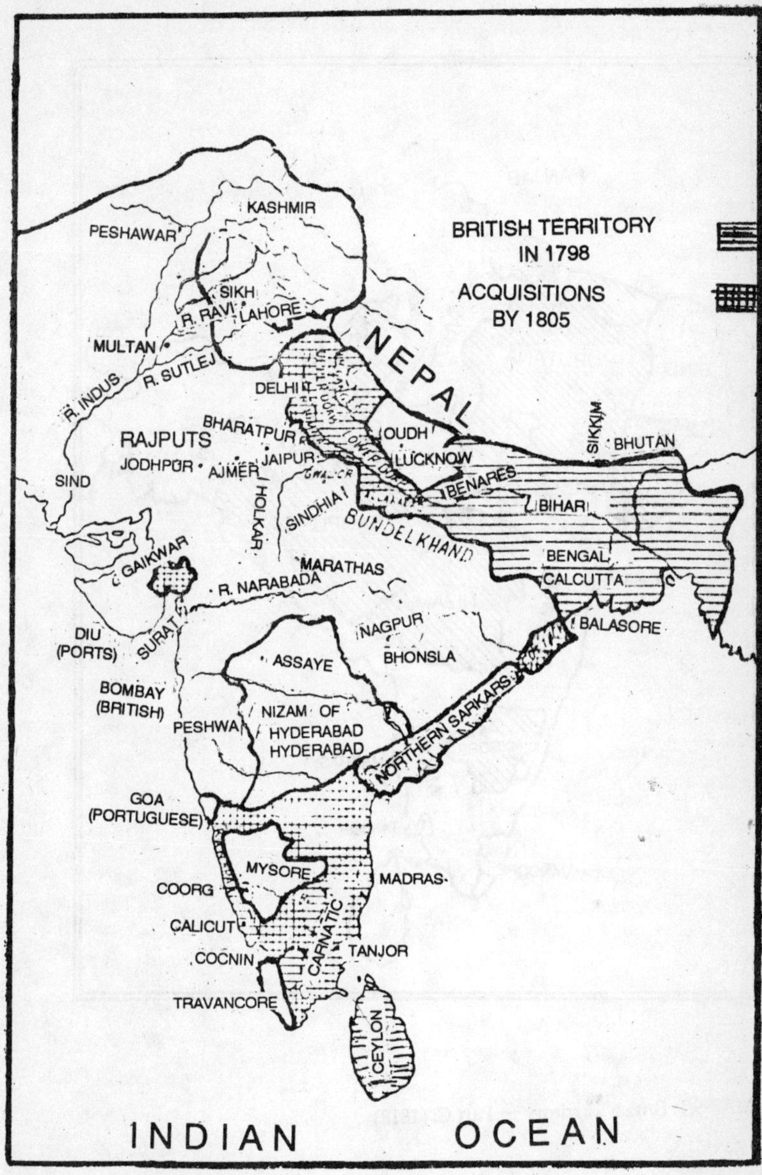

MAP 9.1: British Territory — Part B: (1805)

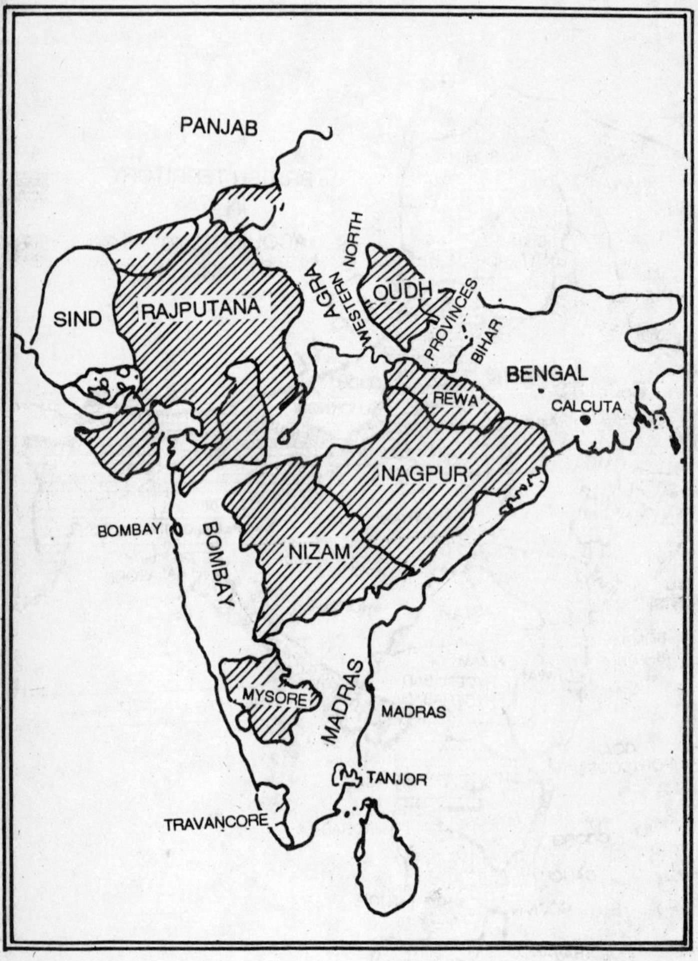

MAP 9.1: British Territory — Part C: (1818)

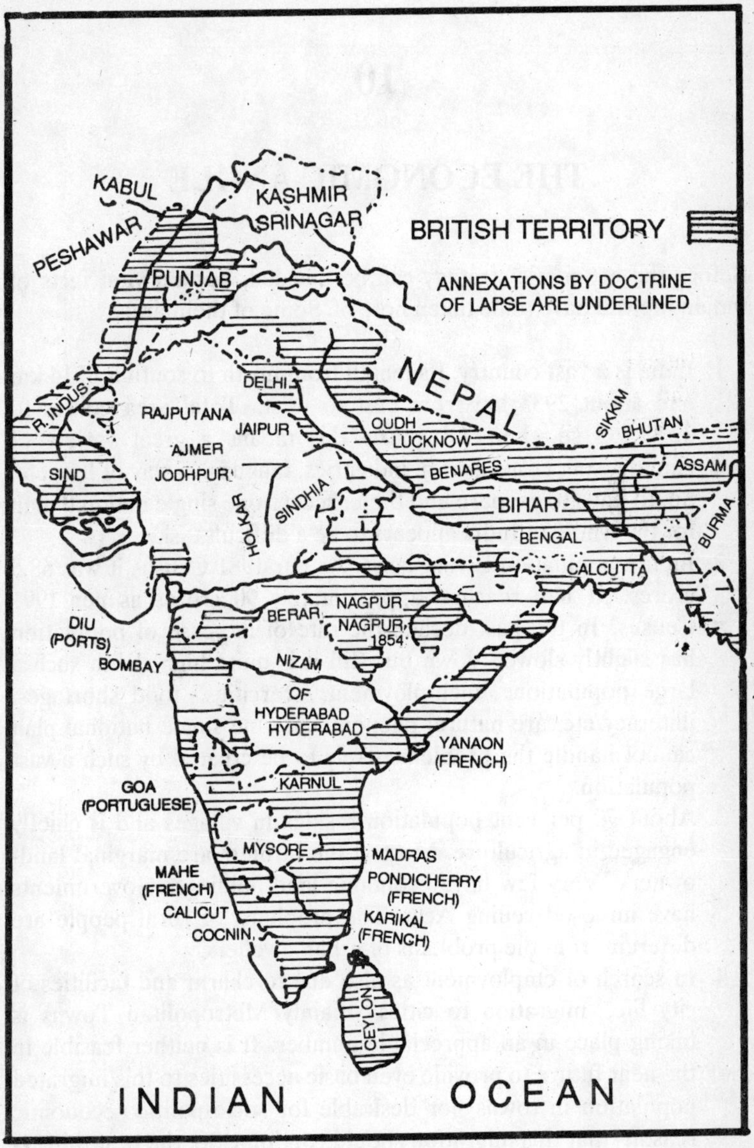

MAP 9.1: British Territory — Part D: (1856)

10

THE ECONOMIC ANGLE

Before the economic strategy can be decided, certain vital facts of Indian life will have to be taken note of. Some of them are:

1. India is a vast country. Its length from north to south is 3214 km and about 2933 km from east to west. Total area comes to 32,87,263 sq. km. Obviously this means a great variety of climate, soil, crops grown, industries, languages, way of life, etc. So, to have to prepare and then execute one single national plan for the whole of India appears to be a difficult task.
2. India's population is very large. As per 1981 Census it was 68.5 crores. It had reached approximately 90 crores as per 1991 Census. In the past decade the rate of increase of population has slightly slowed down but still it is quite high. With such a large population, unemployment, scarcities, food shortages, illiteracy etc. are natural phenomena. One single national plan cannot handle the problems likely to be created by such a vast population.
3. About 70 per cent population resides in villages and is chiefly engaged in agriculture. Most of the farmers are marginal land-owners. Very few have economic land-holdings. Governments have imposed ceiling Acts. The problems of rural people are different from the problems of urban dwellers.
4. In search of employment as also due to charm and facilities of city life, migration to cities, mainly Metropolitan Towns is taking place in an appreciable number. It is neither feasible in the near future to provide even basic necessities to this migrated population in towns nor desirable for socio-politico-economic reasons that this migration should continue. So, the best thing is to provide gainful employment in villages themselves along with all the benefits of city life. Failing that, the scheme of developing "small" and "medium" towns should be taken up.

5. Experience of Western life clearly gives the message that affluence beyond a limit is more harmful, both from individual and social points of view. It, like poverty, has its own problems. Even our past shows that emphasis was not on unreasonable love for matter but on happiness, i.e., *Anand*. Mahatma Gandhi, the Father of the Nation, also pleaded for simplicity, and detachment from the material pursuits. Even our Constitution says:

> "The State shall endeavour to secure, by suitable legislation or economic organisation or in any other way, to all workers, agricultural, industrial or otherwise, work, a living wage, conditions of work ensuring a decent standard of life and *full enjoyment of leisure and social and cultural opportunities* and, in particular, the State shall endeavour to promote cottage industries on an individual or cooperative basis in rural areas.
>
> (Article 43)

This article clarifies:

(i) The workers will get work and a living wage. What this Living Wage means? In Economics, wages may be Minimum Wages, which are equal to Subsistance Wages, Fair Wages and Living Wages. Fair Wage is higher than the Minimum Wage but lower than the Living Wage.

At another place, the Indian constitution says:

Article 39 "The State shall, in particular, direct its policy towards sccuring –

(a) That the citizens, men and women equally, have the right to an *adequate means of livelihood;*"

And yet at the third place, the same Indian Constitution says:

Article 47 "Duty of the State to raise the level of nutrition and the standard of living and to improve public health. . ..

In India, more than 50 per cent population lives below the poverty line. so, the immediate aim is to provide them a Minimum Wage which may ensure the required quantities of nutrition. This, and "adequate means of livelihood" of Art 39 seems to be one and the same thing. So, the ultimate aim seems to be the Living Wage (Art. 43). But this Living Wage should be much lower than the Living Wage of the Western concept. Here in India, by our Constitution, it is a wage which is bound by two conditions, viz., same wage for workers engaged in agriculture, industrial or other places, and also a wage which a cottage industry can provide. Obviously, it should be slightly higher than the Minimum Wage of the Western economists' idea but cannot be a Living Wage of the Western concept. The philosophy of socialism, adopted by India and viewed in the Indian context, cannot afford a more than Fair Wage. It will be more close to a Minimum Wage.

(ii) The workers will get work at their place of residence. Thus, no mass migration of population to urban or industrial areas was contemplated.

(iii) "Enjoyment of leisure" gets importance after the basic requirements of economic life are fulfilled. Emphasis then shifts to "social and cultural activities". Our Constitution does not want to make a man, like the west, an Economic Man.

A reference to the debates in the Constituent Assembly on this article lends support to these conclusions. Shri Mahavir Tyagi said:

". . . the condition of rural areas is very bad today. . . the conditions in the villages are so bad that the artisan classes have all practically come to the towns . . . How will economic democracy come about in the existing state of affairs in the rural areas?

". . . we are not treating the villagers fairly. . . . But the villages are totally neglected. Every man who has the least initiative comes to the town. . . . Now, Sir, it is very good to say that we want economic equality and economic democracy. . . . I am not opposed to big concentration of industries in big towns. Villages have been their recruiting grounds. Villagers come and employ themselves in these big mills only to demoralise themselves in bad atmosphere in towns. . . . The purpose of my placing this amendment before you is that instead of the muscular power going to the machine, I want to carry the machines to the sources of muscular power . . . our party, the Congress Party, has been propagating *Swadeshi* and cottage industries since its very inception, but now that the time has come for making our Constitution if we ignore the villagers, that will be disappointing to the village people. . . . If you want to combine political democracy with economic democracy and translate into life Dr. Ambedkar's maxim, 'one man, one unit', then you should make the villages self-reliant and self-sufficient. Otherwise the millions who are unemployed in the rural areas will never enjoy the fruits of freedom; they will remain slaves of the townsmen as they are today . . . give them cottage industries so that they can live happily with their families in their own happy surroundings. . . ."

Shri T.A. Ramalingam Chettiar said,

"... The only point I want to make is that so far the cottage industries have not been able to make headway for two reasons. One is the competition with the imported and mill made goods and the other want of organisation to help the cottage industries. Raw materials have to be supplied . . . marketing has to be arranged. . . . So the only method that is available and that is open to us is the formation of cooperative societies. . . ."

Shri H.V. Kamath said:

". . . what is economic democracy and what is social democracy? . . . Sir, I would refer to the resolution passed at the Meerut session of the Congress, which gives a definite meaning to this concept of economic and social democracy.

". . . I hope, Sir, the Government will . . . see that in

accordance with the terms of the Article, all workers, industrial or otherwise, are secured work, a living wage and a decent standard of life.

". . . to India through the ages has been given the mission of preaching the noble and sublime ideal, the concept of spiritual democracy, of which political, social and economic democracy are mere off shoots. If true spiritual democracy takes root in our society, there is no doubt that we shall show to humanity a new way of life. . . ."

So, our Constitution wants to ensure a "Living Wage" which means, at best, "Fair Wage" through cottage industries, and does not prefer migration of population to towns in search of jobs.

6. We, in India, have accepted democracy — political, economic and social. Democracy implies decentralisation of power. Democratic Planning means that the people of an area will decide what they want, how they want and what their priorities are. During the last forty years of planning, in the name of democratic planning, we were having central planning of the Russian model. We never tried to know from the persons concerned, their problems, their priorities and their solutions. This has not attracted people's willing and active participation. It has also increased regional imbalances and encouraged greater misuse of our limited resources. So, a scheme is needed which will democratise economic life and decentralise planning in the real sense.
7. We were persuaded to adopt Mahalanobis model. It postulates that higher rate of investment in capital goods will automatically generate increased purchasing power and hence demand for consumer goods which requires comparatively less capital but employs more labour. In this way, a balance is achieved between the investment sector and consumer goods sector. It presumes that establishment of large industrial towns will automatically take care of our problems, specially in the countryside. This model did not succeed.
8. India has limited resources and almost a negligible infrastructure. But in spite of it, we, in our wisdom, had taken several steps which were bound to multiply and intensify our problem:

(i) We realised that to increase the rate of economic development, we need more and more investment in capital goods sector and so bigger and more bigger plans. So, we went on making bigger and bigger plans. We forgot that in Mixed Economy like that one in India, with political democracy tagged, public sector will have greater gestation period and poor efficiency with the result that losses will accrue.

(ii) Bigger plans need resources which we had not. So, we started borrowing on a massive scale, both from within the country and also from outside India. Today, the debt burden has assumed dangerous proportions. We have to take fresh loans to repay back the interest on old loans. It is now becoming more difficult to raise additional loans. Probably the noose of Debt Trap is round the corner.

(iii) To mobilise resources we went on raising rates of taxation without bothering about the elasticities of various taxes. Today a neck-breaking stage seems to have been achieved. It has encouraged corrupt practices and evasion of taxes on an unprecedented scale.

(iv) To meet the requirement of massive plans, we resorted to deficit planning under the false hope provided by "Government Economists" that it will not be inflationary. We tried to conveniently forget all the existing economic literature on the subject to appease our masters.

The result of all this has been that we have forced plan holidays and yet we have not been able to solve even one single problem through planning and in bargain have created many more dangerous problems like two digit price rise, increasing unfavourable balance of payment and stupendous debt burden.

9. The Planners forgot that Human Capital has an important place in any scheme of planning. The plans were for his good and they are implemented with his help. So, it was essential to assess the qualities of the people, specially those associated with implementation work. This was never done. This led to faulty and delayed implementation of plans. The leakages, misdirections and delays became proverbial. A Prime Minister is on

record to have accepted that 85 per cent of money spent on plans is eaten away and only 15 per cent is utilised. It is recently that our planners have given a new slogan of Human Resource Development Strategy. But this simply touches the fringe of this problem. It does not concentrate on character building of Indian variety. Today values — human, social and spiritual, so arduously given to Indian masses by our seers have been ruthlessly destroyed by our politicians by their cheap stunts, aping of Western life and foolish slogans of anti-*Dharma,* pro-secularism and socialism. In the last forty years, the Indian social life has degenerated to dangerous depths. Hardly any one speaks the truth. Villagers do not wish to return back to their villages after sun-set where as earlier they were not prepared to stay at city even after 8 or 9 p.m. Murders, dacoities, bride burning, broken homes, rapes, mafia-kings, rule the roost.

10. The planners did not deem it necessary, for reasons best known to them, to utilise the well-known techniques of *Action Plan* to monitor the results, the problems, the defects and to take corrective steps as the plan moves on. Thus, the targets fixed were hardly achieved and many new problems cropped up.
11. In spite of knowing that our resources are inadequate to meet the requirements of such massive plans, and also knowing that the different regions of India are at different levels of development, it never struck to us that in spite of making All India plans to solve all problems simultaneously, we must make only Regional Plans to solve Regional problems and covering only a part of India, as per our resources. Once this part of the country is taken to take-off stage, it can be left to its own fate and efforts to reach the stage of maturity and thereafter new areas be taken up. This technique might have needed lesser resources and yielded quicker results. It was, however, to the decision of planners to take up the most backward regions first which will need more resources and time to reach take-off stage or select semi-developed areas which would require lesser resources and time.
12. In a vast country like India, the idea of making self-sufficient zones in all matters and small sub-areas in basic requirements was not given a thought even.
13. Life is one. Political life and social life influence economic life and in return get influenced by economic life. Planners, in their

wisdom, did not think it proper to have politico-social plans along with economic plans. So, the economic plans, it appears, helped in lopsided development of human personality resulting in aggravating socio-politico problems. Black-money, for instance, has become a parallel economy and mafia groups are becoming real centres of power.

14. No quick development is possible without proper inputs on infrastructure. So, the basic need is to provide infrastructure. But we must be careful in deciding the priorities of the various infrastructures for each region which we propose to develop. It appears, planners were led more by politicians' cheap slogans than hard-boiled pragmatic decisions. An example will be illustrative.

    In the initial stage of planning, a question of Rural Electrification arose. Research Programme Committee, Planning Commission, New Delhi gave me a project on this subject. My studies revealed that with the meagre resources, it is impossible to electrify each and every village. Moreover, it will not be an economic proposition. Most of the villages have *Kachcha* houses where electricity cannot be given as per law. The incomes and savings of villagers are meagre, their technical know-how is poor, repairing facilities are non-existent and marketing problems are a great hurdle. All this will not permit any appreciable industrialisation in villages. So, rural electrification, if undertaken, will neither be a commercial proposition for the Electricity Boards, nor help the villagers and in bargain, make electricity scarce and costly in towns and hamper the growth of industries. I even estimated the losses that State Tube-wells will give to the state Tube-well Department and also to the State Electricity Board. I suggested that if the money that will be spent on rural electrification is distributed free amongst the farmers for digging wells and irrigating land with the help of their cattle then it will irrigate more land in shorter period, will need no electricity, will make farmer self-sufficient and check yearly losses to the Tube-well and Hydel Departments. But this scientific study was not considered and scheme of Rural Electrification was launched with great fanfare. Today my predictions and fears have proved correct.[1]

15. India has a vast population tagged with mass unemployment

and poverty. So, our priority should have been for the labour intensive techniques instead of capital intensive ones. But in our zeal to follow Western models, we preferred capital intensive methodology. One can certainly question, for example, the necessity of introducing tractor for already cultivated lands when size of land is small and that too fragmented.

16. The towns depend on rural areas and rural areas depend upon towns. So, obvious logic required that the towns and rural areas should be developed as one unit, supplementing and complementing each other. This was not done.
17. Western experts — geographers, economists, sociologists and town planners have developed several theories of spatial structure and urban growth.

For example:

(i) *The Urban Location Theory* was first propounded by Heinrich Van Thunen and later on refined by others. Heinrich Van Thunen showed, on the basis of empirical evidence, that under ideal conditions a city would develop at the centre of this land area and concentric rings of land-use would develop around this central city. In spite of its defects, it established a distance-cost relationship. Today location theory explains the pattern of land-use and also gives a solution to the problem of what is the most rational use of land.

(ii) *The Concentric Zone Theory* of Burgess applies the urban location theory to how to use rural land around a city. This theory is dynamic as it allows for underlying conditions to change continuously such as natural population increase inmigration, economic growth and income expansion.

(iii) *The Sector Theory* of Homer Hoyt is a refinement of Axial Development Theory. It establishes a relationship of a transport use with land-use.

(iv) *The Concentric Zone-sector Theory* of Mann is based on the concentric zone theory of Burgess and appears to be an application only.

(v) *The Multiple Nuclei Theory* of Harris and Ullman, says that in a city, the land-use pattern is built not around a single centre but around several distinct nuclei.

(vi) *The Urban Economic Base Theory* – a crude and outdated one — concentrates on urban employment, additions to the level of employment and multiplying effects upon the total population.

(vii) *The Money Flow Theory* is based on the Keynes circular flow of money theory. It establishes a relationship between total income of the circular flow of money and growth of an urban area.

(viii) *The Human Ecological Approach to Urban Growth* emphasises the importance of human ecology and wants a relationship between urban growth and ecology to be established.

(ix) *The Communication Theory of Urban Growth* of Meier, gives importance to transport and communication in the development and expansion of the cities.

(x) *The City Size and Urban Growth Theory* establishes a relationship between size of industry and growth of a town. It establishes that growth in large cities will be self-generating because large cities have a greater potential for obtaining growth inputs.

(xi) *The Central Place Theory* of Bobeck which was refined by Brian J.L. Berry and others, tries to deal with the question of relation between a city and a rural area and that the city should be in the centre of a productive area. In other words, a city's growth is a function of its hinterland population (and income level).

(xii) *The Growth Centre Theory*: It has been observed that in spite of planned efforts, the rich areas become more rich while backward areas remain backward. To solve the problem of regional imbalances, the Growth Centre Theory was propounded. It suggests that in spite of economic consideration, growth centres should be established in relatively less developed areas. It links the issue to location of industries, urban environment and growth of the area. It favours medium and small towns in place of very big towns. This theory states that growth centres act as poles of attraction for commuters and migrants and generators of spread effects.

These and many useful theories have been developed in the West.

It appears Indian planners did not think it proper to make use of them after Indiansing them. An effort must be made, specially while developing "small" and "medium" towns of a district, to use them.

THE STRATEGY

General Guidelines

1. Experience has shown that India cannot take up a National Plan covering the entire territory of the country due to paucity of national resources. And we cannot wait for another hundred years or more to take the entire country to the take-off stage. So, we must adopt the policy of development bit by bit. The most backward districts of India should be taken up first, either in one lot, or if their number is more than what our resources can afford, then even in two or three lots. Each lot will be given a five year plan. In this five year plan, the entire area will be saturated with the required resources and taken to the take off stage. Thereafter it will be left to develop itself with the momentum given to it and new areas will be covered by a new plan.
2. The aim of these District Plans will be to move towards *Anand*, i.e., an all round integrated and balanced development of the people. Economic development will mean that all the people of the area will be gainfully employed, none will be unemployed, each will have adequate means of livelihood and will be self-sufficient in all the basic needs — water, food, cloth, house etc. They will have the required level of nutrition and good health. There will be minimum uneven distribution of wealth and lot of opportunities of full enjoyment of leisure. This is not possible when the faith is pinned on large scale capital — intensive industries.

   Politically, it will mean that people are patriots par excellence, proud of their cultural heritage, conscious of their duties (not so much rights) and watchful. They will normally not be politically-oriented and will not like to make politics an aim of their life.

   Socially, it will mean that people will lead a moral life based on value system — Human, Social and Spiritual. They will have a rich family life based on love, respect, self-sacrifice, duty, sincerity etc. They will have full faith in the maximum of "Live and Let Live". They will take pride in their culture and try to enrich it further. And this enrichment of social life will depend, to a very great extent, on education, formal and informal. This education will be goal-oriented. The goals of Indian Education will be deep seated in Indian culture, value system, philosophy etc. and at the same time will not ignore modern requirement (not western).

3. India has a rich and unique heritage. Foreign rulers, including our own people, without knowing it and much less understanding it, started condemning it. They started aping the western life style, value system, thought etc. calling it, under a misplaced notion, that it is modern and progressive. This will have to stop. We will have certainly to modernise our own things but not necessarily westernise them. We can modernise them without losing our own roots. Japan has done it. So, the slogan should be 'Modernise India but do not Westernise it'.
4. India has adopted democracy. It means that the Plans should also be democratic. It implies that before preparing a plan, through intensive surveys we should try to know the resources, the problems and their priorities, peoples' suggestions to solve these problems etc. These surveys must be on the basis of house-holds. It is on the basis of this data and aspirations of the people that experts should prepare a plan. Such a methodology is likely to have a better participation of people, right from the planning stage to the execution stage.
5. To make democracy, which means maximum decentralisation of power — political, economic and social, – successful, we have given an idea of District States. So, our one unit of plan will be a district. Suppose, if we have taken one hundred districts for our first plan, then, we will prepare 100 District States' Plans. It will be the duty of the Central Planning Commission to give finishing touches to the District Plans in such a way that while retaining the basis they may become complementary to each other and the whole area, nay the whole country, may move forward in a set pattern, towards a set goal.
6. A District Plan will be an integrated, plan, of the Plan of the District Headquarters, Plan of Tahsils, Plan of Block Headquarters and Plan of Focal village and its command area. All plans will be complementary and supplementary to each

other and make one integrated whole.

(a) A Focal Village will prepare a democratic plan for itself and its command area. It will have a main thrust of the development of agriculture and agro-based industries. It may also develop some other cottage or small scale industries as the resources of the area permit. The Focal Village will act as a mini-township and an Industrial Estate with all the necessary facilities of a city. For example, it will be the responsibility of the Plan of the Focal Village to develop roads connecting it with the villages of the command area and provide all the charm of a city life in this Focal Village.

(b) A Block Headquarters will draw a plan for itself in such a way that it may act as a Focal village for its command area and also a link between Tahsil and District Headquarter's on the one side and Focal Village and their command areas on the other. It will be a *"Small"* Township meeting all the needs of villagers which Focal Villages are not able to meet. For example, it will be the responsibility to lay roads connecting Focal Village with the Block Headquarters etc.

(c) A Tahsil Plan will act as a Focal Village of the command area and will also aim at developing Tahsil as a *"Medium"* township which will be a go-between the Villages, Blocks and the District Headquarters. For Example, it will be its responsibility to connect Block Headquarters with Tahsils with roads and provide all the facilities that could not be provided at Block Headquarters.

(d) A District Headquarter will be an apex town. For example, it will be its responsibility to connect Tahsils and Block Headquarters with the District Headquarter and provide all the facilities which could not be given at Tahsil, Block or Focal Village.

7. A District Plan (Focal Village, Block, Tahsil and District Headquarters Plan) will be of Five Years duration. The time schedule will be divided as below:-

(i) Intensive surveys to know resources, problems, priorities, solution etc. House-hold shall be the unit — 6 months.

(ii) Preparation of Plan at all levels and ensuring that they are complementary and supplementary to each other — 6 months.

(iii) Providing infrastructure such as roads, irrigation, water technical know-how, Financial institutions, Government offices for *'One Window Service'* etc. — 1 year.

(iv) Implementation of plan and simultaneously, on the basis of Action Research, to evaluate and correct Plan — 2 years 6 months.

(v) Finalisation — 6 months.

Total = 5 years

8. (a) The Administrative set-up will fully be decentralised. It means that all the concerned offices will be opened at all levels — Focal Village, Block Headquarters, Tahsils and District Headquarters.

(b) These offices, as far as possible, will be on one campus so that. *'One Window Service'* principle can be followed.

(c) All these offices at all levels, will be put under one Principal Officer, incharge of all offices. This will be a new approach but a very effective one to cut down proverbial delays, corruption, etc. and improve efficiency.

(d) The officers and men of various departments, known for their efficiency and honesty, will be picked up from the whole of the present day 'State' and posted in these Planning Districts. They will be given some extra allowance, if need be, as incentive.

(e) These officers will be given wide powers.

(f) These officers will be made accountable. In case of guilt or fault, transfer will not be a safety-valve for them.

9. Each Focal Village, each Block Headquarter, each tahsil and each District headquarter will have a Planning Advisory Committee.

(i) *Focal Village* — One representative from each village of the command area will be a member. Normally, *Gram Pradhan* will be nominated.

(ii) *Block Headquarters* — One elected representative of each

Focal Village Advisory Committee will be a member of the Block Headquarters' Planning Committee.

(iii) *Tahsil* — One elected representative of each Block Headquarters Advisory Committee will be a member of the Tahsil advisory Committee.

(iv) *District Headquarters* — One elected representative from each Tehsil Advisory Committee will be member of the District Advisory Committee.

If need be, some experts may be nominated at each level by the respective committees.

The work of these Advisory Committees will be to know the Plan of their area, give suggestions, if any, and keep a watch over the execution. If some irregularities come to their knowledge, it will be their duty to bring them to the notice of the chief of the area. They will act as watch dogs.

10. India has surplus of labour but shortage of capital. So maximum of the schemes should be labour-intensive. Of course, obsolete methods, tools etc. will be modernised (not westernised) to suit Indian conditions.

For the development of a District, we should have district plan for:

A Villages
B Towns — Small and Medium.

A brief discussion follows:-

A. Village Plans

How to determine Focal Villages and their Command Areas

India mainly lives in villages. So, villages must be developed. But to develop and modernise 5.76 lakh villages, that India has, is neither easy, nor possible in the near future nor desirable. Hence, the scheme of selecting *Focal Villages,* which may act as a catalyst for a cluster of villages.

These Focal Villages be interconnected with the Block Headquarters, Tahsil Headquarters and District Headquarters so that all may easily interact and help in an integrated and balanced development of the area.

It is rational to select one Focal Village for ten to fifteen villages. It will mean that we will have to develop about forty thousand villages in the whole country. This will not be a small task but still appears to be better manageable.

How to select a Focal Village? Obviously, this can be on the basis of existing inputs and other factors. Some of them are:

1. Population — It is desirable to select a village with large population because it will consist more of all the varieties of people – educated, less educated and illiterate, agriculturists, landless farmers, non-agriculturists such as artisans, service class, businessmen, money-lender etc.
2. Area of the village and distance from other villages of the command area.
3. Connected with road, rail and water transport
4. Canal
5. Seed store
6. Fertiliser store
7. Tube-well
8. F.C.I. centre
9. Village market
10. Cold storage
11. Veterinary hospital
12. Agricultural department — sugarcane, fisheries, etc.
13. Forest department
14. Financial institutions — commercial bank, cooperative bank, land development bank, gramin bank etc.
15. Post office and telegraph office.
16. Primary health centre, maternity and child welfare centre, hospital, etc.
17. *Nayaya Panchayat*
18. Primary school, high school, inter college, technical school.
19. Police station.
20. Industrial estate.
21. Cooperatives — milk, village industries etc.

After selecting a Focal Village, the next question comes: how to determine its command areas? The easiest technique appears that the names of the village of a block may be picked up where maximum of the above facilities exist today. Thereafter through surveys, it may be found out from which nearby villages people come to this village for a particular facility. This will show the command area of that village for that activity. This will give us one ring of villages. A village, which has the maximum number of above mentioned infrastructure facilities thus will give various rings of villages of command areas for various facilities. The villages that are covered by the maximum number of facilities will determine the command area of the Focal village.

To have a practical experience, we selected the Tahsil of Sikandra Rao of the District of Aligarh Map 10.1. And in the Tahsil of Sikandra Rao, we selected the Block of Sikandra Rao, known for its poverty.

Sikandra Rao Block Headquarter is about 39 km from the town of Aligarh. The total area of this block is 262 Sq. km and the population, according to 1981 population census, 96,164. It has 67 villages. Table 10.1 gives the facilities that exist in these villages.

Table 10.1 gives some very interesting information which has a bearing on the development of the area.

The first thing that comes to mind is that during the last forty years of planned development, very little infrastructure could be provided to the villages. With this speed, probably, the next one hundred years will not be able to take these villages to the take-off stage.

Land-Population Ratio

The second thing that becomes apparent is that in these 67 villages 96,164 people reside, i.e., on an average 1435 persons. Only 26 villages have a population of more than 1435. It is surprising to note that two villages, viz., Thatpur (code no. 142) and Sanjarpur (code no. 144) have been shown as deserted villages while the land area attached to them is 223.39 and 50.99 hectares respectively.

The total land area in these 67 villages is 24455.28 hectares. It means that on an average a village has 365 hectares land. A review of the table shows that eight villages have less than 365 hectares land. It is an indicator of the poverty of the inhabitants of these villages.

These 67 villages have a total population of 96,164 and a total land area of 24455.28 hectares. Thus, on an average a person's share comes to 0.29 hectares. Surely, this land is not sufficient to provide a person decent living which the Indian Constitution contemplates.

Transport

Transport facilities are the most important infrastructure for development. A review of Table 10.1 along with the Map 10.2 shows that the Sikandra Rao Block is not placed in an enviable position as far as transport is concerned.

There is no canal big enough to allow water-transport.

Metre gauge railway line connecting Mathura with Kasganj passes through Sikandra Rao. It has only two stations, one at Sikandra Rao and the other at Agsauli. Thus bulk of the Block area on the north side remains uncovered by rail transport. Moreover, since the railway line is meter gauge, its utility becomes still less.

Three *Pucca* roads – Aligarh to Kanpur (G.T. Road), Mathura to Pilibhit and an off route from G.T. Road to Kasganj Road pass through the Sikandra Rao Block. Besides this, there are a few *Kutcha* roads as feeder roads connecting villages, branching off from the *Pucca* road connecting (G.T. Road to Kasganj Road). Looking broadly, this network of road transport cannot help in the rapid development of the area.

Pucca roads pass from 21 villages out of 67 villages. Another 6-7 villages are connected by *Kutcha* roads. Thus, less than 50 per cent villages have facilities of road transport. This is not a happy position looking from the development point of view.

Communication

Twenty four villages out of 67 villages of the Sikandra Rao Block, i.e., 35.8 per cent villages have Post Offices. These 24 post offices cover a population of 96,164, i.e., one post office caters to the needs of 4,000 villagers. Only Sikandra Rao town has a Telegraph Office. There seems to be no facility of telephones.

Most of the Post Offices have been located in villages having large population. (Map 10.3) However, some villages with large population such as Mohamai Salabatnagar (2,417), Nai Nagla Tahar (1,884), Liha Alampur (2,214), Gureda Sultanpur (1,480), Bargawan (2,327) etc., have been left out, while some small villages like Mirpur (547), Bhans Mai (504), Raipur Tappa Agsauli (704) have been provided with Post Offices. This shows the miracle of political pulls.

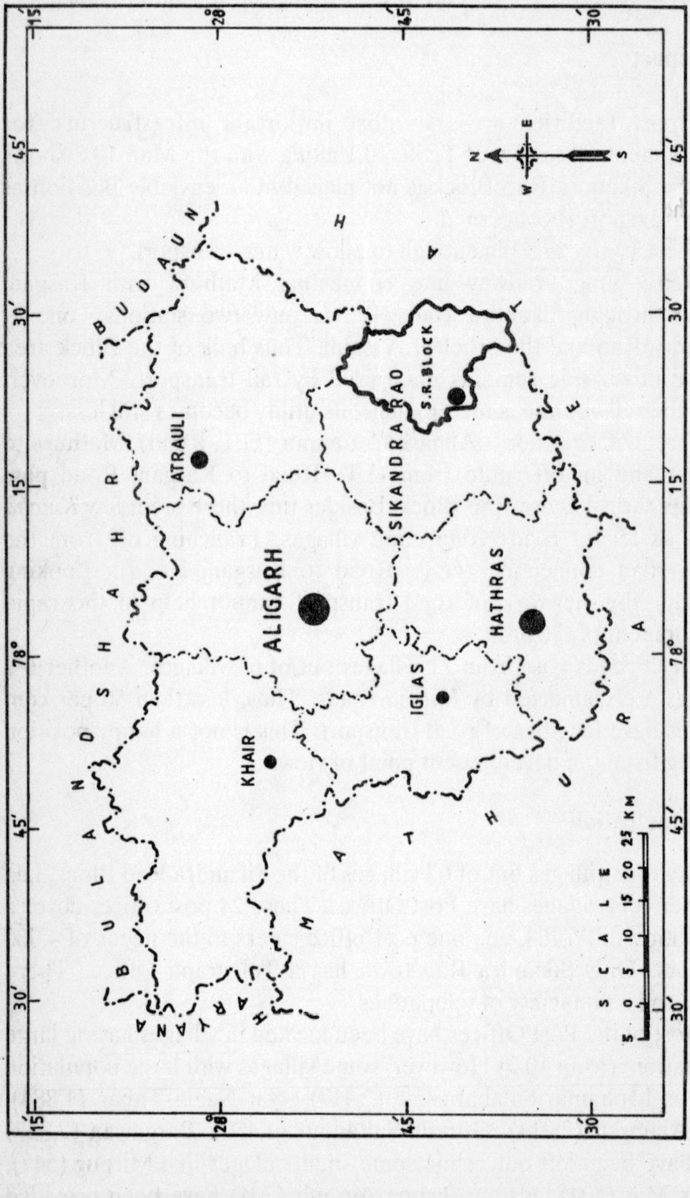

MAP 10.1: District Aligarh

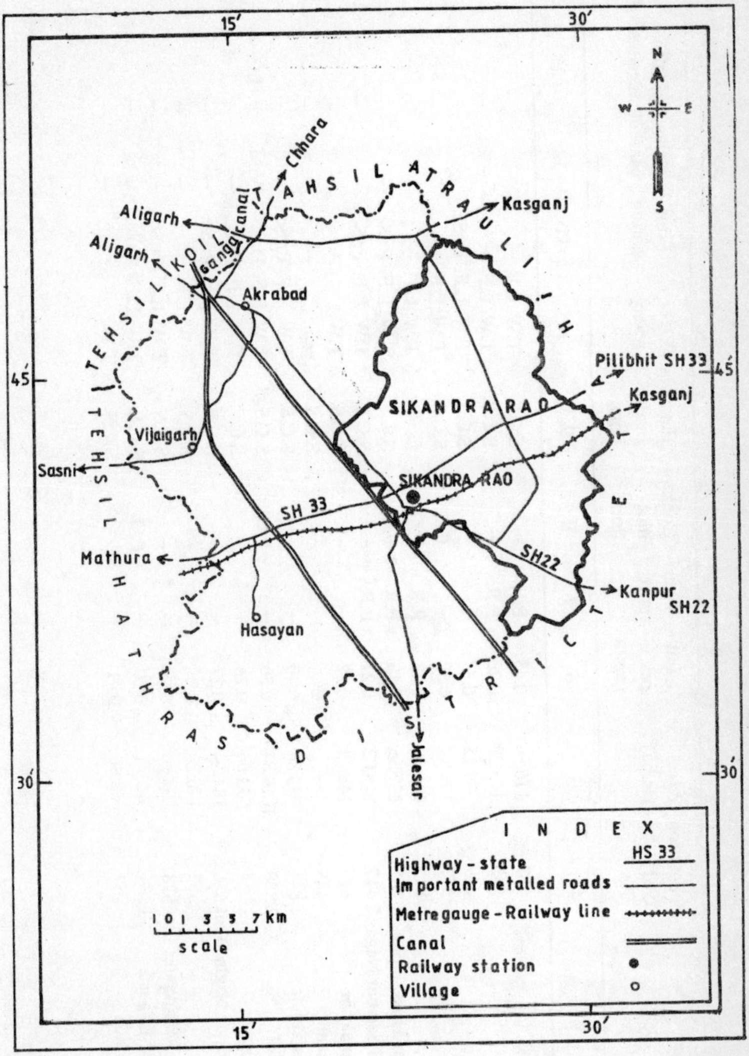

MAP 10.2: Tahsil Sikandra Rao, District Aligarh (Transport)

TABLE 10.1: Infrastructures Provided

Sl. No.	Code No.	Village	Population (1981)	Area (in ha)	Land per capita	Trans-port	Commu-nica-tion	Financial Institu-tions	Elec-tricity	Edu-cation	Village Market	Health Services	Police Posts
1	2	3	4	5	6	7	8	9	10	11	12	13	14
1	88	Paharpur	262	116.96	0.45	P.R.	—	S.C.S.	T.W.,L.F.	—	—	—	—
2.	89	Bilar	568	145.29	0.26	P.R.	—	S.C.S.	T.W.,L.F.	—	—	—	—
3.	90	Udpur	269	99.15	0.37	—	—	S.C.S.	T.W.,L.F.	Pr.Sc.	—	—	—
4.	91	Mirpur	547	176.45	0.32	—	P.O.	S.C.S.	T.W.,L.F.	—	—	—	—
5.	92	Arnot	815	146.10	0.18	P.R.	P.O.	G.Bk.	T.W.,L.F.	—	—	—	—
6.	93	Rattanpur Hussainpur	1,283	237.56	0.19	P.R.	P.O.	S.C.S.	T.W.,L.F.	Pr.Sc.	—	—	—
7	94	Mahamai Salabat Nagar	2,417	518.02	0.21	P.R.	—	S.C.S.	T.W.,L.F.	Pr.Sc.	—	—	—
8.	95	Devar Panakhar	676	148.12	0.22	—	—	S.C.S.	T.W.	—	—	—	—
9.	96	Nagla Chamar	445	—	—	—	—	S.C.S.	—	—	—	—	—
10.	97	Nai Nagla Tahar	1,844	743.84	0.40	—	—	S.C.S.	T.W.	Pr.Sc.	—	—	—
11.	98	Mai Chirail	2,838	1019.84	0.36	—	P.O.	S.C.S.	T.W.,L.F.	H.S.	V.M.	P.H.C.	—
12.	99	Liha Alampur	2,214	573.06	0.26	—	—	S.C.S.	T.W.,L.F.	Pr.Sc.	—	—	—
13.	100	Mahmoodpur Nagla Dhak	676	184.14	0.27	—	—	S.C.S.	T.W.,L.F.	Pr.Sc.	—	—	—
14	101	Esepur	560	120.20	0.21	—	—	S.C.S.	T.W.,L.F.	—	—	—	—
15.	102	Shaimpur Manikpur	678	194.26	0.29	—	—	S.C.S.	T.W.,L.F.	Pr.Sc.	—	—	—
16.	103	Mubrikpur Kapasia	3,484	703.37	0.20	—	P.O.	S.C.S.	T.W.,L.F.	Pr.Sc.	V.M.	—	—
17.	104	Nagla Chhbua	167	68.80	0.41	—	—	S.C.S.	T.W.	—	—	—	—

(Contd.)

TABLE 10.1: *(Contd.)*

1	2	3	4	5	6	7	8	9	10	11	12	13	14
18.	105	Tati Dandia	1,358	411.58	0.30	—	P.O.	S.C.S.	T.W.,L.F.	Pr.Sc.	—	—	—
19.	106	Tikari Buzurg	3,086	758.52	0.25	K.R.	P.O.	S.C.S.	T.W.,L.F.	—	V.M.	P.H.C.,H.	—
20.	107	Bajidpur	1,949	269.93	0.14	—	P.O.	S.C.S., G.Bk.	T.W.,L.F.	Pr.Sc.	V.M.	M.C.W.C.	—
21.	108	Nijra Gokulpur	1,281	248.49	0.19	P.R.	—	S.C.S.	T.W.,L.F.	Pr.Sc.	—	P.H.C.	—
22.	109	Narharpur Dostpur	1,195	231.49	0.19	P.R.	—	S.C.S.	T.W.,L.F.	—	—	—	—
23.	110	Gureda Sultanpur	1,480	252.53	0.17	P.R.	—	S.C.S.	T.W.,L.F.	—	—	—	—
24.	111	Arafpur Bhogpur	825	119.39	0.14	—	—	L.S.S.	T.W.,L.F.	—	—	—	—
25.	112	Bimamai	643	137.19	0.21	—	—	L.S.S.	T.W.	—	—	—	—
26.	113	Khizarpur	1,463	348.45	0.24	—	—	L.S.S.	T.W.,L.F.	Pr.Sc.	V.M.	—	—
27.	114	Bhudia	193	72.44	0.38	—	—	L.S.S.	T.W.	—	—	—	—
28.	115	Dariyapur Urf Nagla Bhanchand	285	55.04	0.19	—	—	L.S.S.	T.W.,L.F.	Pr.Sc.	—	—	—
29.	116	Badhanu	1,443	271.55	0.19	—	—	L.S.S.	T.W.	Pr.Sc.	—	—	—
30.	117	Sujavalpur Haibatpur	1,073	220.16	0.21	—	P.O.	S.C.S.	T.W.,L.F.	I.C.	—	—	—
31.	118	Bhikanpur	325	84.99	0.26	—	—	S.C.S.	T.W.	—	—	—	—
32.	119	Munda Nauzarpur	1,439	280.46	0.19	—	—	S.C.S.	T.W.,L.F.	Pr.Sc.	—	—	—
33.	120	Bhains Mai	504	145.69	0.29	K.R.	P.O.	S.C.S.	T.W.,L.F.	—	—	—	—
34.	121	Dandesri	3,355	698.11	0.21	K.R.	P.O.	S.C.S.	T.W.	—	—	—	—
35.	122	Chhonkra	1,070	212.06	0.20	—	—	S.C.S.	T.W.,L.F.	Pr.Sc.	—	—	—
36.	123	Pachaita	1,258	191.02	0.15	—	—	S.C.S.	T.W.,L.F.	Pr.Sc.	—	—	—
37.	124	Firozpur	370	98.34	0.27	—	—	S.C.S.	T.W.	Pr.Sc.	V.M.	—	—
38.	125	Bartan Khan	1,775	957.92	0.54	P.R.	P.O.	S.C.S.	T.W.,L.F.	Pr.Sc.	—	—	—

(Contd.)

TABLE 10.1: *(Contd.)*

1	2	3	4	5	6	7	8	9	10	11	12	13	14
39.	126	Pachon	3,128	623.24	0.20	P.R.	P.O.	S.C.S.	T.W.;L.F.	Pr.Sc.	V.M.	—	—
40.	127	Nagla Chikna	201	132.74	0.66	—	—	S.C.S.	T.W.	—	—	—	—
41.	128	Raipur Tappa Agsauli	704	79.73	0.11	—	P.O.	S.C.S.	T.W.	—	V.M.	—	—
42.	129	Bhatikara	1,914	244.84	0.13	—	P.O.	S.C.S	T.W.,L.F.	—	V.M.	—	—
43.	130	Mahmoodpur	687	113.72	0.17	—	—	S.C.S.	T.W.,L.F.	—	—	—	—
44.	131	Kheria Tappa Agsauli	501	99.56	0.20	—	—	S.C.S.	T.W.	—	—	—	—
45.	132	Agsauli	5,845	—	—	P.R., R.S.	P.O.	G.Bk. S.C.S.	T.W.,L.F.	Pr.Sc.	V.M.	M.C.W.C.	—
46.	133	Birawar	726	161.07	0.22	P.R.	—	S.C.S.	T.W.	—	—	—	—
47.	134	Khizarpur Casba	430	99.15	0.23	—	—	L.S.S.	T.W.	—	—	—	—
48.	135	Arnia Talesra	572	264.27	0.46	—	—	L.S.S.	T.W.	—	—	—	—
49.	136	Northisseapur	1,734	595.31	0.34	P.R.	P.O.	S.C.S.	T.W.,L.F.	—	—	—	—
50.	137	Bargawan	2,327	663.71	0.29	P.R.	—	S.C.S.	T.W.,L.F.	Pr.Sc.	—	—	—
51.	138	Kachora	5,847	1,305.97	0.22	P.R.	P.O.	L.S.S, C.Bk.	T.W.,L.F.	Pr.Sc.	V.M.	M.C.W.C., C.P. P.H.C.	
52.	139	Anandpur	211	225.42	1.07	—	—	L.S.S.	—	—	—	—	—
53.	140	Ganthri Shahpur	2,412	699.73	0.29	—	P.O.	S.C.S.	T.W.,L.F.	Pr.Sc.	—	—	—
54.	141	Takari Khurda	1,382	339.14	0.25	—	—	S.C.S.	T.W.,L.F.	Pr.Sc.	—	—	
55.	142	Thatpur	—	223.39	—	—	—	S.C.S.	T.W.	—	—	—	—
56.	143	Ainchola Sahadatpur	793	163.09	0.21	P.R.	—	S.C.S.	T.W.	—	—	—	
57.	144	Sanjorpur	—	50.99	—	—	—	S.C.S.	T.W.	—	—	—	—
58.	145	Rampur Nagla Chatoe	473	173.62	0.37	P.R.	—	S.C.S.	T.W.	—	—	—	—
59.	146	Nawalilarpur	1,136	50.99	0.04	P.R.	—	L.S.S.	T.W.,L.F.	—	—	—	—

(Contd.)

TABLE 10.1: *(Contd.)*

1	2	3	4	5	6	7	8	9	10	11	12	13	14
60.	147	Sikandra Rao	2,667	1636.20	0.61	P.R. R.S.	P.O. T.O.	L.S.S. C.B.K.(3)	T.W.,L.F.	I.C.	V.M.	H.	P.S., C.P.
61.	148	Ikbalpur	1,456	455.69	0.31	P.R.	—	L.S.S.	T.W.,L.F.	—	—	—	—
62.	149	Kheria Khurd	522	181.31	0.35	—	—	L.S.S.	T.W.	—	—	—	—
63.	150	Barai Shahpur	3,012	613.53	0.20	P.R.	P.O.	L.S.S., G.Bk.	T.W.,L.F.	Pr.Sc.	—	H.	—
64.	151	Pipalgawan	5,595	1,705.00	0.30	P.R.	P.O.	—	T.W.,L.F.	Pr.Sc.	—	—	—
65.	152	Agrana Jarara	3,075	752.34	0.24	—	P.O.	S.C.S.	T.W.,L.F.	Pr.Sc.	—	—	—
66.	153	Bhisimirzapur	2,333	1,172.01	0.50	P.R.	P.O.	S.C.S.	T.W.,L.F.	—	—	—	—
67.	154	Dighawan	368	369.01	1.00	—	—	S.C.S.	T.W.,L.F.	Pr.Sc.	—	—	—
Total			96,164	24,455.28	0.25								

R.S.	Railway Station	C	Canal
P.R.	*Pucca* Road	Pr.Sc.	Primary School
K.R.	*Kutcha* Road	H.S.	High School
P.O.	Post Office	I.C.	Inter College
T.O.	Telegraph Office	V.M.	Village Market
S.C.S.	Service Cooperative Society	P.H.C.	Primary Health Centre
L.S.S.	Large Scale Cooperative Society	M.C.W.C.	Maternity Child Welfare Centre
G.Bk.	Gramin Bank	H	Hospital
C.Bk.	Commercial Bank	P.S.	Police Station
T.W.	Tube Well	C.P.	Check Post
L.F.	Light and Fan		

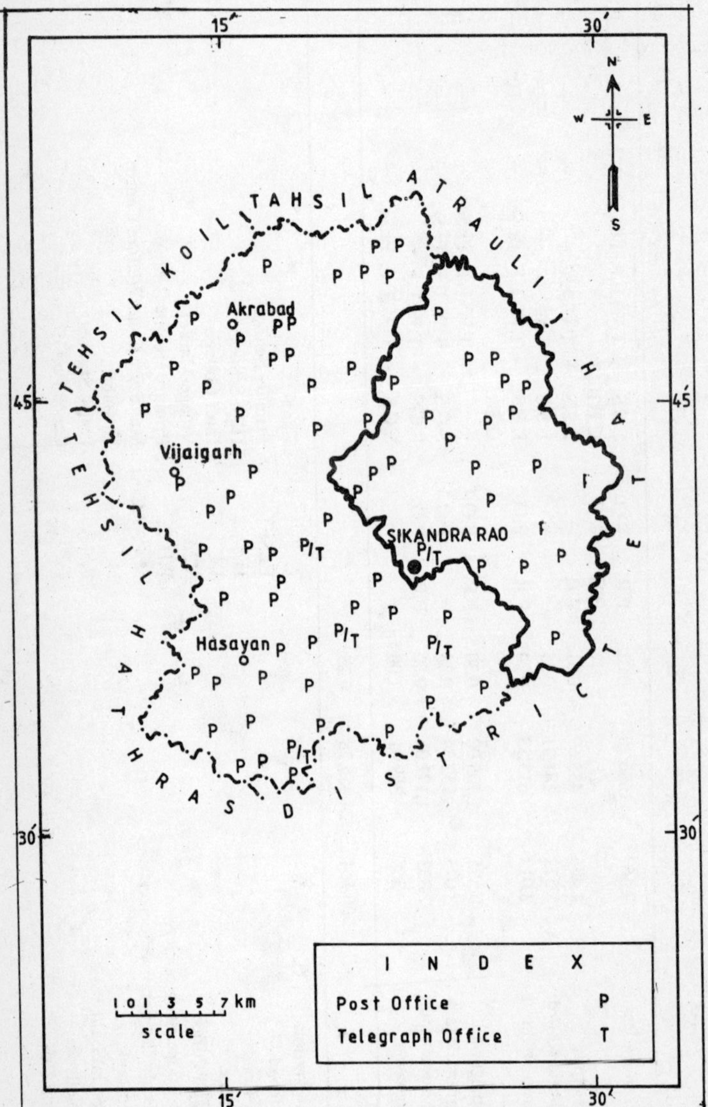

MAP 10.3: Tahsil-Sikandra Rao, District Aligarh (Communication)

Absence of telephone and telegraph services is also not conducive to the development of the block.

This poor state in matters of communication is not conducive to rapid development.

Financial Institutions

Canara Bank is the Lead Bank for the District of Aligarh. The Bank's

survey (Map 10.4) of 1990 reveals that Sikandra Rao Block has branches of Gramin Bank at 4 villages, viz., Arnot (92), Bajidpur (107), Agsauli (132) and Barai Shahpur (150) and of Commercial Banks at 2 villages, viz., Kachora (138) and Sikandra Rao (147). At Sikandra Rao, three Commercial Banks – Punjab National Bank, Canara Bank and State Bank of India have their branches. These 7 banks cover the entire Block of Sikandra Rao comprising 67 villages. Certainly, this picture shows over doing and a cut throat competition to get more business.

Besides the Gramin Bank and Commercial Banks, the Block has a net work of cooperative societies. They are of two types:

1. *Large Size Cooperative Societies* (L.S.S.) – fourteen villages are covered by L.S.S. which provide Credit, Seeds, Manure, etc.
2. *Service Cooperative Societies* (S.C.S.) – fifty villages have a S.C.S., 2 villages, viz., Arnot (92) and Pipalgaon (151) have no S.C.S. These service cooperatives are of small size and mainly deal with credit.

This study of financial institutions of the villages gives a very rosy picture but seeing to the rate of economic development it can be stated that there seems to be something seriously wrong.

Electrification

In Sikandra Rao Block, out of 67 villages, except two villages, the rest are electrified (Map 10.5). These two unfortunate villages are Nagla Chamar (Population 445, code 96) and Anandpur (population 211, code no. 139). This amply testifies to our passion for rural electrification for political ends.

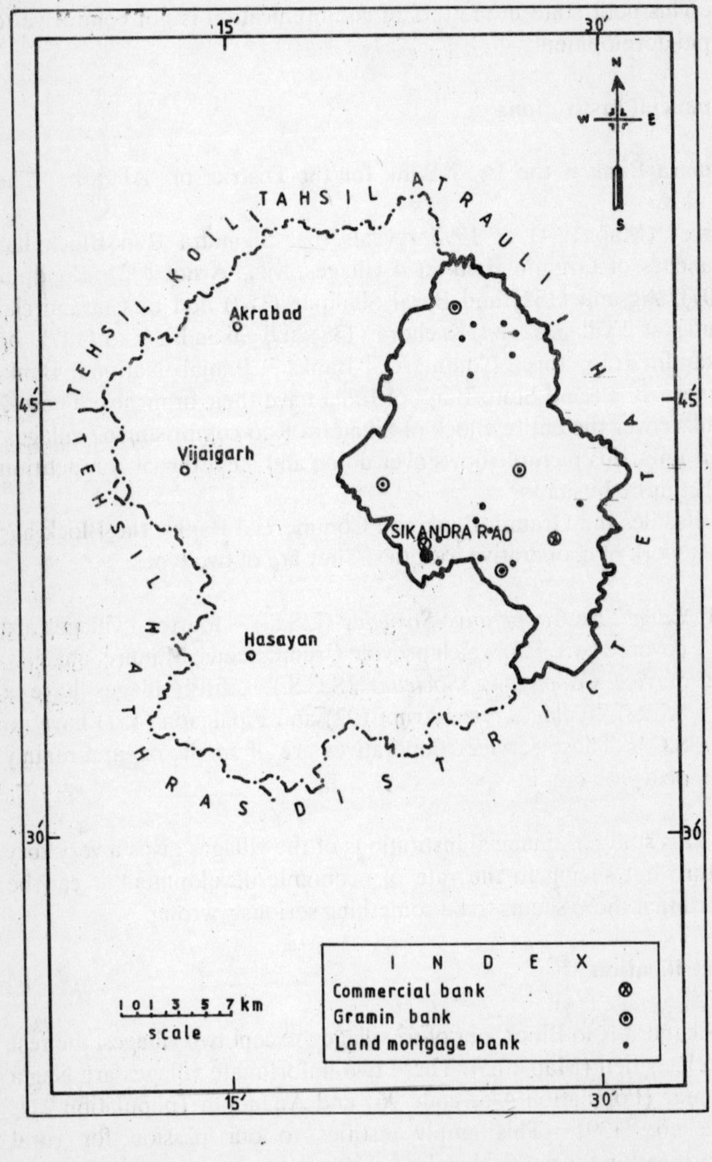

MAP 10.4: Tahsil Sikandra Rao, District Aligarh (Financial Institutions)

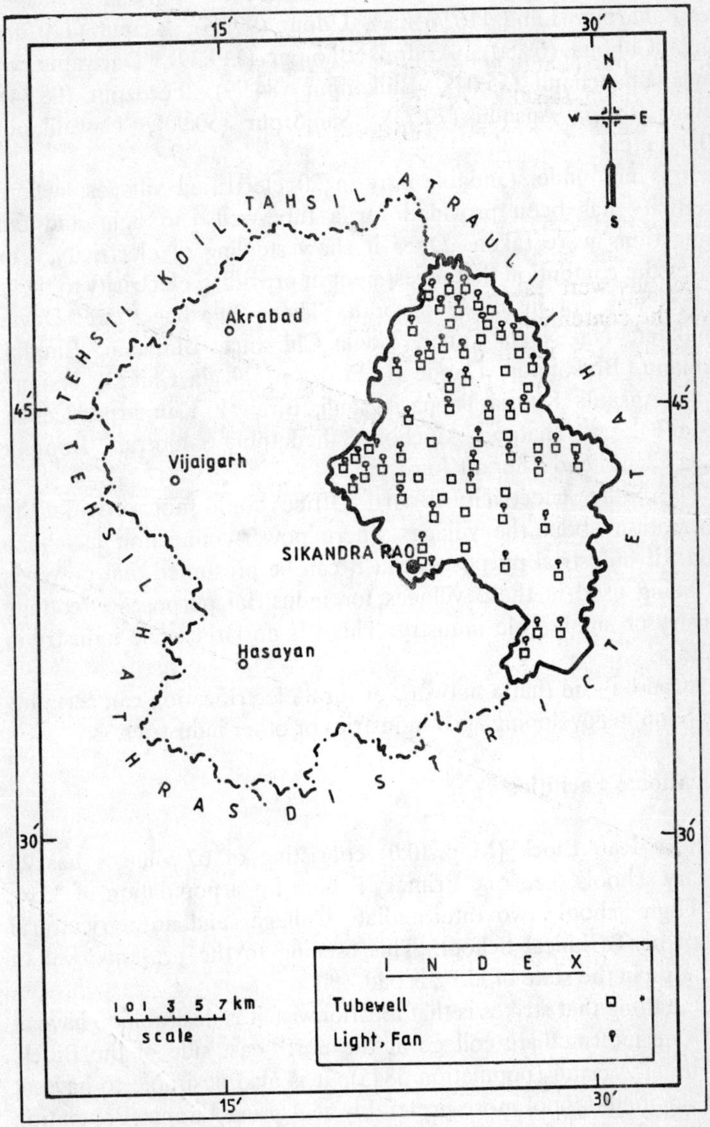

MAP 10.5: Tahsil Sikandra Rao, District Aligarh (Electrification)

The author could not follow the logic of connecting a tube-well in those village, where total land of a village was less and the sub-division and fragmentation is a known fact. Some such villages are: Paharpur (Land 116.96 ha.), Udpur (99.15), Esapur (120.20), Nagla Chhbua (68.80), Arafpur Bhojpur (119.39), Dariyapur *urf* Nagla Bhanchand (55.04), Bhikanpur (84.99), Ferozpur (98.34), Raipur Tappa Agsauli (79.73), Sanjorpur (50.90), Nawalilapur (50.99) etc.

It is not understandable why in 20 electrified villages, where electricity has been provided for a tube-well, no light and fan connections were taken. Does it show stealing of electricity, or proves the contention that investment in providing electricity to these villages was not justified, or both. These 20 villages are: Devar Panakher, Nai Nagla Tehar, Nagla Chhubua, Bimamai, Bhudia, Badhanu, Bhikanpur, Dandesri, Firozpur, Nagla Chikna, Raipur, Tappa Agsauli, Kheria Tappa Agsauli, Birawar, Khirzarpur Casba, Arnia Talesra, Thatpur, Ainchola Sahadatpur, Sanjorpur, Rampur Nagla Chatol and Kheria Khurd.

The State Electricity Board Office could not provide the information about the villages where power-connection has been given for industrial purposes. But it can be presumed that power is not being used in these villages for industrial purposes – cottage industry or small scale industry. There is no large scale industry in the area.

It can be said that a network of rural electrification can certainly be a boon in developing agro-industries or other industries.

Educational Facilities

Sikandra Rao Block (Map 10.6) consisting of 67 villages has 29 primary schools, i.e., one Primary School for a population of 3316, one High School, two Intermediate Colleges and no Agricultural School or Technical School. This, seeing to the present level of education in the state of U.P., is bad.

One thing that strikes is that locationwise it is desirable to have at least one intermediate college at the north-east side of the Block, may be at Agsauli (population 5845). It is also desirable to have at least one high school more preferably at Agrana Jarana (Population 3075) or Pipalgawan (population 5595).

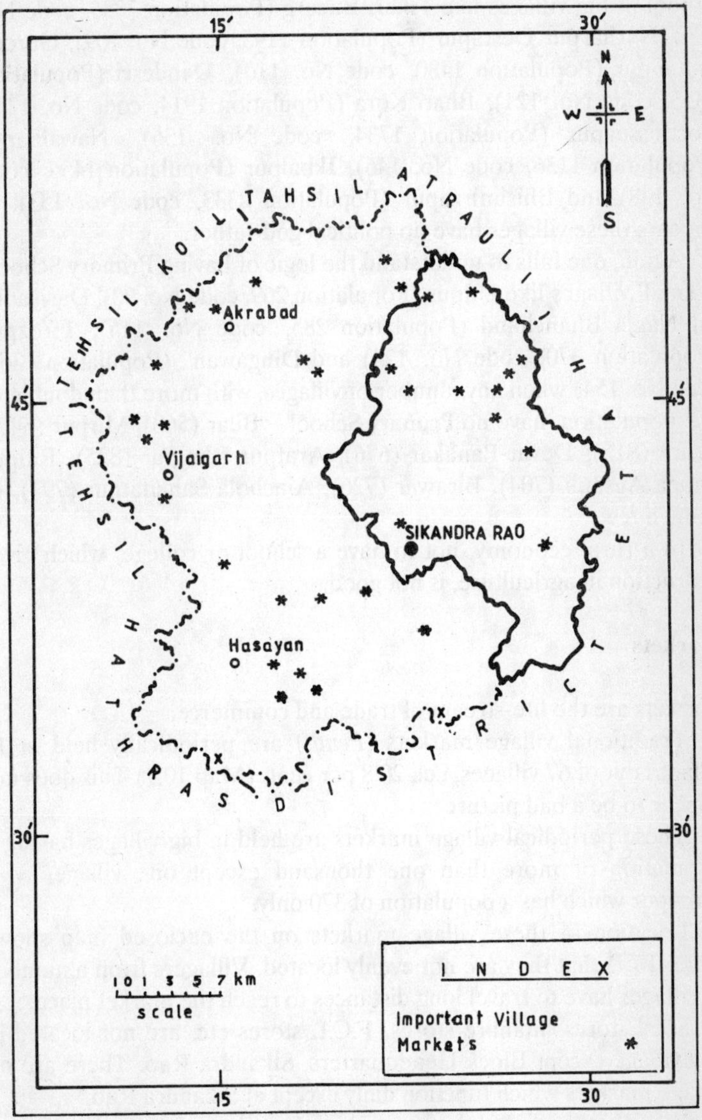

MAP 10.6: Tahsil Sikandra Rao, District Aligarh (Educational Facilities)

One could not understand the logic of not having even a Primary School at big villages like Tikari Buzurg (Population 3086, code No. 106), Narharpur Destapur (Population 1195, code No. 109), Gureda Sultanpur (Population 1480, code No. 110), Dandesri (Population 3355, code No. 121), Bhati Kora (Population 1914, code No. 129), Northisseapur (Population 1734, code No. 136), Nawalilapur (Population 1136, code No. 146), Ikbalpur (Population 1456, code No. 148) and Bhisimirzapur (Population 2333, code No. 153). It appears these villages have no political god-father.

Again, one fails to understand the logic of having Primary Schools at small villages like Udpur (Population 269, code No. 90), Dariyapur urf Nagla Bhanchand (Population 285, code No. 115), Firozpur (Population 370, code No. 124) and Dihgawan (Population 368, code No. 154) when any number of villages, with more than double of this population, have no Primary School – Bilar (568), Mirpur (547), Arnot (815), Devar-Panakar (676), Arafpur Bhojpur (825), Raipur Tappa Agsauli (704), Birawar (726); Ainchola Sahadatpur (793), to name a few.

In a rural economy, not to have a school or college, which gives instruction in agriculture, is not good.

Markets

Markets are the life-stream of trade and commerce.

Traditional village markets *(Penth)* are periodically held in 12 villages out of 67 villages, i.e., 20.8 per cent. (Map 10.7) This does not appear to be a bad picture.

These periodical village markets are held in big villages having a population of more than one thousand except one village, viz., Firozpur which has a population of 370 only.

Location of these village markets on the enclosed map shows (Map 10.7) that they are not evenly located. Villagers from a number of villages have to travel long distances to reach the market place.

Seed stores, manure stores, F.C.I. stores etc. are not located in any village except Block Headquarters, Sikandra Rao. There are no village markets which function daily except at Sikandra Rao.

It can be concluded that from the sale and purchase point of view, much is needed.

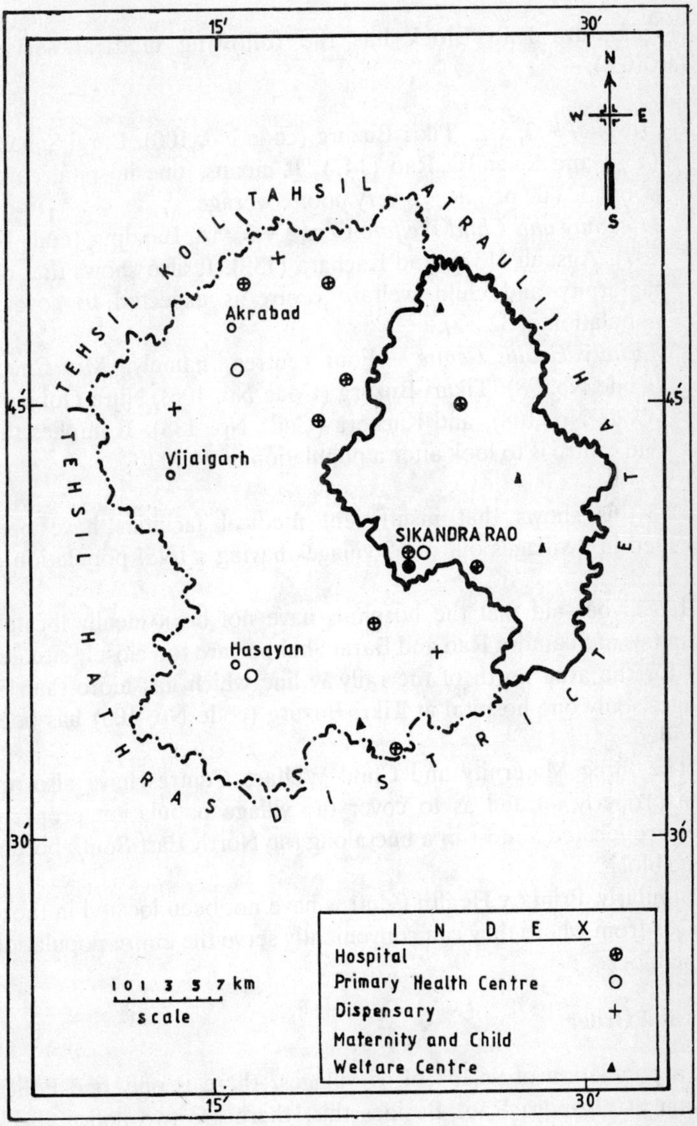

MAP 10.7: Tahsil Sikandra Rao, District Aligarh (Markets)

Health Services

The Sikandra Rao Block has the following medical services (Map 10.8): –

1. *Hospital* – 3, viz., Tikri Buzurg (code No. 106), Barai Sahapur (150) and Sikandra Rao (147). It means, one hospital covers about 32,000 people – a very poor coverage.
2. *Maternity and Child Welfare Centre* – 3, viz., Bajidpur (code No. 107), Agsauli (132), and Kachara (138). It also shows that one maternity and child welfare centre is expected to cover a population of 32,000.
3. *Primary Health Centre* – Four centres, namely, Mia Chirail (Code No. 98), Tikari Buzurg (Code No. 106), Nijra Gokulpur (Code No. 108), and Kachera (Code No. 138). It implies that one centre is to look after a population of 24,000.

All this shows that insufficient medical facilities have been provided in 8 villages out of 67 villages having a total population of 96,164.

It can be said that the hospitals have not been ideally located. Hospitals at Sikandra Rao and Barai Shahpur are too closely situated and for the area north of the railway line which has more than 50 villages, only one hospital at Tikri Buzurg (code No. 106) has been provided.

The three Maternity and Child Welfare Centres have also not been properly located as to cover the village population properly. They are located almost in a line along the North-East-South border of the block.

Similarly, Primary Health Centres have not been located in those villages from where they can conveniently serve the entire population of the block.

Law and Order

For a population of 96,164 of 67 villages, there is only one Police Station at Sikandra Rao. Besides this, there are two police check posts, one at Sikandra Rao (Code No. 147) and another at village Kachora (Code No. 138). Both these check posts have been established by the District Administration on its own and have not yet been approved by the Government of U.P. (Map 10.9).

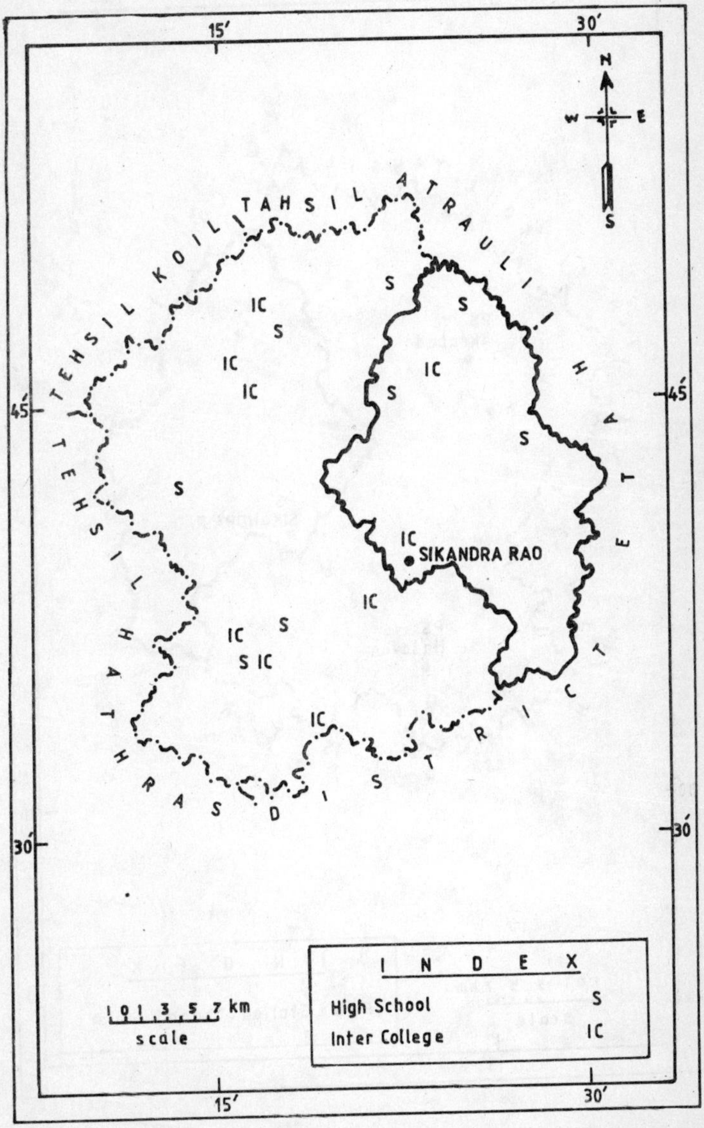

MAP 10.8: Tahsil Sikandra Rao, District Aligarh (Health Services)

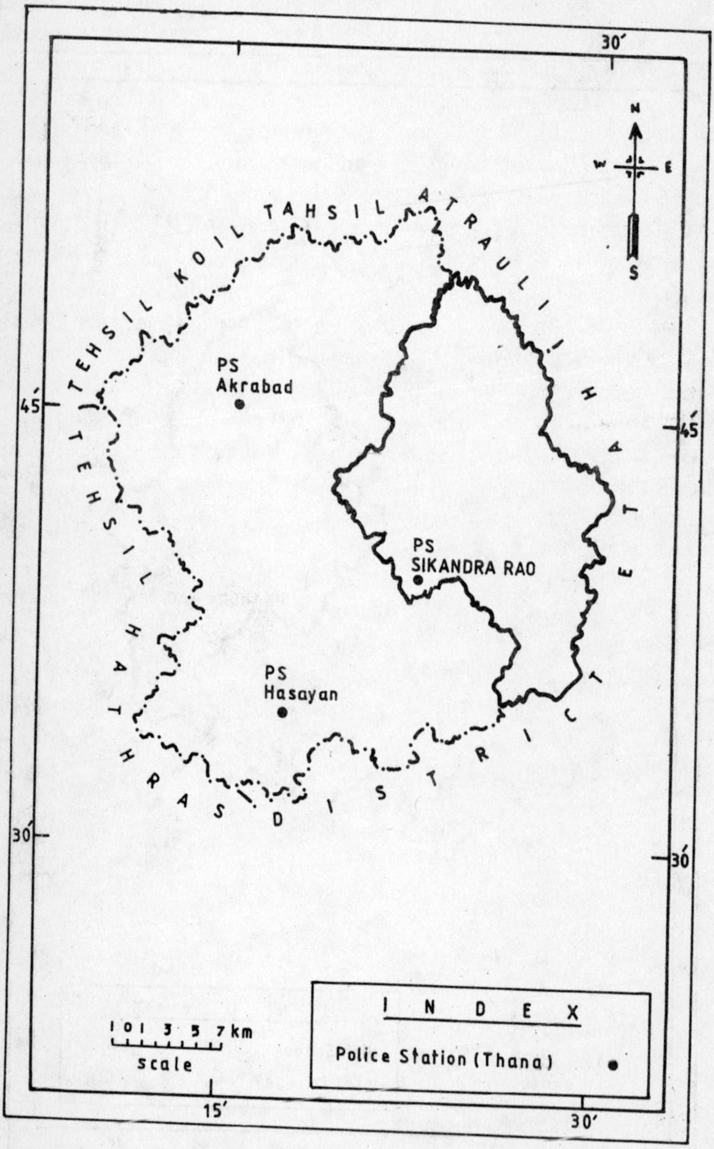

MAP 10.9: Tahsil Sikandra Rao, District Aligarh (Law and Order)

A glance at the map clearly demonstrates that there is no police station or even a check post in the Northern portion of the road connecting Mathura and Pilibhit. This means that about 40 villages out of 67 have no nearby police station.

With the increase in crime-number and quality, this arrangement of the Law Enforcing Machinery apparently is very inadequate.

On the basis of Table 10.1 and discussion, it is not possible to select Focal Villages because it is apparent that very meagre infrastructure facilities have been provided in the villages. Further, even these facilities which have been provided, have no scientific basis. It appears to be a handy work of politicians. So, our efforts to select Focal Villages on the basis of the existing facilities and then determine their command areas failed.

Under the circumstances, the only alternative appeared to divide the whole Sikandra Rao Block into five command areas and select five Focal Villages. This was done primarily on the basis of central location of a big village having infrastructure facilities, and situated, as far as possible, on a road. Here are our findings. Obviously, they are only illustrative and not final for want of intensive surveys.

	Focal Village	Command Area
1.	Sikandra Rao (147)	88, 89, 90, 91, 92, 93, 94, 95, 134, 135, 142, 143, 144, 145, 146, 148, 149, – 18 villages.
2.	Mubarakpur Kapasia (103)	96, 97, 98, 99, 100, 101, 102, 104, 116, 141. – 11 villages
3.	Bajidpur (107)	108, 109, 110, 111, 112, 113, 114, 115, 117, 118, 119, 120, 121, 122, 123 – 16 villages
4.	Agsauli (132)	105, 106, 124, 125, 126, 127, 128, 129, 130, 131, 133, 136, 140 – 14 villages
5.	Kachara (138)	137, 139, 150, 151, 152, 153, 154 – 8 villages

Map 10.10 shows these Focal Villages and their command areas.

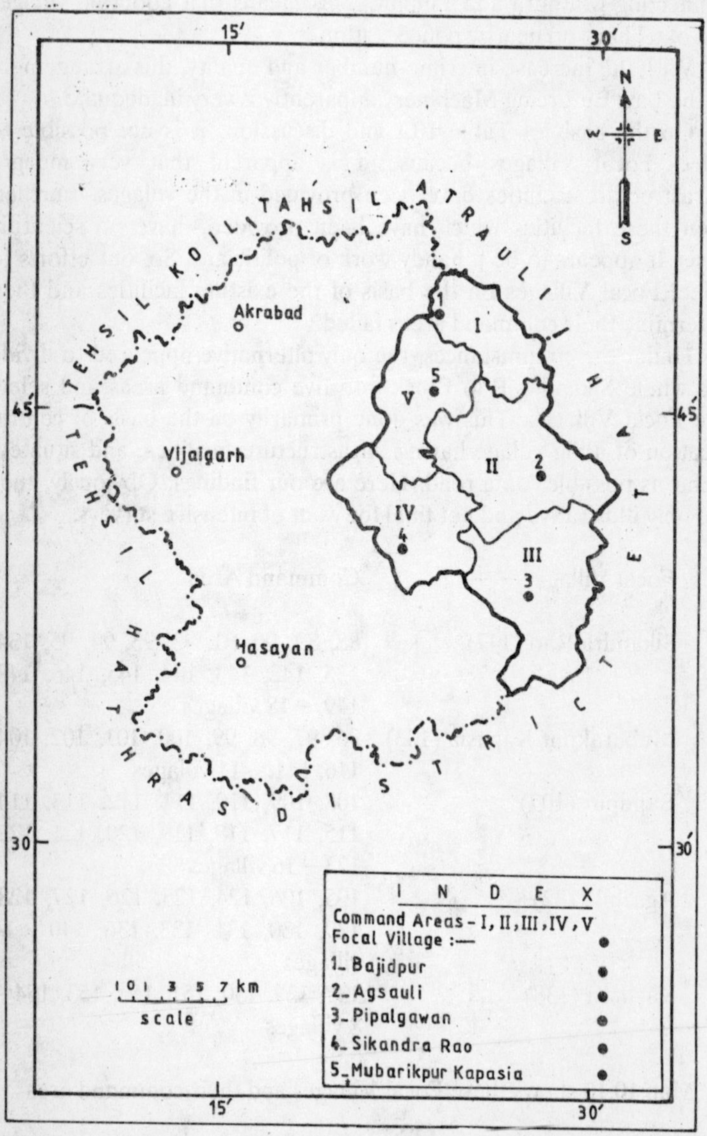

MAP 10.10: Tahsil Sikandra Rao, District Aligarh (Focal Villages and Command Areas)

Some Experiments and Some Lessons

I became a Principal of a Post-Graduate College in 1974. Soon after, Emergency was clamped down. So, I, on my own and also under the compulsion of Emergency made some experiments with village life. The results were very beneficial.

The scheme of N.S.S., I discovered, was more confined to papers. There was hardly any orientation of students and certainly no benefit accrued to anybody. It was a clear case of wastage of money and energy. I tried to make it educational. So, I ordered that we must select only one village, instead hopping from village to village every year, and try to make it meaningful, both for students as well as villagers.

I suggested that the students of N.S.S. – about one hundred in number – must be grouped in batches and required to do resource survey of each and every house-hold. Separate batches should be made of girl-students who will go and talk with ladies of each house. This enabled students to know the problems of the villagers. This was a unique experience for both the students and villagers. It also created a rapport between the two. For example, the people belonging to scheduled castes, specially untouchables, had a feeling that students will not visit their houses. But when they visited them, they were surcharged with emotions only to be seen to be believed. In the night, students had cultural programmes at village *Chaupal* to which villagers were invited. They enjoyed it and slowly started participating in them. This helped in breaking barriers. The suspicion that city students have come to village to enjoy or for a political purpose or for some other gain started giving way. And when students took the work of cleaning or laying the drains of the lanes, repairing the roads, digging the pits where unclean water of the houses accumulated and empty the pit in the morning, all the barriers just vanished. Full confidence was restored. Even the villagers came forward to give a helping hand. This was the miracle of the ten days camp.

It was decided that contact with the village will be maintained. So, religiously the Prof. in-charge of N.S.S. along with a few students visited the village at least once a week to know their problems and how the college can share their problems.

One day the news came that the sugar-cane crop has caught some disease and something must be done. I sent a team of those N.S.S.

students who had offered Botany as one of their subjects along with a senior teacher of the Department. My surprise was limitless when I was told that in order to know the disease some laboratory tests will have to be made. Thereafter, I was informed that the sugar-cane has a particular disease. On my enquiry, I was told, after a weeks consultations, that a particular type of medicine must be sprayed. The college purchased the spraying kit and the medicine. The students went and did the needful. After a week the S.O.S. came from the village that the disease is persisting. It meant that either the diagnosis was wrong or the medicine ineffective. So, I consulted the Cane Inspector. He was sent to the village. He told me that the diagnosis of the disease and the medicine selected were correct but the method of spraying the medicine was wrong. He did the job. But it vividly revealed how shallow is our education. What will these first class Botanists be able to do? It convinced me that education should not be confined to classroom laboratories but extended to open laboratories of the village. Nevertheless, it helped in strengthening the villagers' confidence in the college.

In the rainy season, Malaria took an epidemic form. The college sent N.S.S. boys regularly with a doctor to distribute free medicines and suggest preventive measures. The village had much less incidence of Malaria as compared to neighbouring villages.

During the days of Emergency, one day I decided myself to visit the village. It was my first visit. The villagers were informed earlier. To our shock and surprise, not even one had come outside the village to meet us as promised. A visit to the village revealed that no male was in the village. All had fled and would return only at night. We were told that earlier, a police Inspector had come and taken away with him three males including one bachelor and one old man of above 60 years. They were operated upon for sterilisation. The fear of the police visit had done this miracle. With great difficulty I was told that the village, by its own sweet will, would give the required number of males and females for operations provided they are not hunted and arrested. I contacted the Sub-Divisional Officer and The Police Superintendent It was decided that no one — Police, *Lekhpal* or any other officer — would touch residents of this village and it would be the duty of the college to provide the required number of cases. We did our best to educate villagers of the advantages of sterilisation. The fact that none of the government officers harassed the villagers, helped us. So, more than the double number of cases were selected. They were invited to come to the college and stay. The Blood Test of these cases revealed that almost half of the persons were suffering from diseases like itching, etc. and so should not be operated upon. They were allowed to go back to their village after they were provided medicines and lessons in hygiene. The rest were operated upon. They were happy, we were happy and the administration was happy. This was the result of right approach.

The college advised the villagers to settle their civil suits out of court. They agreed. A Retired District Judge was persuaded to hold an open court in the village and decide the cases on the spot. Quite a few cases were decided. But soon village group politics tried to spoil the atmosphere. Our mirage was over.

These experiments revealed that for speedy execution of plans, people's cooperation can go a long way. And this cooperation and confidence can be won by honest and sincere actions and not by mere sweet talks or promises or dirty politics. Promises and speeches do not keep company for long.

Types of Village Plan

These village upliftment plans will have several distinct components:

1. Agricultural Development Plan.
2. Industrial Development Plan.
3. Health and Hygiene Development Plan.
4. Social and Moral Upliftment Plan.

Before we take up these Development plans, it will be desirable to think of a Focal Village's administrative set-up.

Administrative Set-up of a Focal Village

As a teacher of economics, I was guiding research. I decided to give such topics to my Ph.D. students which were connected with village upliftment. To one I gave Techno-Economic Survey of a Tahsil, to another a study of Trysem Scheme in Rural Development, to the third, Economics of Dairy Industry, to the fourth Impact of Commercial Banks in Rural Development, to the fifth, Inter-Regional Disparities and Imbalances in Agricultural Transformation etc. I was also associated with evaluation work of some rural district plans. As a senior teacher, I was called upon to evaluate Ph.D. theses of a few Universities. All this added to my knowledge, my experience and gave a line of thinking. On the basis of this, the following Administrative Set-up can be suggested.

1. Focal Village will have to be developed as a progressive village with most of the facilities of a city life because it will have a demonstrative effect on the village of the command area. So, the village *Panchayat Ghar* should have a decent building, where facilities of open meetings, cultural programmes, small library, display of video pictures, guest house, *Nayaya Panchayat* office, etc. should be provided.
2. Adjacent to the village *Panchayat*, a campus be developed. This campus must house all those agencies which are connected with village development, such as agricultural office with all its sub-departments such as soil testing, various inspectors incharges of different activities viz. sugarcane, cotton, groundnut etc. It must also have Canal and Tube-well Departments, Electricity Department, P.W.D. Department, Seed Store, Fertiliser Store, Fisheries Department,

   F.C.I. Department, Forest Department, Post Office including Telegraph Office, Police Station, Cooperative Societies' offices such as Cooperative Banks, Village Industries etc. All these offices should have their Departmental Incharges stationed at Focal Village itself with the authority to take on the spot decision. And a senior person should also be appointed who may be over-all Incharge with powers to direct any officer of any department.
3. Next to the campus of Government offices should be the campus of Financial Institutions. Cooperative Bank, Land Mortgage Bank, Gramin Bank, Industrial Bank, L.I.C. etc. located at one place. There should be no competitive spirit in these financial institutions as is seen today in the towns. As far as possible, duplication should be avoided.
4. Next to this campus another campus must be of Primary Health Centre (PHC), Maternity and Child Welfare Centre, Hospital and Veterinary Hospital.
5. There must be the fourth campus of Primary School, High School, Inter College and Technical College.
6. There must be a different campus of Industrial Estate and

Repairing Workshop with spare parts shop, and cooperative marketing stores.

7. The Focal Village must develop a Games-cum-picnic spot where swimming and rowing facilities, facilities of out-door games etc. should be provided.

1. Agricultural Development Plan

It we really want to develop the countryside fast, we have, first of all to provide all the infrastructure at top priority like roads, railway stations, irrigation facilities, training centres, repairing shops, marketing cooperatives, power etc.

During the past forty years of plan period, we have done sufficient to develop our agriculture. What is needed today is to differentiate between marginal and sub-marginal land-owners and big land-owners. We must enhance facilities available to the land-owners so that they may get more yield per acre and at the same time, try to provide more income yielding crops to the marginal land-owners.

It appears that in spite of our best efforts, we have not been able to make every inch of land irrigated. It is desirable to provide money, even on unreturnable basis, to farmers for digging wells and installing a *pur* or persian wheel. This will revolutionise agriculture. The existing State Tube-wells should be sold to private people. This will save loss of crores of rupees to the Government given by the State Tube-Well Department and the State Electricity Board. Through soil testing, the farmers must be told which fertiliser should be used and in what doses.

Botanists must tell the farmers, specially the marginal land-owners, which new commercial crops can be grown by them. For example, today Sun Flower is a very paying crop. Similarly many oil giving crops can be found out and introduced. Medicinal plants like *Tulsi* and roses are in great demand. They can be grown. The nursery business is also very profitable. Orchards can be another good business. For example, Sasni, a *Kasba* at Aligarh-Agra road, has become famous for Guava and Bera which are exported. Marginal and sub-marginal land-owners can be persuaded to take up these and many more high income yielding crops.

2. Industrial Development Plan

On the basis of resource survey, villagers should be encouraged to set up some cottage or small scale industries. For example:

(a) Every village has a tailor. He can stitch clothes but his misfortune is that he has not sufficient work. In towns, craze for readymade garments is increasing. They are very costly also. So, a cooperative society should be set up for the villages of the Focal Village and its command area to encourage garment industry. Industrial Estate of the Focal Village will train up tailors. Cooperative society shall provide them sewing machines and all the required raw materials. It will also provide designs, colour schemes, sizes of clothes to be stitched etc. It will have a strict quality control. The garments will be marketed by the cooperative society.

(b) Today embroidery including patch-work, has become a fashion. It has demand even in foreign markets. Ladies of the village can be trained, provided with raw materials, designs, colour schemes etc. and the readymade goods can be marketed. The Industrial estate, cooperatives, banks have a role to play.

(c) Every village has a shoemaker. The shoes have become very costly. Let this industry be also developed as a cottage industry on the same pattern as the garment industry.

(d) On the same pattern any number of cottage industries can be set up such as Dairy Industry, Carpet Making Industry, *Dari* Industry, Earthen Pots Industry (after modernisation), Poultry Farm, Conduit pipe's two point, three point or four point junction boxes, lock industry etc.

(e) Fish breeding and frog breeding can be a very profitable business in villages. In Bihar it is a prosperous business.

Thus, through cooperatives and village Industrial Estate, a series of cottage and small scale industries be developed in a very short span of two or three years. The lessons of TRYSEM Scheme can be profitably utilised in evolving a better and more effective scheme for each area, as outlined above.

3. Health and Hygiene Development Plan

Villagers live in open spaces with very little pollution of city life. They, per force, do a lot of physical exercise. So, they are normally healthier. In post-independence period, they have become more health conscious and so consult a physician soon after they fall ill and take lot of medicines. They prefer injections. But in spite of these plus points, contact with village life revealed the following bad points:[2]

1. Normally, drinking water is polluted. The villagers take their bath within the ring of the well with the result that dirty water goes back inside the well and pollutes the water. The water of village pools or tanks is dirtier still. All the filth goes in them.
2. The villagers do not habitually wash their clothes. They have very few spare clothes also. When they wash them, they do not get clean water and soap. The washerman of the village washes these clothes in the dirty water of the village pool. These clothes are carriers of several skin diseases.

   The bedding and other useable clothes are equally dirty and susceptible to diseases.
3. The villagers seldom use bathing soaps and the old practice of using *Multani Mitti, Reetha* etc. have been given up long back.
4. The space where animals are kept is very near the living space. They are dirty. So they become breeding places of flies, fleas, and mosquitoes which carry germs of diseases.
5. The villagers have no concept of a balanced diet. Their intake of vegetables, pulses, fruits and raw vegetables is almost negligible. My studies have revealed that with intake of pulses and vegetables, the consumption of cereals automatically decreases. It gives a better balanced diet at almost the same cost. The idea needs propagation.
6. The knowledge of Family Planning and Child Welfare has increased but it has yet to be adopted.
7. Village lanes are narrow, full of pits, dirt and pools of dirty water outflowing from houses etc.
8. The villagers, habitually have dirty habits. They are not civic conscious also. They do not hesitate, for example, to throw the dirt of their houses on open lanes.

A village plan to educate people and more so, to provide necessary facilities is needed. It is unfortunate that during the last forty years of planning period we have not been able even to provide the basic necessities like neat drinking water to villagers. It must be given top priority. The special arrangements are to be made of providing clean water where washermen can wash clothes. The video films can sell the message of cleanliness, civic awareness and responsibility and balanced diet at low cost. This can follow with debates and discussions on village *Chaupals*.

The experience of the author has shown that if handled properly villagers will come forward themselves to assist in cutting down their illegal platforms (*Chabutras*) and broaden the lanes, filling in the pits and make *Kutcha* drains. It should be the duty of planners to lay brick paved lanes including drains if nothing better can be done.

4. Social and Moral Upliftment Plan

An Indian villager, by nature and age old training and culture, was god-fearing, meek, truthful, honest, law-abiding, respectful to elders, contented, hardworking etc. Unfortunately, last forty years' planning, westernisation in the name of modernisation, democracy and elections specially of *Panchayat* etc. have changed the village life completely. Today, the average villager has become a law-breaker, untruthful, dishonest, greedy, bold and fearless (in Morarji's terminology), lover of gold instead of God etc. He has developed criminal mentality. Today, murders, rapes, fights, robberies and dacoities, bride-burning, kidnapping, elopments have become common features of a village life. Because of this deteriorating law and order position, good people want to migrate to towns.

A village upliftment plan must try to stop this rot. Old value-based life, round a sweet family life, should be revived. The modern media can play an effective role. Family, formal and informal education and social and national festivals have an important role to play. They can be modernised if need be, keeping the ancient roots intact. It will be wrong to throw them out, under the impact of westernisation, as we have done today. Ancient culture with modernisation is the only solution of our present day ills.

It is essential that healthy recreation facilities should be provided to the villages. The Indian games cost much less. They, mixed with selected western games, picnic spots, open cinema houses etc. should be provided at least in each Focal Village. When crores can be spent on schools and colleges in the name of games, where most of it goes waste, why not some money can be diverted to organise village games.

Temple culture (it includes mosque and church also) and *Tirth* culture (Pilgrimage) should be revived. With it "Knowing India" through visits to historical, religious and beauty spots be added. This will make people patriots.

The age old tested method of grandmothers narrating value-oriented short stories to the children needs to be revived.

Video films have come. They must be used with discretion. Sexy pictures, crime-oriented pictures, vulgar pictures are not conducive to raising morals and making life value-oriented. For this, good stories, which are in abundance in our ancient literature and new ones can also be produced, as needed. These stories must give lessons in different values – Human, Social and Spiritual. This will be modernisation of old techniques.

It is essential to tell people the meaning of patriotism, the need to be patriots and how to become a patriot. Family life, social life, social and national festivals – all should create an atmosphere in which character and patriotism may flourish. Mere empty sermons from politicians, whose own lives give opposite lesson, cannot achieve the desired results.

5. Town Development Plan

In the west, efforts have been made to know the causes of the growth of a town, its relationship with the hinterland and the way a town should be allowed to grow. The various theories, mentioned earlier, show it.

They clearly stress two aspects of a town. First, how a town is to be planned so that it may provide all the facilities to its residents. Secondly, what should be its functional relationship with the hinterland on one side and the national level on the other.

These theories of Urban Growth and Development envisage a five tier hierarchy of growth centres:

(a) Central villages at the local level
(b) Service centres at the micro-regional level
(c) Growth points at the sub-regional level
(d) Growth centres at the regional level
(e) Growth poles at the national level.

In India, some towns are growing at a tremendous speed, God knows why, while others, are almost static. We have established, to give an impression of a planned development of a town, the Town Development Authorities. But these Town Planners are busy in planning new colonies. They do very little to beautify the town or check its haphazard growth. They have hardly any concept of the relationship of a town and its hinterland and how should a town be helped to grow.

While preparing a Town Development Plan, we must be very clear on the following points:

1. We should avoid, as far as possible, the establishment of very big towns like Delhi, Calcutta, Madras etc. They defeat the very purpose of an orderly development and have a great socio-economic cost first to establish them and thereafter to maintain them.
2. We should encourage the development of Focal Village Towns, Block Headquarters Towns, Tahsil Towns and District Towns, in the light of the studies in the West of growth of towns. Focal Village Town should be a "very small town", Block Headquarters and Tahsil towns should be "small" towns and District Headquarters must be a "medium" town. They, amongst themselves, must be able to adjust surplus labour or displaced labour force.

   "Very small", "small" and "medium" towns should be developed into centres of industrial growth and "bring the adjoining rural areas into the vortex of agro-industrial complexes for rapid development". The objective of 'very small', 'small' and 'medium' towns has to be achieved within the balanced regional development perspective. They should generate optimal employment. They should, therefore, be developed to provide infrastructural and socio-economic facilities. 'Very small' and 'small' towns should also become the processing industrial centres of agricultural raw materials.
3. The District Headquarters should be a 'medium' township. It should be an innovative and propulsive centre with a strong manufacturing base. It should have secondary activities, tertiary activities and a strong agro-industrial sector. This 'medium' township should be developed more as an industrial town. It should cater to the need of the area.
4. Each type of town-'very small', 'small', and 'medium' – must provide all the modern facilities to make life of citizens happy

and peaceful – good and cheap houses, cheap and in abundance the basic facilities like water, electricity, transport, schools, hospitals etc., lot of park and picnic spots, very good social life etc.

5. Administrative set-up of Block Headquarters, Tahsil Headquarters and District Headquarters should be set-up, with necessary variations, on the line of Administrative set up of Focal Villages.

In short, a philosophy of town development in relation to area growth be developed.

NOTES

1. S.S. Gupta, Utilisation of Electricity in the Villages, R.P.C. Planning Commission, D.S. College, Aligarh, 1969.
2. These observations are based mainly on the study of villages of U.P. But probably, it is true for rest of the country also.

SELECTED BIBLIOGRAPHY

BOOKS

Maslov, A.H. and Bela Mittelmann, *Principles of Abnormal Psychology*, Harber and Bros. Publishers, New York, 1951.

Atal, Yogesh, *The Changing Frontiers of Caste*, National Publishing House, Delhi, 1968.

Kapoor, A.C., *Constitutional History of India, 1875-1975*, S. Chand and Co, Delhi, 1976.

Appadorai, A., *The Substances of Politics*, Oxford University Press, Madras, 1971.

Imtiaz, Ahmad (ed), *Caste and Social Stratification among Muslims in India,* Manohar, New Delhi, 1978.

Imtiaz, Ahmad (ed), *Rituals and Religion among Muslims in India*, Manohar, New Delhi.

Nadwi, Abdul Hassan Ali, *Muslims in India* (Translated from Urdu to English by Mohammad Ali Kidwai), Academy of Islamic Research and Publication, Lucknow, 1960.

Nanda, B.R. (ed), *Indian Women from Purdah to Modernity*, Vikas Publisher, New Delhi, 1976.

Grover, B.L. *et al.*, *Adhunik Bharat Ka Itihas* (Hindi). S. Chand and Co., Delhi, 1988.

Upadhyay, Deen Dayal, *Bharatiya Arth Niti : Vikas Ki Aik Disha*, Rashtra Dharma Publication, Lucknow, 1975 (in Hindi).

Upadhyay, Deen Dayal, Shri Guruji and D.B. Thengdi, *The Integral Approach,* Deen Dayal Research Institute, Delhi, 1979.

Upadhyay, Deen Dayal, *Vichar Darshan* : Seven volumes : Different Writers, Saruchi Prakashan, New Delhi, 1986 to 1987 (in Hindi).

Basu, Justice Durga Das, *Introduction to the Constitution of India*, Prentice-Hall of India P. Ltd., New Delhi, 1987.

Hobman, D.L., *The Welfare State.*

Dhengdi, Dattopant, *Comniunism (Hindi)*, Rashtra Dharma Pustak Prakashan, Lucknow.

Hurlack, Elizabeth B., *Child Development*, McGraw-Hill Book Co. Inc., Japan, 1956.

Coker, F.W., *Recent Political Thought*.

Fredrick, L. Scuman, *International Politics*, McGraw-Hill Book Co. Inc. 1948.

Ghurye, G.S., *Caste and Class in India*, The Popular Book Dept., Bombay, 1950.

Hassnain, S.E., *Indian Muslims, Challenges and Opportunities*, Lalva Publishing House, Bombay, 1968.

Hunter, W.W., *The Indian Musalmans*, Premier Book House, Lalva, 1964.

Jack, Homer A., (ed), *World Religions and World Peace*, Beacon Press, Buston.

Huttan, J.H. *Caste in India*, Cambridge University Press, London, 1946.

Clay Lindgren Henry and Donn Byrne, *Psychology: An Introduction to a Behavioural Science*, John Wiley and Sons Inc., 1971.

Laski, Haorold J., *The State: In Theory and Practice*, George Allen and Unwin Ltd., London, 1951.

Laski, Harold J., *A Grammar of Politics*, George Allen and Unwin Ltd., London, 1973.

G. Marx Jr., Harbert (ed), *The Welfare State*.

Margenhan, Hans J., *Politics Among Nations*, Scientific Book Agency, Calcutta.

Coleman, James C., *Abnormal Psychology and Modern Life*, D.B. Taraporevala Sons and Co. P. Ltd., Bombay, 1969.

Kapadia, K.M., *Marriage and Family in India*, Oxford University Press, Bombay, 1947.

Vaid, K.N., *State and Labour in India*, Asia Publishing House, Bombay, 1965.

Kautilya, *Arthshastra* (in Hindi)

Subramanian, K.N., *Wages in India*, Tata McGraw-Hill Publishing Co. Ltd., New Delhi, 1977.

Vishwanathan, K.E., *A New World Order: Economic Democrism*, International Socio-Economic Research Bureau, Madras, 1986.

Antonova K., *et al.*, *A History of India*, Progress Publishers, Moscow, 1978.

Markhandan, K.C., *Directive Principles in the Indian Constitution*, Allied Publishers P. Ltd., Bombay, 1966.

Watson, Lyall, *Supernature*, Bantam Book, New York, 1974.

Maciver and Page, *The Society*, MacMillan and Co. Ltd., London, 1957.

Kagzi, M.C.J., *The Constitution of India*, Metropolitan Book Co. P. Ltd., Delhi, 1987.

Jhingran, M.L., *The Economics of Development and Planning*, Konark Publishers, P. Ltd., Delhi, 1988.

Bruce, M., *The Coming of Welfare State*, Babsford, London, 1961.

Spahr, Margaret, *Readings in Recent Political Philosophy*.

Malhotra, O.P., *The Law of Industrial Dispute*, Vol. I. N.M. Tripathi P. Ltd., Bombay, 1985.

Gauba, O.P., *An Introduction to Political Theory*, Macmillan India Ltd., Delhi, 1981.

Robert, P.E., Translated by Ram Krishan Sharma, *British Kalin Bharat Ka Itihas* (Hindi), S. Chand and Co., Delhi, 1969.

Prabhu, P.N., *Hindu Social Organisation*, Popular Book Depot, Bombay, 1954.

Tompkins, Peter and Christopher Bird, *The Secret Life of Plants*, Aven Publishers of Bard, New York, 1974.

Radhakrishnan, S., *The Hindu View of Life*, Allen and Unwin, London, 1947.

Doshi, Ramji Manek Chand (ed), *Moksh Shastra*, Shri D. Jain Swadhayaai Mandir Trust, Songarh, 1954.

Radhakrishnan S., *Indian Philosophy*, Vol. I and II, Allen and Unwin, London, 1927.

Sethi R.R. *et al.*, *Constitutional History of India*, S. Chand and Co., Delhi, 1956.

Shri Niwan, M.N., *Religion and Society Among the Coorg of South India,* Oxford University Press, Bombay, 1952.

Shri Niwan, M.N. *Social Change in Modern India*, Orient Longman, Bombay, 1972.

Singh, Yogendra, *Modernisation of Indian Tradition*, Thomson Press, Delhi, 1973.

Swami Daya Nanda Saraswati, *Satyarth Prakash (in Hindi)*, Sarvdeshik Arya Pratindihi Sabha, New Delhi.

Gupta, S.S., *Communalism, Secularism And India*, Concept Publishing Co., New Delhi, (in Press).

Gupta, S.S., *A Draft Plan of the Indian Education*, Acharan Prakashan, Delhi, 1980.

Gupta, S.S., *The Economic Philosophy of Mahatma Gandhi*, Ashok Publishing House, Delhi.

Gupta S.S., *et al.*, *Vālmiki Ramayan me Rajya, Samaj Avam Arth Vyavastha*, (in Hindi), Bharat Prakash Mandir Ltd., Aligarh, 1976.

Gupta, S.S., *Utilisation of Electricity*, R.P.C., Planning Commission, D.S. College, Aligarh, 1969.

Gupta, S.S., *Varna, Castes and Scheduled Castes*, Concept Publishing Co., New Delhi, 1991.

Sturmay, S.C., *Income and Economic Welfare.*

Tara Chandra, *History of Freedom Movement in India*, Govt. of India, New Delhi, 1970.

Marshall, T.H., *Citizenship and Social Classes.*

Kent, T.W., *Welfare State.*

Tewari, Uma Kant, *The Making of the Indian Constitution*, Central Book Depot, Allahabad, 1974.

Giri, V.V., *Labour Problems in Indian Industry*, Asian Publishing House, Bombay, 1972.

PAMPHLETS

Naik, Yashwant S., *Some Lessons of Planning in India*, Forum and Free Enterprise, Bombay, 1984.

Ganguly, A.S., *Managing Economic Changes in India*, Forum and Free Enterprise, Bombay, 1986.

Brahmanda, P.R., *An Analysis of India's New Economic Policy*, Forum and Free Enterprise, Bombay, 1986.

Chelliah, Rajendra J., *Reflections on Indian Political Economy and Development,* Forum and Free Enterprise, Bombay, 1986.

Singh, Bhanu Pratap, *Time to Change Rural Policies*, Forum and Free enterprise, Bombay, 1986.

Gandhi, Indira, *No Centre-State Conflict in Planning*, Government of India, New Delhi, August 1984.

Gandhi, Rajiv, *Planning for Development*, Government of India, New Delhi, 1986.

The Nutritive Values of Indian Food, I.C.M.R. No. 42963.

Hand Book on Diabetes, Mellitus.

GOVERNMENT PUBLICATIONS

District Gazette, Aligarh.

District Population Census, Vol. I and II.

District Credit Plan, Aligarh Distt. 1990-91, Canara Bank. 1990.

Constituent Assembly Debates Vol. VI Book I, Lok Sabha Secretariat, 1989.

Constituent Assembly Debates Vol. VII Book II, Lok Sabha Secretariat, 1989.

Constituent Assembly Debates Vol. VIII Book III, Lok Sabha Secretariat, 1989.

Constituent Assembly Debates Vol. IX Book IV, Lok Sabha Secretariat, 1989.

Constituent Assembly Debates Vol. X-XII Book V, Lok Sabha Secretariat, 1989.

Indian Constitution

Report of the Third Pay Commission, 1973, Vol. I.

MAPS

1. U.P. State Electricity Board for Sikandra Rao Tahsil.
2. U.P. State Irrigation Department for Sikandra Rao Tahsil.
3. U.P. State P.W.D. Department for Sikandra Rao Tahsil.

JOURNALS

Srivastva, G. P., Beyond Westminster Model — Restructuring, Indian Political System for General Goal Achievement, *Journal of Indian Institution of Public Administration*, New Delhi, November 3, 1985.

Rowe W.L., The Marriage Net Work and Structural Changes in a North Indian Community, *South-Western Journal of Anthropology*, U.S.A.

Vinod Kumar, Position of the President under the Indian Constitution, *Law Journal*, 1962.

NEWSPAPERS

Hindustan Times

	Date	Author	Title
1.	15.2.1987	Sandhya Jain	Decline of the Bureaucracy
2.	1.12.1987	D.H.Pai Panandiker	A Cost-Plus Society
3.	19.5.1988	J.D. Sethi	Strategy for Eighth Plan Part I

4. 20.5.1988 J.D. Sethi — Strategy for Eighth Plan Part II
5. 24.12.1990 Prafull Gardia — Case for Small States.
6. 27.3.1991 K. Ganeshan — Threat From Ministers and Musclemen.
7. 15.4.1991 P. Tharyan — A Bomb or a catalyst?
8. 16.4.1991 L.K. Advani — Stability, Nationalism Is the Key?

Indian Express

1. 11.11.1983 J.D. Sethi — Prices, Poverty and the Plan
2. 8.2.1985 L.C. Jain — Leading upto 2001 A.D.
3. 3.3. 1985 Nani A. Palkhivala — The Union Budget and After
4. 15.4.1985 Swaminathan S. Aiyer — The Decline of Poverty Part I
5. 16.4.1985 Swaminathan S. Aiyer — The Decline of Poverty Part II
6. 21.1.1987 A.G. Norrani — Political Parties V. Constitution
7. 30.1.1987 L.P. Singh — The P.M. and Civil Servants
8. 31.1.1987 A Correspondent — Direct Elections of P.M. suggested
9. 14.2.1987 A Correspondent — Plea for Presidential form of Government
10. 15.2.1987 B.K. Nehru — Is it time for a change
11. 16.2.1987 L.P. Singh — The Man, not the system
12. 26.2.1987 Jogindra Singh — Making the Bureaucracy efficient, responsive
13. 13.5.1987 B.G. Vergese — The Other Side of the Coin
14. 15.6.1987 Lt. Gen. S.K. Sinha — A Fractured Democracy
15. 20.6.1988 L.C. Jain — Developing Backward Areas
16. 29.11.1988 B.M. Bhatia — Why Farmers Are unhappy
17. 17.3.1989 Lt. Gen. S.K. Sinha — Evolving A National Alternative
18. 26.5.1989 A Correspondent — Autonomy For D.D., A.I.R.
19. 23.7.1989 Rajiv Dhavan — Panchayat Raj and Rajiv Raj
20. K.K.G. Nambiar — Should Small Units Be Propped up
21. Swaminathan S. Aiyar — Less Planning, More Growth
22. Michal Peter — The Relevance of Corporate Planning, I to IV

Nav Bharat Times (Hindi)

1. 7.4.1985 Rajendra Mathur — Albida, Prof, Mahalonobis

Organiser

1. 18.9.1983 Dattopant Thengadi — Modernisation without Westernisation
2. 30.10.1983 P.B. Thengadi — Why Man-Moulding Deserve Highest Priority
3. 27.12.1987 M.M. Sankhdher — Integral Humanism Versus Radical Humanism
4. 27.12.1987 M. Mehta — Blind Craze for High-Tech is Destroying our Economic Fabric
5. 21.8.1988 J.A. Naik — Reshaping the Hindu Type
6. 12.3.1989 Daya Krishna — High Concentration and Continuation of Poverty in Rural Sector

7.	12.3.1989	Baij Nath Rai	Labouralisation is the Need of the Hour
8.	4.6.1989	Daya Krishna	Growing Disparities in Income — Most Potent Threat to National Unity Part I
9.	18.6.1989	Daya Krishna	Part II
10.	27.8.1989	Daya Krishna	India Continues to Grapple with Poverty
11.	10.2.1991	M.V. Kamath	Wanted a Presidential Form of Government
12.	7.3.1991	S. Gurumurth	Secularism in the Hindi Psyche
13.	24.3.1991	D.B. Thengadi	Dharma and Secularism
14.		P.K. Nijhawan	Secularism — Search for a New Paradigm (6 Articles)

Statesman

1.		N.R. Madhav Menon	Judicial Reforms Part I, II
2.		S. Sahay	A close look, Government, Judges and Lawyers.

Times of India

1.	9.6.1988	Meher C. Nanavatty	District Planning, Some Lessons

Tribune

1.	21.8.1988	Niti Paul Mehta	Moral Voice

MAGAZINE

Akhand Jyoti (Hindi), Mathura.

INDEX